Gender, Nature, and Nurture

Gender, Nature, and Nurture

Richard A. Lippa
California State University, Fullerton

LAWRENCE ERLBAUM ASSOCIATES, PUBLISHERS
2002   Mahwah, New Jersey   London

Senior Editor:	Debra Riegert
Textbook Marketing Manager:	Marisol Kozlovski
Editorial Assistant:	Jason Planer
Cover Design:	Kathryn Houghtaling Lacey
Textbook Production Manager:	Paul Smolenski
Full-Service & Composition:	Pre-Press Company, Inc.
Text and Cover Printer:	Hamilton Printing Company

This book was typeset in 10/12 pt. Cheltenham
The heads were typeset in Stone Sans Bold

Lawrence Erlbaum Associates, Inc., Publishers
10 Industrial Avenue
Mahwah, New Jersey 07430

Library of Congress Cataloging-in-Publication Data

Lippa, Richard A.
    Gender, nature, and nurture / Richard A. Lippa
       p. cm.
    Includes bibliographical references and index.
    ISBN 0-8058-3605-5 (alk. paper)
    1. Sex differences (Psychology) 2. Gender identity. 3. Nature and nurture. I. Title.
BF692.2 .L555 2001
    155.3'3--dc21   2001033505

*In loving memory of my aunt and uncle, Mitzi and Ed Levy,
who lived their lives to the fullest
and who faced illness with dignity and courage.*

Contents

Preface

I don't know about you, but throughout my life I have been puzzled by the behavior of both men and women. When I go to the gym, I am bemused by men's animated conversations about football games and cars, and when I go to the local gift shop, I am equally bemused by women who endlessly discuss how "darling" various ceramic figurines are. I don't think I am alone in finding both men and women somewhat inscrutable, each in their own way. And I'm certainly not alone in pondering the nature and nurture of gender.

Most of us try hard to understand what makes individual boys, girls, men, and women "tick," so most of us constantly grapple with gender, either consciously or unconsciously. We live and work and play with members of both sexes, and inevitably, we love and loathe individual males and females. If nothing else, the topic of gender carries immense egocentric appeal, for we all possess gender, in one form or another. And of course, the topic of gender is intimately tied to other favorite topics—like love, sex, and romance. In a more serious and political vein, our personal views of gender are linked to other important attitudes—about affirmative action, sexual harassment, women in the military, and a host of other topics. For all these reasons, gender is a "hot" topic—in everyday conversations, on talk shows, and in popular books.

Gender is also a hot topic among scientists. It has long been the focus of a veritable cottage industry of empirical research in the social and biological sciences. And after decades of concerted effort, scientists now have a lot to say about the causes and consequences of gender. The book you are about to read—*Gender, Nature, and Nurture*—presents a straightforward and accessible summary of scientific findings on gender. It offers a balanced, fair-minded account of what science currently does and does not know about the behavior of males and females, and it describes the major theories that attempt to explain gender differences, gender similarities, and gender variations.

Because *Gender, Nature, and Nurture* is, on one level, a "primer" of gender research, it is ideally suited for classes on the psychology of women, the psychology of men, sex roles, and gender. It can also serve as a stimulating accompaniment to introductory psychology and critical thinking classes, for it addresses a host of mainstream topics in psychology (personality, social behavior, cognitive abilities, biological psychology, behavioral genetics, evolutionary psychology) from the vantage point of a single unifying theme—gender. Students who read the book will exercise their critical thinking skills as they evaluate competing theories and integrate complex strands of empirical evidence. They will also see how scientific research applies to public policy questions. They will come to appreciate that science is an ongoing debate as much as a fixed and finished body of "facts."

Gender, Nature, and Nurture should appeal to the general reader, too, because it provides a readable, up-to-date summary of research on a topic that affects us all. In addition to presenting scientific findings, the book tackles many important real-life questions: Should boys and girls be reared alike? Should mothers be granted custody of young children more often than fathers? Is sexual violence a male rather than female problem, and does it have biological roots? Should corporations treat male and female employees the same? What roles should women and men assume in the military? Consideration of these questions demonstrates that scientific research can have important social consequences and that the nature-nurture debate is not just an academic exercise.

Writing a book is a complex process that involves many people. DiAnn Herst provided able assistance in conducting computer searches and obtaining library materials. Thanks to Joshua Pruett for creating the delightful cartoons that grace this book. The following reviewers read early chapter drafts, and their comments improved the quality of my ideas and writing: Diane F. Halpern of California State University, San Bernardino; Michael Bailey of Northwestern University; James Archer Jr. of the University of Florida, Gainesville; and John E. Williams of Georgia State University. Thanks to Debra Riegert, senior editor at Lawrence Erlbaum Associates, for guiding this project from inception to completion. Thanks to Larry Erlbaum for suppporting this project and to the other staff at Lawrence Erlbaum Associates who helped to transform a set of word processing files into an attractive finished book. And most of all, thanks to the many scholars who have ceaselessly probed the nature and nurture of gender. Their work encourages us all to celebrate the amazing diversity of men and women and to appreciate the common humanity of all people, regardless of their sex or gender.

Richard Lippa
Psychology Department
California State University, Fullerton

Introduction

The phrase "nature and nurture" is a convenient jingle of words, for it separates under two distinct heads the innumerable elements of which personality is composed. Nature is all that a man brings with himself into the world; nurture is every influence from without that affects him after his birth. The distinction is clear: the one produces the infant such as it actually is, including its latent faculties of growth of body and mind; the other affords the environment amid which the growth takes place, by which natural tendencies may be strengthened or thwarted, or wholly new ones implanted.

—*English Men of Science: Their Nature and Nurture*
Francis Galton

Ever since Sir Francis Galton coined one of science's few bona fide sound bites—"nature versus nurture"—the nature-nurture debate has reverberated through the halls of academia. To what extent *are* important human characteristics innate or learned? Nowhere is this debate more contentious than in the study of gender.

Given that gender is the topic of this book, it is perhaps ironic to start with a quote from Galton, who didn't even deign to include women in his purview ("Nature is all that a *man* brings with *himself* into the world..."). Although Galton is credited with originating the nature-nurture debate in psychology, he also is sometimes criticized for being sexist and racist. Whatever Galton's ideologies, his words are an appropriate starting point, for they not only set the tone for the nature-nurture debate, but they also hint at the political and ideological overtones that would come to inflame that debate.

Today, to ask whether there are biological factors that lead to gender differences is not just to pose a scientific question. It is to scrape open old wounds inflicted by sexist ideologies, and to confront stubborn prejudices on all sides. Biological theories of gender *have* been used to belittle and oppress women in the not-so-distant past, and thus, it is no wonder that contemporary feminists view such theories with suspicion. Phrases such as "anatomy is destiny" and "heredity is destiny" have served too often as predictions of positive destinies for in-groups (e.g., men) and negative destinies for out-groups (women).

Still, no one can doubt that men and women *are* biological creatures. Though unique in many ways, humans are animals, and like other animals, we have been molded by evolutionary forces that sometimes produce sex differences. We are not just encultured men and women; we are also embodied men and women. Too often in the study of gender, biological theories have been relegated to the category of "politically incorrect" or even, "reactionary."

Unfortunately, partisans on both sides of the nature-nurture debate have often talked past one another. Sometimes, they have even resorted to hurling invectives at one another. So why write a book that places itself (not to mention its author) in the crossfire of such a rancorous debate? One simple answer is that the nature-nurture controversy—whether applied to gender or to other topics—is fascinating. It touches upon a host of important real-life questions: To what extent can parents influence their children's personalities and intellects? What are the limits of educational enrichment? Are geniuses born or made? Is sexual orientation innate, learned, or "chosen"? Can mental illness be "in our genes"? Does violence come from "bad blood" or bad environments?

Like Galton, we want to know how much a person's environment can "strengthen or thwart" preexisting tendencies. Is it possible to imagine a society, for example, in which women murder more than men? Or one in which women like to watch football more than men do? Like Galton, we wonder whether the proper environment can "implant wholly new tendencies" in people. Could we rear a generation of women who are as interested as men in being engineers, or a generation of boys who play with babydolls as much as girls do?

One thing is clear. Over a century of research on the nature-nurture question has produced an explosion of new methods and findings. Were Galton alive today, he would be amazed by the complex mathematical techniques and huge database of modern behavioral genetics (this, despite the fact that he was the originator of the twin method in psychology). He would likely be overwhelmed by advances in biological psychology, neuroscience, and molecular genetics. He might even find himself modifying some of his strong hereditarian beliefs after examining 100 years of social scientific research.

Today, to understand the nature and nurture of gender, we must look to a multitude of disciplines: genetics; molecular biology; neuroanatomy; ethology; anthropology; sociology; and many branches of psychology. But before we can sift though all the data, we must first pose a preliminary and deceptively simple question: What is it that we are trying to explain? That is, what is *gender*? This question is the central focus of Chapters 1 and 2. Chapter 1 ("What's the Difference Anyway?") summarizes scientific findings on sex *differences* in people's behavior and traits, and Chapter 2 ("Masculinity and Femininity: Gender within Genders") summarizes research on gender-related individual differences *within each sex*. Chapter 3 ("Theories of Gender") presents prominent theories that have attempted to explain these two sides of gender.

Chapters 4 and 5 present research evidence on the nature and nurture of gender. Chapter 4 ("The Case for Nature") argues strongly for the power of biological evolution, genes, hormones, and neural structures to produce sex differences in behavior and gender-related individual differences within the sexes. Chapter 5 ("The Case for Nurture") argues just as strongly for the power of culture, social roles, social learning, stereotypes, and social settings to produce the very same phenomena. Chapter 6 ("Cross Examinations") presents an imagined debate between a personified "Nature" and "Nurture." Each side attempts to pick apart the other side's case and to sow doubts in the reader's mind about both strong nature and strong nurture accounts of gender.

The final chapter ("Gender, Nature, and Nurture: Looking to the Future") strives for a theoretical synthesis, and it examines how the nature-nurture debate affects real-life public policy debates. Offering a *cascade model* of gender, Chapter 7 proposes that biological and social factors trace out an interdependent causal cycle over the course of an individual's life and that gender is a phenomenon that can be explained only from a developmental perspective. From the vantage point of Chapter 7, nature and nurture are the inseparable "yin" and "yang" of gender development.

Chapter 7 then applies the cascade model to broader public policy questions. Should parents rear boys and girls alike? Is same-sex education beneficial or harmful? Should employers offer men and women the same parental benefits? Should judges in child custody cases treat mothers and fathers alike? Are men and women biologically destined to experience conflicts in their intimate relationships? Do biological or social factors lead to male sexual violence and coercion? Why do men hold elective office more than women do, and do women bring different leadership styles than men to government and business? Should the military treat men and women alike?

None of these questions is trivial. Some will require a Solomon-like wisdom to resolve. Research on the nature and nurture of gender can help us frame these questions more precisely and perhaps, to answer them more wisely. More broadly, research can help us to understand better the nature of each sex and to nurture that which is admirable in both.

Gender, Nature, and Nurture

1

What's the Difference Anyway?

"Tell me, how does the other sex of your race differ from yours?"

He looked startled and in fact my question rather startled me; kemmer brings out these spontaneities in one. We were both self-conscious. "I never thought of that," he said. "You've never seen a woman." He used his Terran-language word, which I knew.

"I saw your pictures of them. The women looked like pregnant Gethenians, but with larger breasts. Do they differ much from your sex in mind behavior? Are they like a different species?"

"No. Yes. No, of course not, not really. But the difference is very important. I supposed the most important thing, the heaviest single factor in one's life, is whether one's born male or female. In most societies, it determines one's expectations, activities, outlook, ethics, manners—almost everything. Vocabulary. Semiotic usages. Clothing. Even food. Women . . . women tend to eat less. . . . It's extremely hard to separate the innate differences from the learned ones. Even where women participate equally with men in the society, they still after all do all the childbearing, and so most of the child-rearing. . . ."

"Equality is not the general rule, then? Are they mentally inferior?"

—The Left Hand of Darkness
Ursula K. Le Guin

In her award-winning science fiction novel, *The Left Hand of Darkness*, Ursula K. Le Guin describes the planet Gethen, where all the people are hermaphrodites capable of both fathering and mothering a child. The people of Gethen cannot comprehend the difference between male and female. When the Terran ambassador, Genly Ai, visits Gethen, he must negotiate with people who have never experienced gender. As a result, he is forced to examine all the preconceptions he carries with him, as a man from a world in which people definitely do have gender.

The question that Genly Ai tries to answer is one that we all grapple with: How do men differ from women? Although fascinating, this question raises many scientific and political controversies on our own planet Earth. Throughout recorded history, men and women have often been seen as different. However, different has rarely been considered equal. Cultural stereotypes have held that men are more intelligent, logical, courageous, mature, and moral than women are. In times past women have even been regarded as chattel—that is, possessions—of men. It is no wonder then that many feminist scholars are suspicious of research on sex differences, for they suspect that research on sex differences may serve to legitimize sexist beliefs and to reinforce pernicious stereotypes about men and women.

Must research on sex differences promote inequality between the sexes? Not necessarily. Even if there are actual differences between men and women, this does not need to imply that one sex is better than the other. Psychologist Diane Halpern (1997) notes that although no one would deny that female genitals differ from male genitals, it is silly to ask whether women's genitals are "superior" to men's or vice versa. Differences are differences. *How* they are viewed is a matter of values.

But can we really remove values from the study of sex differences? Feminist theorists often note that in sexist societies (which probably includes most societies) what is male or masculine tends to be valued, and what is female or feminine tends to be devalued (see Crawford & Unger, 2000). At the very least, the study of sex differences requires that scientists constantly examine the ways in which society uses or misuses their findings. Researchers who study sex differences must guard against biases in evaluating and explaining their findings. Too often, lay people and scientists alike assume that sex differences—to the extent that they do exist—reflect "wired in," biologically innate and immutable differences between males and females. But this need not be true. Though there may be significant (that is, statistically reliable) differences between the sexes, the reasons for these differences are open to debate.

Research findings on sex differences can be viewed from two opposing points of view (Eagly, 1995; Hare-Mustin & Marecek, 1988). The first emphasizes *differences*. Some popular books argue that "men are from Mars, women from Venus" (Gray, 1992), and some feminist scholars argue that men and women speak with "a different voice" and possess different moral outlooks and communication styles (Gilligan, 1982; Maltz & Borker, 1982; Tannen, 1990). Those who emphasize sex *differences* may sometimes mistakenly portray women and men as "opposite sexes." The very phrase, "opposite sex," embodies a common misconception—that men and women differ dramatically, that the two sexes differ in kind rather than in degree. The truth is that boys and girls, and men and women, are rarely if ever the "opposite" of each other. Men may be on average more physically aggressive than women, for example. Still, most people—regardless of their sex—do not assault or murder other people (Bussy & Bandura, 1999). Thus men and women may be more similar than different in their homicidal aggression, even if we grant that they show an on-average difference.

The second, opposing perspective on sex differences tends to minimize differences. According to this "minimalist" perspective, most sex differences are small to negligible in magnitude, and even when they do occur, they are often ephemeral—now you see them, now you don't (Deaux, 1984; Deaux & LaFrance, 1998). The minimalists argue that sex differences appear in some situations but not in others; they occur in some studies but not in others. This variability is taken to imply that sex differences in behavior are created by social settings (for example, by business organizations that assign more power to men than to women), and that sex differences can therefore be eliminated by changing social settings. The minimalist perspective generally holds that human sex differences *are not* due to innate biological differences between males and females.

The minimalists further suggest that when sex differences in behaviors *are* found, they often result from gender stereotypes and from wrongheaded research methods. Consider, for example, the common finding that men report more sexual partners than women do (see Wiederman, 1997, for a review). Does this reflect a real sex difference, or does it indicate instead that when responding to surveys, men and women respond in ways that conform to gender stereotypes? If common stereotypes portray men to be more "promiscuous" and interested in sex than women, then perhaps men and women describe themselves consistent with these stereotypes. Men's tendency to report more sexual partners than women may also indicate that men boast (and perhaps lie) more than women do about their sexual "conquests."

Similar sorts of problems may affect many other studies that look at sex differences in self-reported behaviors (such as helping, aggression, risk taking). Despite these problems, researchers continue to study sex differences. After all, the very concept of "gender" is partly defined by *differences* between the sexes—differences in men's and women's dress, grooming, occupational choices, communication styles, aggression, and nonverbal behaviors.[1] As we shall see in chapter 2, gender is also partly defined in terms of variations *within each sex*—variations in individuals' masculinity and femininity. To analyze how much biological and environmental factors contribute to gender, we must first examine these two different faces of gender: (a) sex differences in behavior and (b) individual differences in masculinity and femininity within each sex.

This chapter focuses on the first face of gender—sex differences. Our first order of business is to decide which sex differences do in fact exist. Do the sexes differ in their personality traits? Do women take fewer risks than men do? Are men more physically aggressive than women? Are women more altruistic and helpful than men? Do women use different "body language" than men do? Do men and women prefer different kinds of occupations and hobbies? Do women and men differ in their sexual behaviors and mate choices? Is there a male advantage in math? Do women show better verbal skills than men do? Do men and women display different kinds of mental illness? The goal of this chapter is to answer these sorts of questions, based on the best current research evidence.

As we will see, the findings are varied and complex. Sex differences are large in some domains and small to nonexistent in others. Some kinds of sex differences vary over time and across cultures, and others are more stable. Some sex differences depend heavily on situational factors, some do not. As we wend our way through the findings, it is important constantly to remind ourselves that whether they are strong or weak, consistent or variable, the mere fact that sex differences exist does not necessarily tell us *why* they exist.

THE STUDY OF SEX DIFFERENCES

To understand research on sex differences, it is important first to understand a bit about the statistical methods used to study sex differences. (This discussion is easy to understand and light on technical details, I promise.) When psychologists study variations in human traits such as height, intelligence, or personality, they often plot people's scores in the form of frequency distributions. Such distributions show the proportion of people who take on various values for a given trait. Figure 1.1, for example, displays the distribution of height in a particular group of people.

For large populations, trait distributions often take the approximate form of an idealized curve called the *normal distribution* (again, see Fig 1.1). This distribution takes the shape of the familiar bell-shaped curve. The normal distribution has a precise mathematical definition, but that need not concern us here. Normal distributions often arise in nature when a trait—height, for instance—results from many small, random factors that "add up" to produce the trait. For example, an individual's height depends on many factors, such as the effects of individ-

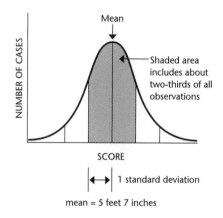

FIG. 1.1 Height as a Normally Distributed Trait

ual genes, nutritional factors, exposure to infectious diseases and environmental chemicals, and so on.

A normal distribution can be characterized by two important numbers: its *mean* and its *standard deviation*. The mean is the average value of the distribution. Since normal distributions are symmetric (the right side is the mirror image of the left side), the mean of a normal distribution is at its center. The standard deviation is a measure of how narrow or spread out a distribution is. Distributions that are very spread out have large standard deviations, whereas distributions that are very narrow have small standard deviations. In a normal distribution, about two thirds of all values are in a range between one standard deviation below the mean and one standard deviation above the mean (see Fig. 1.1).

The following example should make this clearer. A study by Gillis and Avis (1980) found the average height of a sample of 98 American men to be 70 inches (5 feet, 10 inches), and the average height of a sample of 98 American women (the men's wives) to be 64 inches (5 feet, 4 inches). Of course, these are just averages. Some women (half, to be exact) were taller than the average woman, and half were shorter than the average woman. In Gillis and Avis's study, the standard deviation (which, you'll recall, is a measure of the spread of a distribution) was 2.3 inches for each sex. Because men's and women's heights were approximately normally distributed, about two thirds of all men were between 67.7 and 72.3 inches in height (between 5 feet, 7.7 inches, and 6 feet, 0.3 inches), and two thirds of all women were between 61.7 and 66.3 inches in height (between 5 feet, 1.7 inches, and 5 feet, 6.3 inches). If you look at the idealized normal distributions of men's and women's heights, which are shown in Fig. 1.2, you will see that most men were taller than most women.

Graph shows the distribution of women's and men's heights. The computed value
of *d* is very large, indicating that men are noticeably taller than women on average
and that the two distributions do not overlap much.

(a) *d* = 2.6 (very large)

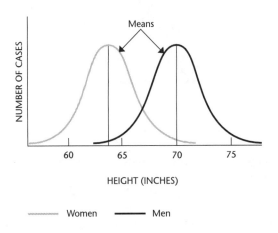

HEIGHT (INCHES)

---------- Women   ———— Men

d values of 2.6 are very rare in psychological research. For psychological data, Cohen (1977)
describes *d* values of .8 as "large," values of .5 as "medium," and values of .2 as "small."

FIG. 1.2 Distributions of Men's and Women's Height in Inches

The difference between the height of men and women can be quantified in the following way, which will prove to be very useful in our subsequent discussions of sex differences: Subtract the mean of the
women's heights from the mean of the men's heights, and then divide
this difference by the standard deviation of each distribution. The resulting number is the *d* statistic (sometimes called Cohen's *d* statistic, in
honor of the statistician Jacob Cohen, who advocated its use; Cohen,
1977). In Gillis and Avis's (1980) study, d = (men's mean height −
women's mean height) / the standard deviation = $(70 − 64) / 2.3 = 2.6$.

The *d* statistic takes into account two things when estimating how big
the difference is between two distributions: (a) the difference between
the means of the two distributions and (b) the standard deviations of the
two distributions. (If the standard deviations of the two distributions differ, then the average standard deviation is used.) Stated a bit differently,
the *d* statistic considers the difference in the means of two distributions
in relation to the standard deviations of those distributions.

Why is it important to take the standard deviation (i.e, the spread of
the distributions) into account? The following example should make

this clear. Suppose I develop a new test that tries to measure how successful people are at pacifying crying babies. Each person who completes my test is given, in succession, five squalling babies to rock and cuddle, and I measure with a stopwatch how long it takes each comforted baby to stop crying. The person's "score" is the average time it takes the five babies to stop crying. After collecting data for 500 men and 500 women, I am interested in determining whether there is a meaningful sex difference in "baby pacification ability." Suppose I find that, on average, women pacify babies more quickly than men do—30 seconds more quickly, to be precise. Is this a "big" or a "small" difference? The key point to understand is that this difference does not mean much until it is compared to the standard deviations of the distributions (see Fig. 1.3).

If the standard deviations are small (that is, the distributions are "narrow" about their means), then a 30-second difference might be quite large and meaningful (the left side of Fig. 1.3). However, if the standard deviations are large (the distributions are "spread out"), the observed 30-second difference may not mean much at all (right side of Fig. 1.3). In the first case, the two distributions do not overlap much and are distinct. The difference between them is quite apparent to the naked eye. In the second case, the two distributions overlap substan-

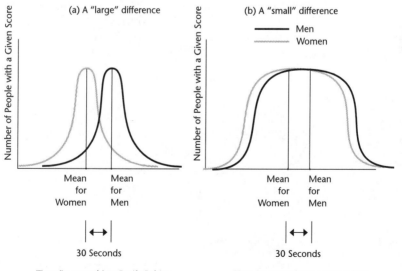

FIG. 1.3 Male and Female Distributions for a Hypothetical Test of "Baby Pacification Ability"

tially and are not very different at all. In a sense, the *d* statistic assesses how much the two distributions *overlap*, not simply the degree to which the *means* of the two distributions differ.

Let's return to Gillis and Avis's (1980) study of the heights of men and women. We computed *d* to be 2.6. Is this large or small? Jacob Cohen (1977), the statistician who first promoted the use of the *d* statistic, offered the following rough guidelines for psychological research: Values of around 0.2 are "small," values of around 0.5 are "moderate," and values of around 0.8 are "large." (See Fig. 1.4 for an illustration of these different values of *d*.) Here is another way to think about this. When *d* = 0.2, the two distributions overlap substantially, and although the difference between the means may be statistically significant (that is, not due to chance), the difference may nonetheless be small in terms of practical significance, and it is unlikely to be very noticeable in everyday life. When *d* = 0.5, however, the difference becomes large enough to be noticed in everyday life, and when *d* = 0.8, the difference is grossly apparent in everyday life; you don't have to do fancy studies to be aware of it. By Cohen's guidelines, the difference between men's and women's heights in Gillis and Avis's study (*d* = 2.6) is huge, and you'll probably agree that the height difference between men and women is readily apparent in everyday life. You don't need to be a scientist to know that men are generally taller than women.

Why is the *d* statistic important to researchers who study sex differ-

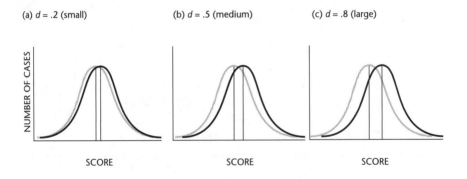

Note: To simplify the discussion, we have assumed that the normal distributions for both men and women have equal standard deviations. This assumption is not always warranted, however. For example, in measures of intellectual abilities, men's scores often have a greater spread (larger standard deviation) than women's scores do—that is, there are more very low-scoring and very high-scoring men than women. However, *d* can still be computed for such distributions.

FIG. 1.4 Small, Moderate, and Large Differences Between Two Groups

ences? First of all, it provides a standard way to compute sex differences. As we will see, this statistic provides a way of averaging sex differences from different studies. Despite its usefulness to statisticians, however, the meaning of the d statistic may not always be obvious to lay people. Therefore, it is often useful to translate the d statistic into more common-sense kinds of information. In this chapter, I do the following translation: I convert the d statistic into the percentage of men who score higher than the average woman, or the percentage of women who score higher than the average man, on a particular trait or behavior.

How does this translation work for men's and women's heights? For a d value of 2.6, we want to know what percentage of women are taller than the average man. Assuming that height is normally distributed for men and for women, the answer for Gillis and Avis's (1980) sample is that only about one half of one percent of women would be taller than the average man. (This is consistent with the fact that the two distributions do not overlap very much; see Fig. 1.2.)

As this chapter reviews evidence on sex differences in personality traits, aggression, interests, and cognitive abilities, you are presented with many d statistics. To make them easier for you to understand, I frequently translate the d statistic into the more commonsense notion of what percentage of men score higher than the average woman or what percentage of women score higher than the average man. Most psychological sex differences prove to be much smaller than differences between men's and women's height.

COMBINING THE RESULTS OF MANY STUDIES: META-ANALYSIS

It is a truism in science that no single study can definitively answer any question, and this is certainly true in the study of sex differences. Are men more physically aggressive than women? No single study can answer this question. Still, many individual studies *have* addressed this question, either directly or indirectly. To complicate matters, though, various studies have measured different kinds of aggression, and even when they have measured the same kinds of aggression, various studies may have measured aggression differently and with different degrees of precision. For example, some studies have asked people to report their levels of aggression on questionnaire scales. Psychology experiments have sometimes placed college men and women in settings where they deliver what seem to be painful electric shocks to obnoxious partners during experimental games. Studies of children have asked their parents and teachers to rate them on aggressiveness. Still other studies have analyzed statistics about sex differences in real-life aggressive behaviors, such as criminal assaults and murders.

Therefore, when trying to summarize observed sex differences in aggression, social scientists face a problem of trying to combine apples and oranges—different results based on different measures of aggression, which have been obtained in different studies, from different populations, under different circumstances.

This "apples and oranges" problem is not insurmountable. In trying to summarize the results of various studies, researchers can focus their attention on a uniform group of studies (for example, on just experimental studies of aggression conducted on adult participants). Whichever studies are to be summarized, it is important that researchers "scale" sex differences the same way across studies. This is why the d statistics are so important. In various studies, if groups of men and women (or boys and girls) have been measured on aggression, it is generally possible to compute a d statistic. Then researchers can average the d statistics from the various studies to see what the average findings are. This technique of quantitatively combining (i.e., numerically averaging) the results of many different studies is called *meta-analysis*. Over the past 20 years, meta-analysis has become a very important method for reviewing and synthesizing research findings in the social and biological sciences (Hunt, 1999).

In one meta-analysis of 64 studies on sex differences in aggression, psychologists Alice Eagly and Valerie Steffen (1986) computed the average value of d across studies to be 0.29, with men tending to be more aggressive than women. This value of d implies that, on average, about 39% of women are more aggressive than the average man, or conversely, that 61% of men are more aggressive than the average woman. Sex differences in aggression were sufficiently consistent across the 64 studies for Eagly and Steffen to conclude that these differences were very unlikely to be due to chance. In the language of statistics, the overall sex difference in aggression was found to be *statistically significant*. We can therefore conclude with some confidence, based on this synthesis of 64 studies, that men are on average somewhat more aggressive than women in experiments on aggression.

Meta-analysis is useful not only because it provides us with the average results of many studies. It is also useful because it can help us to understand why results vary across studies. As noted before, studies investigating sex differences in aggression differ from one another in their subjects, methods, settings, and measures of aggression. Such differences can be coded (that is, assessed and quantified based on the published research reports) and then included as factors to be analyzed in a meta-analysis. For example, meta-analyses of sex differences in aggression have coded studies based on whether they studied physical or verbal aggression. Their results show that sex differences (that is, d values) are larger in studies that measure physical aggressiveness ($d = 0.40$) and smaller in studies that measure verbal aggressiveness ($d = 0.18$). Thus, meta-analyses conclude that men are particularly more *physically* aggressive than women.

At about the same time that Eagly and Steffen published (1986) their meta-analysis, University of Wisconsin psychologist Janet Shibley Hyde (1986) published another meta-analysis on sex differences in aggression. Hyde reported a somewhat larger mean sex difference in aggressiveness ($d = 0.50$). For this value of d, only 30% of females are more aggressive than the average male, and 70% of males are more aggressive than the average female. Why the difference between Hyde's findings and those of Eagly and Steffen? One answer is that Hyde's meta-analysis included studies of children, whereas Eagly and Steffen's meta-analysis looked only at studies of adolescents and adults. Indeed, in an earlier meta-analysis, Hyde (1984) broke down studies by subjects' ages, and she found that sex differences in aggression were large in children ages 4 through 5 ($d = 0.86$), moderate in children ages 9 through 12 ($d = 0.54$), and small for college-age subjects ($d = 0.27$). Findings such as these begin to offer hints about factors that influence sex differences in aggression.

This tale of two meta-analyses makes an important point: The results of meta-analyses depend in part on the studies that are "cranked into" them. One of the first steps in conducting any meta-analysis is to identify the studies to be reviewed, which ideally include all the studies ever conducted on a given research topic. Identifying studies has been made easier by computerized citation searches. Using a computerized search, a researcher could, for example, search for any study ever published over the past 10 years that includes in its abstract terms such as *gender differences, sex difference, aggression, hostility,* and so on. (An abstract is the brief summary of findings that begins a published research article.) Computer searches, however, are unlikely to locate *all* the studies carried out on a given topic. Some studies are never published. And some studies on aggression have looked at sex differences only incidentally, thus the sex differences they find may not be reported in the study's abstract. Inevitably, computerized searches miss some relevant studies.

Another way to track down studies on a particular topic is to look up all the articles cited in the reference lists of articles you *do* locate, and then determine if *they* report sex differences in aggression. Then continue this process of tracking down studies cited in reference lists until you come up with no new studies on sex differences in aggression. As you can imagine, this process of tracing your way through networks of research citations can be quite time-consuming.

WHAT DO META-ANALYSES TELL US ABOUT SEX DIFFERENCES?

It's time now to turn to evidence about sex differences. To make our discussion manageable, the evidence will be organized by the following topic areas: personality, risk taking, social behaviors, nonverbal behavior and perceptiveness, sexuality and mate preferences, occupational preferences interests, cognitive abilities, and physical abilities (such as grip strength and throw velocity). Finally, we will look at sex differences that have not been well summarized by meta-analyses: sex differences in mental illness, emotional experience, self-concept, and childhood friendship patterns.

Are There Sex Differences in Personality?

Personality traits can be defined as internal factors—partly determined by experience and partly determined by heredity and physiology—that cause individuals' characteristic patterns of thought, feeling, and behavior (see Funder, 1997). Personality traits lead people to show consistencies in their behavior, both over time and across settings. For example, an extraverted person will probably continue to be extraverted a month from now (consistency over time). Furthermore, an extraverted person likely shows his or her extraversion in many different situations: at work, at parties, and at home with family members (consistency over settings). Trait theories typically assume that people vary along a measurable dimension—for example, a dimension of introversion-extraversion.

What are the key trait dimensions of personality, and how many different personality traits are there? The answer to this question depends in part on whether you focus on very broad or very specific traits. Over the past two decades, personality psychologists have reached a consensus that, at the broadest level of description, human personality can be characterized by five traits, which are termed, appropriately enough, the *Big Five* (Wiggins, 1996). The Big Five traits are extraversion, agreeableness, conscientiousness, neuroticism, and openness to experience.

Although these labels may seem straightforward, the traits they refer to are sometimes broader than their labels might suggest, and each Big Five trait comprises a number of subtraits, or facets. People who are highly extraverted, for example, are sociable, bold, assertive, spontaneous, cheerful, and energetic, and introverted people are just the opposite. Agreeable people are warm, kind, polite, friendly, and good-natured, whereas disagreeable people are cold, irritable, hostile, vindictive, and unfriendly. Conscientious people are careful, serious, and responsible; they manage their impulses well and abide by social rules and norms. In contrast, people who are low on conscientiousness are unreliable; they have difficulty controlling their impulses and sometimes "act out" and break social rules. People who are high on neuroticism are nervous, depressed, tense, and suffer from low self-esteem, whereas people who are low on neuroticism are calm, well adjusted, self-assured, and confident. Thus people who are high on neuroticism suffer from many negative emotions, and indeed, another label for neuroticism is "negative affectivity" or "negative emotionality." Finally, people who are high on openness to experience are imaginative, curious, creative, and liberal. They take pleasure in intellectual and artistic experiences and love variety in food, travel, friends, and acquaintances. People who are low on openness tend to be closed minded, conventional, and set in their ways. They do not value introspection or aesthetic experiences.

Do men and women differ on the Big Five personality traits? Yale psychologist Alan Feingold (1994) conducted a meta-analysis to answer this question. Much of the data Feingold reviewed came from large samples assessed to develop norms for standardized personality tests. Thus the data were not collected specifically for the purpose of studying sex differences.

Feingold (1994) found that the traits showing the largest sex differences were facets of extraversion and agreeableness. The extraversion component that showed the largest sex difference was assertiveness ($d = 0.50$, with men more assertive than women). The agreeableness component that showed the largest sex difference was tender-mindedness ($d = 0.97$, with women more tender-minded than men). In terms of Cohen's (1977) guidelines, these sex differences are moderate and large, respectively. The sex difference in assertiveness implies that 69% of men are more assertive than the average woman, and the sex difference in tender-mindedness implies that 83% of women are more tender-minded than the average man is.

Feingold's (1994) meta-analyis found a modest gender difference in anxiety, a neuroticism facet ($d = 0.28$, with women more anxious than men). There were negligible gender differences in conscientiousness and openness to experience (although it's worth noting that Feingold did not examine all possible facets of these traits). Feingold also summarized the results of a number of studies on self-esteem, and though he found a slight difference favoring men ($d = 0.16$), this difference was small and not of great practical significance. A more recent meta-analysis similarly found a small sex difference in self-esteem favoring men ($d = 0.21$), and this sex difference proved to be largest in studies of late adolescents ($d = 0.33$; Kling, Hyde, Showers, & Buswell, 1999).

There are two additional traits worth mentioning before we leave the topic of personality: authoritarianism and social dominance orientation. Both of these personality traits are related to prejudice. Authoritarianism refers to the degree to which people defer to authority, follow traditional societal norms and conventions, and feel hostility to people who are seen as outsiders (Adorno, Frenkel-Brunswik, Levinson, & Sanford, 1950; Altemeyer, 1981, 1988, 1998). Social dominance orientation refers to the degree to which people feel that some groups are better than others (Pratto, Sidanius, Stallworth, & Malle, 1994). People who are high on social dominance view the social world in terms of haves and have-nots—and they think that inequality is "the way things should be."

Are there sex differences in authoritarianism and social dominance orientation? Although there have been no meta-analyses on the topic, recent studies find that men and women do not differ much on authoritarianism (Altemeyer, 1998). In contrast, men and women do differ in social dominance, with men scoring higher than women (Lippa & Arad, 1999; Sidanius, Pratto, & Bobo, 1994). The d value for sex differences in social dominance orientation (based on my own summary of a number of recent studies) is around 0.6. Assuming this ballpark estimate, about 27% of women score higher on social dominance orientation than the average man does, or conversely, 73% of men score higher on social dominance orientation than the average woman does. Largely because of this difference, men tend to hold somewhat more prejudiced attitudes toward minority groups than women do (Altemeyer, 1998).

Are There Sex Differences in Risk Taking?

Three University of Maryland researchers—James Byrnes, David Miller, and William Schafer (1999)—conducted a meta-analysis that summarized 150 studies on sex differences in risk taking. Some of these studies measured risk taking via self-reports, and others observed actual risk-taking behaviors (see Table 1.1). In general, men proved to take more risks than women did ($d = 0.13$), but this difference is quite small. A d value of 0.13 implies that 45% of women take more risks than the average man does, and 55% of men take more risks than the average woman does.

An examination of Table 1.1 shows, however, that sex differences were larger for some kinds of risk taking than for others. For example, men reported engaging in riskier driving practices than women did ($d = 0.29$). This value implies that 39% of women reported riskier driving practices than the average man, whereas 61% of men reported riskier driving practices than the average woman. Men also took greater risks than women did in exposing themselves to danger in ex-

TABLE 1.1
Mean Sex Differences in Risk Taking by Kind of Behavior

Task	Mean d Value
Self-Reported Behavior	
Smoking	−0.02
Drinking/drug use	0.04*
Sexual activities	0.07*
Driving	0.29*
Observed Behavior	
Physical activity	0.16*
Driving	0.17*
Gambling	0.21*
Experiment	0.41*
Intellectual risk taking	0.40*
Physical skills	0.43*

Note. *Positive* d *values occur when men take more risks than women, and negative values occur when women take more risks than men. The asterisk indicates that the mean* d *value is significantly different from zero. From "Gender Differences in Risk Taking," by J.P. Byrnes, D.C. Miller, and W.D. Schafer, 1999,* Psychological Bulletin, 125, *p. 377. Copyright 1999 by American Psychological Association. Adapted with permission.*

periments, exposing themselves to intellectual risks, and in games of physical skill. The average *d* value for these sex differences was about 0.4. Thus, about 66% of men took greater risks in these sorts of tasks than the average woman did. Byrnes, Miller, and Schafer (1999) reported a tendency for sex differences in risk taking to decrease with age. They also noted that sex differences in risk taking have decreased somewhat in recent years.

Are There Sex Differences in Social Behaviors?

Social psychologists study behaviors such as aggression, helping, conformity and susceptibility to persuasion, and behavior in groups and leadership. Are there sex differences in these sorts of social behaviors?

Aggression.   As noted before, two meta-analyses found moderate gender difference in aggression favoring males, with *d* statistics ranging from 0.29 to 0.50. In a more recent meta-analysis, which included some newer studies, Ann Bettencourt and Norman Miller (1996) found a mean gender difference of *d* = 0.23. This meta-analysis, like the earlier one by Eagly and Steffen (1986), included only studies of adolescents and adults, and its results were quite similar to Eagly and Steffen's.

Bettancourt and Miller's (1996) meta-analysis further showed that sex differences in aggression were larger in studies of unprovoked aggression ($d = 0.43$) than in studies of provoked aggression ($d = 0.06$). (In case you are wondering what counts as a provocation, some examples are insults, physical attacks from another, and frustration.) However, specific kinds of provocation did lead to sex differences in aggression. The kinds most likely to goad men to be more aggressive than women were physical attacks ($d = 0.48$) and insults about one's intelligence ($d = 0.59$). So, when physically attacked, 68% of men were more aggressive than the average woman was when similarly attacked.

Helping Behavior. Social stereotypes hold that women are "nicer" and more nurturant than men (Eagly, Mladinic, & Otto, 1991). But are women truly more helpful than men? This may depend in part on the kind of helping studied. Some kinds of helping, such as giving money to charities and making soup for a sick friend, are common in everyday life and not risky to the helper. Other kinds, such as running into a burning house to rescue a child or jumping into icy water to save a drowning victim, are rare, dramatic, and very risky. Social psychologists have tended to study risky and dramatic forms of helping—termed "emergency interventions"—more than commonplace, everyday kinds of helping, and this may have biased their findings somewhat in favor of finding men more helpful than women.

You may recall from our discussion of personality that women report being more tender-minded than men. A similar finding comes from studies of self-report measures of empathy. Women report that they are more empathetic than men are ($d = 0.27$; Eisenburg & Lenon, 1983). However, a meta-analysis of 182 studies that actually observed the helping behaviors of men and women in both laboratory and field settings found men, on average, to be a bit more helpful than women ($d = 0.34$; Eagly & Crowley, 1986). A difference of this size implies that 63% of men help more than the average woman does. (Again, it is worth noting that this difference favoring men may in part reflect the kinds of helping social psychologists have studied most—emergency interventions.)

Sex differences in helping varied considerably across studies, however. Eagly and Crowley (1986) observed that men were more helpful than women particularly when they were being observed by others ($d = 0.74$) and when the person they assisted did not directly request help ($d = 0.55$). Furthermore, men were more helpful to *women* in need than they were to *men* in need. Putting these findings together, it seems that men are more helpful than women particularly in public settings and when assisting women. A flattering interpretation might be that men wish to be chivalrous to "women in distress." A more cynical interpretation might be that men wish to look heroic before a public audience, especially if that audience consists of women. Men's tendency to be more helpful than women when help is not directly requested may reflect men's greater assertiveness and perhaps greater intrusiveness.

Conformity and Susceptibility to Persuasion.

Conformity refers a person's tendency to shift his or her opinions to be more like those of a group, presumably because of pressure from the group. Think of teenagers who dress like their friends, or church members who espouse the same religious beliefs as other members of their congregation. Solomon Asch (1956) conducted classic early studies of conformity in which college students were asked to make obvious perceptual judgments, like judging which of three lines was equal in length to a fourth line. On some judgment trials, the answers that students believed to be correct were openly contradicted by a unanimous group of peers. Asch observed how often students would "cave in" and go along with the crowd when other peers openly disagreed with their judgments. Since Asch's time, hundreds of additional studies have investigated when and why people conform.

Two meta-analyses have examined sex differences in Asch-type conformity experiments (Becker, 1986; Eagly and Carli, 1981). Their findings are quite similar: On average, women conform a bit more than men do ($d = 0.32$ and 0.28 in the two respective meta-analyses). A d value of 0.3 implies that about 38% of men conform more than the average woman does, or that 62% of women conform more than the average man does. Sex differences in conformity are strongest in face-to-face settings, like those employed in Asch's studies, when subjects are in the direct presence of peers who exert pressure on them to conform.

Becker (1986) and Eagly and Carli (1981) also summarized evidence on sex differences in people's degree of attitude change after hearing or reading persuasive messages. Women proved to be slightly more persuaded on average than men were ($d = 0.11$ and 0.16, respectively). Assuming a d value of 0.16 (which is probably the better estimate because of the better statistical procedures used by Eagly and Carli), then 56% of women were more influenced by persuasive messages than the average man was—a small difference, to be sure.

Group Behavior and Leadership.

For over half a century, social psychologists have studied behavior in various kinds of groups: therapy groups, work groups, juries and other kinds of decision-making groups. Small group research has identified two basic kinds of group behaviors: *social-emotional* behaviors and *task-oriented* behaviors. Social-emotional behaviors—such as telling a joke to relieve group tension or praising another group member who does a good job—are focused on maintaining personal relationships in groups. Task-oriented behaviors—such as offering information or asking for solutions to problems—are focused on achieving the work goals of the group.

Do men and women differ in the amount of social-emotional and task-oriented behaviors they show in groups? In the early 1980s, two meta-analyses examined this question (Anderson & Blanchard, 1982; Carli, 1982). Both found similar results. On average, men engage in more task-oriented group behaviors than women do ($d = 0.59$ in Carli's meta-analysis), and women engage in more social-emotional group behaviors than men do (again, $d = 0.59$). This implies that 72% of men engage in more task-oriented group behaviors than the average woman does, and similarly, 72% of women engage in more social-emotional group behaviors than the average man does.

Other meta-analyses have studied sex differences in leadership. According to a meta-analysis by Alice Eagly and Steven Karau (1991), men are somewhat more likely than women to emerge as leaders of unstructured laboratory groups ($d = 0.32$). This difference implies that 37% of women are more likely to emerge as leaders in small groups than the average man is, and conversely, that 63% of men are more likely to emerge as leaders than the average woman is.

Group leaders can be experts in either social-emotional behaviors or task-oriented behaviors, or sometimes both. The social-emotional leader tends to be liked, has good "people skills," and excels at reducing group tensions and managing group emotions. The task-oriented leader is "hard-nosed" and focuses on getting the job done and achieving group goals. Eagly and Karau (1991) found that men are more likely than women to emerge as task leaders of groups ($d = 0.41$), whereas women are more likely than men to emerge as social-emotional leaders ($d = 0.18$). In another meta-analysis, Alice Eagly and Blair Johnson (1990) found that women on average show a more democratic leadership style in groups, whereas men show a more autocratic style ($d = .22$). This difference implies that 59% of women are more democratic in their leadership style than the average man is.

Yet another kind of group behavior is negotiation. In a meta-analysis of 21 studies, Alice Stuhlmacher and Amy Walters (1999) found that men on average achieved slightly better outcomes in negotiations than women did ($d = 0.09$). This very small difference implies that 54% of men negotiated better outcomes than the average woman did. The difference favoring men was strongest in studies in which the negotiator had a high degree of power ($d = 0.25$) and in studies in which the negotiation was a "zero-sum game," in which only one of the negotiators could come away with positive outcomes ($d = 0.20$). Although sex differences in negotiation appear to be small, Stuhlmacher and Walters argue that the *cumulative* effects of such differences could be larger. For example, over the course of many years, employees may negotiate salaries, working conditions, and promotions many times. As a result, small negotiating advantages favoring men could build up with repetition, and this cumulative effect could contribute the greater number of men than women found in positions of power in government and business organizations.

Are There Sex Differences in Nonverbal Behavior and Nonverbal Perceptiveness?

People convey a huge amount of information to one another, both intentionally and unintentionally, through behaviors such as eye contact, smiling, facial expressions, speech intonation, gestures, and the use of personal space. Researchers have studied the nonverbal behaviors people display to one another and people's ability to "read" one another's facial expressions and body language.

Northeastern University psychologist Judith Hall (1984) conducted meta-analyses that summarized sex differences in nonverbal behavior and in people's ability to decode (that is, to understand or read) nonverbal behaviors. Table 1.2 presents some of her findings. In general, women are better than men at decoding nonverbal information ($d =$

TABLE 1.2
Sex Differences in Nonverbal Behaviors and in the Ability
to Decode Nonverbal Behaviors

Measure	Median d Value	Number of Studies
Decoding skill	0.43	64
Face recognition skill	0.34	12
Judgeability of emotions	0.52	35
Facial expressiveness	1.01	5
Social smiling	0.63	15
Gaze	0.68	30
Distance in approaching others in natural settings	−0.56	17
Distance approached by others in natural settings	−0.95	9
Body restlessness	−0.72	6
Expansiveness	−1.04	6
Bodily expressiveness	0.58	7
Speech errors	−0.70	6
Filled pauses ("ah's," "er's," and "um's")	−1.19	6

Note. *Positive* d *values occur when women score higher than men, and negative values occur when men score higher than women. Adapted from* Nonverbal Sex Differences: Communication Accuracy and Expressive Style *(p. 142), by J.A. Hall, 1984, Baltimore, MD: Johns Hopkins University Press. Copyright 1984 by The Johns Hopkins University Press. Adapted with permission.*

0.43). A difference of this magnitude implies that 67% of women are better at judging nonverbal information than the average man is, and conversely, only 33% of men are better than the average woman is. Women are also better than men at posing emotions with their facial expressions ($d = 0.52$), which implies that 70% of women are better at posing facial emotions than the average man is. Women tend to be more facially expressive than men ($d = 1.01$), and this means that 84% of women are more facially expressive than the average man is. (Note that this finding refers to *natural* facial expressiveness, not *posed* facial expressions.)

Men and women differ in specific kinds of nonverbal behavior. For example, women smile more than men do in social settings ($d = 0.63$). Thus 74% of women smile more than the average man does. Women gaze more at others than men do ($d = 0.68$), which implies that 75% of women gaze more at others than the average man does. Hall (1984) also reported that mutual gaze (i.e., eye contact) occurs at much higher levels between women than between men. Men maintain more personal space (i.e., physical distance) between themselves and others, both when approached by others ($d = 0.56$) and when approaching others ($d = 0.95$). A d value of 0.95 implies that 83% of men maintain more distance from others than the average woman does. Men are more restless ($d = 0.72$) and expansive ($d = 1.04$) in their body movements than women are. Thus 85% of men show more expansive movements and gestures than the average woman does.

Women also tend to have more expressive gestures than men ($d = 0.58$), and this means that 72% of women have more expressive gestures than the average man does. Perhaps because of women's greater expressiveness, their emotions are judged more accurately than men's emotions are ($d = 0.52$) and this is true both for judgments based on vocal and facial information. Finally, men show more speech errors (e.g., stammers and stutters) than women do ($d = 0.70$). Similarly, men show more "filled pauses" (e.g., "ah's," "er's," and "um's") in their speech than women do ($d = 1.19$). Thus, 88% of men produce more filled pauses than the average woman does. Many of the sex differences observed in nonverbal behaviors are quite large.

Are There Sex Differences in Sexuality and Mate Preferences?

Sexual relations constitute perhaps our most intimate form of social behavior. Mary Beth Oliver and Janet Shibley Hyde (1993) conducted a meta-analysis of 177 studies that investigated sex differences in various kinds of sexual behavior and attitudes. Some of their results are presented in Table 1.3.

Here's a summary: Men hold more positive attitudes toward casual sexual intercourse than women do ($d = 0.81$), and they hold more sexu-

TABLE 1.3
Sex Differences in Sexual Behavior and Attitudes

Measure	Mean d Values	Number of Studies
Attitude toward casual intercourse	0.81	10
Attitude toward intercourse in a committed relationship	0.49	10
Attitude toward intercourse in an engaged couple	0.43	5
Sexual permissiveness	0.57	39
Anxiety, fear, or guilt about sex	−0.35	11
Incidence of intercourse	0.33	135
Intercourse at earlier age	0.38	?
Number of sexual partners	0.25	12
Frequency of intercourse	0.31	11
Incidence of masturbation	0.96	26
Incidence of homosexuality	0.33	19

Note. *Positive* d *values occur when men score higher than women, and negative values occur when women score higher than men. From "Gender Differences in Sexuality," by M.B. Oliver and J.S. Hyde, 1993,* Psychological Bulletin, 114, *p. 43. Copyright 1993 by American Psychological Association. Adapted with permission.*

ally permissive attitudes than women do ($d = 0.57$). This implies that 71% of men regard casual intercourse more positively than the average woman does. Men report masturbating much more than women do ($d = 0.96$). A difference of this magnitude implies that 83% of men masturbate more than the average woman does.

Oliver and Hyde (1993) also reported a number of smaller sex differences. Men hold more positive attitudes than women do toward engaging in sexual intercourse in the context of committed relationships ($d = 0.49$) and in the context of marital engagements ($d = 0.43$). Women report more fear and guilt about sex than men do ($d = 0.35$). Men report engaging in sexual intercourse more than women do ($d = 0.33$), engaging in sexual intercourse at an earlier age than women do ($d = 0.38$), and having sex with a greater number of sexual partners than women do ($d = 0.25$). Finally, men report a higher incidence of homosexual behavior than women do ($d = 0.33$). In short, men on average report engaging in sex somewhat more than women do, and they also seem to *want* to engage in sex more than women do.

One striking aspect of sexuality is not addressed by Oliver and Hyde's (1993) meta-analysis—namely, the degree to which people are sexually attracted to men or to women. As far as I know, there have been no meta-analyses on this topic. I conducted a study in which I asked 285 college men and 429 college women to rate on 7-point scales how sexually attracted they were to men and to women (Lippa, 2000). Not surprisingly, men reported on average being much more sexually

Do men and women have different attitudes toward sex?

attracted to women than women were ($d = 3.52$), and women reported on average being much more sexually attracted to men than men were ($d = 3.99$).

Differences of this magnitude imply that almost all men are more sexually attracted to women than the average woman is, and that almost all women are more sexually attracted to men than the average man is. The d statistic may be misleading in this case, however, because "sexual attraction to men" and "sexual attraction to women" are not continuous variables in the same sense that, say, smiling or aggression are. Most men are sexually attracted to women and are not sexually attracted to men. However, there is a minority of men—gay and bisexual men—who *are* sexually attracted to men. Similarly, there is a minority of women—lesbians and bisexual women—who are sexually attracted to women. Nonetheless, the d statistics illustrate the basic point, that sexual attraction to men and sexual attraction to women show huge sex differences, on average.

Psychologist Roy Baumeister (2000) recently compiled evidence showing that women and men may show another fundamental difference in sexuality: women's sexuality seems to be more flexible, variable, and responsive to social norms, whereas men's sexuality seems more fixed, urgent, and unresponsive to social norms and settings. One piece of evidence in support of this view is that individual women report more variability over the course of their lives, both in sexual activity levels and in sexual orientation, than do individual men. In a sense, Baumeister argues that women's sexuality may by molded relatively more by nurture and men's sexuality more by nature.

Do men and women look for the same characteristics in a mate? Alan Feingold (1992) conducted a meta-analysis on this question. He found that women rated social class and ambitiousness to be more important in a mate than men did ($d = 0.69$ and 0.67, respectively). This implies that about 75% of women rate class and ambitiousness to be more important in a mate than the average man does. Women also rated the traits of character and intelligence to be more important in a mate than men did, but these differences were more modest ($d = 0.35$ and 0.30, respectively). There were still smaller sex differences in how important humor and personality were rated to be in a mate ($d = 0.14$ and 0.08, respectively, with women rating these more important than men).

Are there some traits that men rate to be more important in a mate than women do? Physical attractiveness is one (Feingold, 1990). In questionnaire studies, men rate a mate's physical attractiveness to be more important than women do ($d = 0.54$). And in studies that analyze the content of personal ads, men list attractiveness as a characteristic they are seeking in a romantic partner more than women do ($d = 0.47$). A d value of about 0.5 implies that 69% of men consider a mate's physical attractiveness to be more important than the average woman does. Men's greater preference for physical attractiveness in a mate proves to be quite consistent across many different cultures (Buss & Schmitt, 1993).

Another trait more preferred in a mate by men than by women is youth. There is a strong norm in most cultures that, when there is an age difference in a marriage or couple relationship, the man should be older than the woman. Across cultures, as men age, they increasingly prefer women who are younger and younger, whereas as women age, they seem to consistently prefer mates who are about their own age (Kenrick & Keefe, 1992).

Are There Sex Differences in Occupational Preferences and Interests?

Despite the fact that many studies have investigated sex difference in occupational preferences, no comprehensive meta-analysis has been conducted on this topic (see Ashmore, 1990). To remedy this, I conducted a meta-analysis of six studies that collected occupational preference data from more than 14,000 participants (Lippa, 2001).

According to vocational psychologist John Holland (1992), there are six main kinds of occupations: realistic, investigative, artistic, social, enterprising, and conventional (1992, pp. 19–23). Realistic occupations (e.g., mechanic, carpenter, plumber, and farmer) involve work with machines, tools, equipment, or farm animals. Investigative occupations (e.g., physicist, biologist, chemist) entail investigating physical, biological, behavioral, or cultural phenomena. Artistic occupations (e.g., painter, actor/actress, writer) involve manipulating physical, verbal, or human materials to create artistic products. Social occupations (e.g., minister/rabbi/priest, teacher, counselor) require a person to train, develop, counsel, manage, teach, or direct other people. Enterprising occupations (e.g., salesperson, politician, stockbroker) involve manipulating other people to achieve organizational goals or to make money. Finally, conventional occupations (e.g., accountant, file clerk, or bookkeeper) require people to operate business machines, process data, or keep records.

Do men and women differ in their preferences for these six types of occupations? The results of my meta-analysis showed that men prefer realistic occupations much more than women do ($d = 1.06$). This difference implies that 86% of men prefer realistic occupations more than the average woman does. In contrast, women prefer social and artistic occupations more than men do ($d = 0.62$ and 0.63, respectively). Differences of this size imply that about 73% of women are more interested in social and artistic occupations than the average man is. Men are a bit more interested than women in investigative occupations ($d = 0.32$), and women are a bit more interested than men in enterprising occupations ($d = 0.27$). Men and women do not differ much in their preferences for conventional occupations ($d = 0.06$).

Are There Sex Differences in Cognitive Abilities?

Most psychologists agree that there are no meaningful sex differences in general intelligence (Halpern, 1992, 1997, 2000; Jensen, 1998). However, sex differences are sometimes found for specific kinds of mental abilities. On average, men perform somewhat better than women on tests of math ability ($d = 0.43$, based on reanalyses of data from Hyde, 1981, by Becker & Hedges, 1984, and Rosenthal and Rubin, 1982). In contrast, women perform somewhat better than men do on tests of verbal ability: $d = 0.11$ according to Hyde and Linn's (1988) estimate, and $d = 0.24$ according to Hyde's (1981) estimate. Thus 67% of men perform better than the average woman does on math tests, and 54% of women perform better than the average man on verbal tests (using Hyde & Linn's smaller estimate).

Although the female advantage in general verbal ability appears to be small, there are some specific verbal tasks—such as spelling and verbal fluency—in which women show a more substantial advantage over men (see Halpern, 1992, 1997, 2000, for reviews). Verbal fluency refers to one's ability to quickly generate words that possess a certain meaning or feature. For example, in two minutes, try to think of as many words as you can that mean the same thing as *hard.* Another example of verbal fluency is quickly generating words with a certain sound or spelling feature. For example, in two minutes, try to think of as many words as you can that begin with the letter, *K.*

On average, men score higher than women on many kinds of visual-spatial tests ($d = 0.45$; Linn & Petersen, 1986; see also Voyer, Voyer, & Bryden, 1995), and this difference is particularly strong for tests of mental rotation ($d = 0.73$ in Linn & Petersen; $d = 0.56$ for all ages and 0.66 for participants over 18 in Voyer et al.). A d value of 0.73 implies that 77% of men score higher on mental rotation tests than the average woman does. Mental rotation tests assess how well a person can mentally turn around sketched three-dimensional objects to determine if they are the same as the same object presented in a different orientation. Men also do better than women on water-level tests, which ask participants to estimate the surface created by water in containers that are turned to various orientations ($d = 0.42$ in Voyer et al.). However, women outperform men on tests of spatial location memory, which ask participants to remember, for example, where various objects are located throughout a room after brief observation (Eals & Silverman, 1994).

Are There Sex Differences in Physical Abilities?

Several meta-analyses have summarized sex differences in physical abilities (Eaton & Enns, 1986; Thomas & French, 1985). On average, men show higher activity levels than women do ($d = 0.49$). However, women show better fine eye-hand coordination than men do ($d = 0.21$), and their joints and limbs are more flexible than men's ($d = 0.29$). Men can throw objects faster, farther, and more accurately than women can ($d = 2.18, 1.98$, and 0.96, respectively). The sex difference in throw velocity indicates that some 99% of men can throw faster than the average woman can, and the difference for throw distance indicates that about 98% of men can throw farther than the average woman can. Seventy-seven percent of men can throw objects more accurately than the average women can. On average, men's grip strength exceeds that of women ($d = 0.66$). Men also perform better than women on tests of sit-ups, short run speeds, and long jumps ($d = 0.64, 0.63$, and 0.54, respectively). A d value of around 0.6 implies that 73% of men perform better than the average woman does. Many of these findings reflect the fact that men have greater upper-body strength than women do.

BEYOND META-ANALYSES: OTHER POSSIBLE SEX DIFFERENCES

Although meta-analyses have helped synthesize huge research literatures on sex differences, there are many important sex differences that have not been summarized by meta-analyses. Certain kinds of sex differences (for example, sex differences in mental disorders) cannot be easily tallied with the d statistic, because the behaviors under study are not continuous. For example, people are either clinically depressed or they are not. Although sex differences in the incidence of depression may be real, such differences are better captured by sex ratios (i.e., the ratio of men to women who suffer from depression) than by d statistics. In this final section, we consider some additional ways in which males and females may differ. We address the following questions: Are there sex differences in mental illness? Do men and women experience emotions somewhat differently? Are the self-concepts of men and women organized differently? Do boys and girls differ in their friendship patterns and styles of play?

Sex Difference in Mental and Behavioral Disorders

Table 1.4 summarizes evidence on sex differences in various kinds of behavior problems and mental disorders, in both children and adults (see Hartung & Widiger, 1998). The information comes from the Diagnostic and Statistical Manual of Mental Disorders, published by the American Psychiatric Association (the most recent version is DSM-IV, published in 1994).

As Table 1.4 shows, boys are much more likely than girls to suffer from mental retardation, reading disorders, stuttering, autism, attention deficit disorder, and Tourette's syndrome (a neurological condition characterized by compulsive movements and, sometimes, abusive verbal exclamations). In adolescence and adulthood, males are more likely than females to abuse various substances, including alcohol, amphetamines, marijuana, hallucinogens, and opioids. Among adult mental disorders that show a tilt in favor of men are many sexual disorders, gender identity disorders, and antisocial, compulsive, schizoid, and narcissistic personality disorders.[2] Disorders that show a tilt in favor of women are major and minor depressions, phobias, generalized anxiety disorders, conversion disorders, dissociative disorder (multiple personalities), eating disorders, and borderline and histrionic per sonality disorders.[3]

There is considerable controversy surrounding the topic of sex differences in mental disorders. Some researchers argue that observed differences may reflect biases in diagnostic practices and criteria more than real sex differences. Others argue that the differences are real. Despite the possibility of bias, it is likely that many of the sex differences

TABLE 1.4
Sex Ratios for Selected Behavior and Mental Disorders

Disorder	Sex Ratio (Male-to-Female)
Childhood Disorders	
Mental retardation	1.5 to 1
Reading disorders	1.5–4 to 1
Stuttering	3 to 1
Autism	4–5 to 1
Attention deficit disorder	4–9 to 1
Tourette's syndrome	1.5–3 to 1
Substance-Related Disorders	
Alcohol, amphetamines, marijuana	Male rate greater than female
Hallucinogens	3 to 1
Nicotine (smoking)	Male rate greater than female
Opioids (e.g, heroin)	3–4 to 1
Mood, Anxiety, and Adjustment Disorders	
Major depression	1 to 2
Dysthymia (minor depression)	1 to 2–3
Manic depressive disorder	1 to 2
Panic disorders	1 to 2–3
Conversion disorders	1 to 2–10
Dissociative identity disorder (multiple personality disorder)	1 to 3–9
Anorexia nervosa	1 to greater than 9
Bulimia	1 to greater than 9
Nightmare disorder	1 to 2–4
Sexual and Gender Identity Disorders	
Sexual masochism	20 to 1
Gender identity disorders	2–3 to 1
Fetishism	Male greater than female
Pedophilia	Male greater than female
Personality Disorders	
Schizotypal personality disorder	Male greater than female
Antisocial personality disorder	Male greater than female
Borderline personality disorder	1 to 3
Histrionic personality disorder	Female greater than male
Narcissistic personality disorder	1–3 to 1
Compulsive personality disorder	2 to 1

Note. *Adapted from "Gender Differences in the Diagnosis of Mental Disorders: Conclusions and Controversies of the DSM-IV," by C.M. Hartung and T.A. Widiger, 1998,* Psychological Bulletin, 123, *pp. 261–262. Copyright 1998 by American Psychological Association. Adapted with permission.*

reported in Table 1.4 (such as sex differences in childhood autism, childhood speech and reading disorders, depression, and antisocial personality disorders) are real and large.

Sex Differences in Emotional Experience

Meta-analyses have shown that women are slightly more self-disclosing than men are ($d = 0.18$; Dindia & Allen, 1992). That is, women share more personal information about their lives, thoughts, and feelings than men do. However, these differences depend in part on who does the disclosing and who is the target of disclosure. For example, most people (both men and women) are more self-disclosing with women than with men. Self-disclosure also depends on the kinds of emotions expressed. Women express negative feelings—such as sadness and depression—more than men do (Zeman & Garner, 1996), whereas men express anger more than women do (Clark & Reiss, 1988).

Not only do men and women express emotions somewhat differently, they also seem to experience them somewhat differently. James Pennebaker (Pennebaker & Watson, 1988; Roberts & Pennebaker, 1995) found that men infer their emotions more from internal physiological cues (e.g., heart rate and blood pressure), whereas women infer their emotions more from the social setting and context (e.g., deciding you are happy because you are in an audience with laughing people). Men prove to be more accurate than women are in estimating internal physiological cues such as heart rate, and this may be one reason why they use such cues more to infer their emotions.

A related finding is that men tend to "internalize" their emotions more than women do. Men may not show their emotions facially as much as women do; however, they may "churn" more internally. In contrast, women "externalize" their emotions more than men do. They show their emotions in facial and verbal expressions, and perhaps as a result, they don't have such strong physiological arousal as men do (Buck, Savin, Miller, & Caul, 1972).

University of California psychologist Shelley Taylor and her colleagues (2000) recently compiled evidence showing that when stressed, men are more likely to show a "fight or flight" response, whereas women are more likely to show a "tend-and-befriend" response. Men are more likely to respond to threatening situations with aggression, whereas women are more likely to tend to others (e.g., their friends and children) and seek social support.

Sex Differences in the Self-Concept

Psychologists Susan Cross and Laura Madson (1997) proposed that the self-concepts of men and women are organized somewhat differently. Men have a more independent view of themselves. They view themselves more in terms of their individual achievements, traits, values, and abilities—the ways in which they are unique and separate from other people. In contrast, women have a more interdependent and connected sense of self. They view themselves more in terms of their relations with others and in terms of social roles and obligations.

In recent years, this distinction between the "independent" versus the "interconnected" self has been studied by cross-cultural psychologists, who argue that the independent view of self is more common among people who live in individualistic countries like the United States (see Markus & Kitayama, 1991). People from such cultures often view themselves in terms of their autonomous principles, traits, values, and abilities. For example, an American might describe herself as "honest, intelligent, interested in cultural activities and the arts, and good at statistics." In contrast, the interconnected view of self is more common in traditional, collectivist cultures, which are frequently found in Asia, Africa, and Latin America. People from collectivist cultures view themselves more in terms of their social roles and relations to others. A traditional Japanese woman might describe herself as a "wife, mother, a good daughter to her aging parents, and a loyal employee." Cross and Madson (1997) argue that men have self-concepts that are more typical of people from individualistic cultures, whereas women have self-concepts that are more typical of people from collectivist cultures.

Robert Josephs, Hazel Markus, and Romin Tafarodi (1992) reported several experiments that also are consistent with Cross and Madson's (1997) hypotheses. In these studies, college men's self-esteem proved to be more strongly linked to their accomplishments and women's to their personal relationships. Furthermore, men's self-esteem was more threatened when they were challenged about their achievements and abilities, whereas women's self-esteem was more threatened when they were challenged about their nurturance and responsiveness to others.

Elaborating on this difference, Roy Baumeister and Kristin Sommer (1997) have argued that both women and men view themselves in relation to other people. However, women conceive of themselves more in terms of warm, one-on-one, intimate relations (e.g., daughter, spouse, best friend), whereas men conceive of themselves more in terms of social groups and hierarchical relationships (boss, member of sports team, American). Baumeister and Sommer (1997) put the matter succinctly: "female sociality is dyadic, whereas male sociality is tribal" (p. 39). Gabriel and Gardner (1999) conducted a number of studies that supported this proposed difference in men and women's conceptions of relatedness.

Sex Differences in Children's Friendship Patterns

Most of this chapter has focused on sex differences in adults' behaviors. However, to paraphrase the words of poet William Wordsworth, if the boy is the father of the man and the girl is the mother of the woman, then it is important to consider children's behaviors as well. Much recent research has documented sex differences in children's play patterns and social interaction (see Maccoby, 1998; see also Chapter 5 of this book). For example, male toddlers get into trouble more and have more difficulty controlling their impulses than female toddlers do. Older boys play in groups more than girls do, and boys' groups are independent of adult supervision more than girls' groups are. Girls play in same-sex dyads (one-on-one pairs) more than boys do.

Boys' group-oriented social lives center on dominance, hierarchy, and competition more than girls' one-on-one social lives. (Think of boys' stickball games and cowboy-and-Indian fights and girls' playing house.) Boys test one another's strength and toughness more than girls do. They also test and break adults' rules more than girls do. Boys tend to have somewhat higher activity levels than girls, and they engage in more rough-and-tumble play, which sometimes degenerates into physical fighting. In contrast, girls' aggression often takes more verbal forms than boys' aggression does. Girls sully one another's reputations when they want to be hostile; boys confront, shove, and punch. Boys get what they want more through dominance, challenge, and physical combat, girls more through negotiation and verbal influence.

Boys' fantasy lives center more around enacting heroic figures (superheroes, sports figures, cops, and warriors), whereas girls' fantasy lives center more around enacting reciprocal social roles (mother-child, teacher-student, doctor-patient), often with other girls (see Maccoby, 1998, for a review). On average, boys and girls play with different kinds of toys. Boys play more with mechanical toys (trucks, cars, erector sets), and girls play more with dolls and domestic toys (tea sets, dollhouses). Boys enjoy toys that allow them to role-play aggression (e.g., guns, swords, tanks) more than girls do. Perhaps all these childhood sex differences set the stage for the different interaction and communication styles of adult men and women, with men more verbally assertive and competitive and women more verbally collaborative and accommodating (see Tannen, 1990).

All the childhood sex differences just cataloged likely contribute to probably the most dramatic and consequential of all sex difference observed in children—sex segregation of friendships and playmates. Starting at around age 3, children interact more with members of their own sex than with children of the other sex, and as childhood progresses, children play and socialize more exclusively with members of their own sex (Maccoby, 1998). Sex segregation is a very strong phenomenon. Indeed, if plotted in the form of frequency distributions, boys' and girls' amounts of interaction with boys (or with girls) would form two largely nonoverlapping distributions. Boys "hang out" mostly with other boys, typically in groups, and girls hang out mostly with other girls, often in pairs or in small friendship clusters. Childhood sex segregation does not dwindle until puberty approaches and children begin to experience the romantic and sexual attractions that will entice most of them back into frequent interactions with the opposite sex.

SUMMARY

The study of sex differences is contentious and controversial. Some scholars exaggerate sex differences, others minimize them. The truth probably lies somewhere in between. Meta-analytic reviews, which quantitatively summarize sex differences using the d statistic, have documented some fairly large sex differences in specific domains. For example, men and women differ substantially in the personality trait of tender-mindedness, on many nonverbal behaviors, in some kinds of occupational preferences, in some kinds of sexual behaviors and attitudes, in some kinds of mate preferences, and in at least one cognitive ability (mental rotation). Sex differences in many social behaviors (aggression, helping, conformity, persuasion, group behavior) are small to moderate, and they often vary depending on situational factors. For many personality traits (e.g., conscientiousness, openness to experience, self-esteem), cognitive abilities (e.g., general intelligence, general verbal ability), and social behaviors (e.g., self-disclosure, negotiation outcomes) sex differences are small to negligible.

The incidence of some mental disorders (e.g., depression, antisocial personality disorder) and behavior problems (e.g., reading and speech disorders) show substantial sex differences. Men and women may express and experience emotions somewhat differently, with men more sensitive to internal cues and women more sensitive to external social cues. In response to stress, men may be more likely to show a "fight or flight" response and women a "tend and befriend" response. Men's self-concepts may be organized more in terms of the independent characteristics emphasized by individualistic cultures, and women's self-concepts may be organized more in terms of the interdependent characteristics emphasized by collectivist cultures. Women's relatedness to others is conceived more in terms of personal, one-on-one relationships, and men's relatedness is conceived more in terms of social groups and social hierarchy.

Boys and girls show a number of robust behavioral differences. Boys' social lives are more hierarchical and group-centered, and boys engage in more competitive, aggressive, and rough-and-tumble play. Girls' social lives are more one-on-one, and girls engage in more reciprocal, verbal, and negotiated kinds of play. Boys fantasize more about heroic individual achievements, and girls fantasize more about family and reciprocal social roles. All these childhood sex differences contribute to the sex segregation commonly observed in children's friendship and playgroups. This segregation begins at around age three, grows stronger through middle childhood, and does not wane until opposite-sex romantic and sexual attractions emerge in preadolescence.

ENDNOTES

1. Some researchers have argued that the word *sex* should be used to refer to the biological status of being male or female, whereas the word *gender* should be used to refer to all the socially defined, learned, constructed accoutrements of sex, such as hairstyle, dress, nonverbal mannerisms, and interests (Crawford & Unger, 2000; Unger, 1979). However, it is not at all clear to what degree differences between males and females are due to biological factors versus learned and cultural factors. Furthermore, indiscriminate use of *gender* tends to obscure the distinction between two different topics: (a) differences between males and females, and (b) individual differences in "maleness" and "femaleness" that occur within each sex.

   Accordingly, in this chapter, I use the term *sex differences,* for the goal here is to contrast two biological groups: males and females. My use of *sex differences* implies nothing about the causes of these differences. In the next chapter, I will use the terms *masculinity* and *femininity* to refer to individual differences within each sex in how male-typical or female-typical individuals are.

2. *Personality disorders* refers to long-term patterns of abnormal behavior that are deeply rooted in the individual's personality. People who suffer from antisocial personality disorders are sometimes also referred to as sociopaths or psychopaths. They are deceitful, manipulative, and sometimes violent. Because

they lack a conscience, they experience no remorse over despicable deeds. Those suffering from compulsive personality disorders engage in rigid, ritualized, and overcontrolled behaviors, whereas people with schizoid disorders are reclusive, antisocial, and show what most consider strange and eccentric behaviors. People with narcissistic disorders are excessively self-centered and self-aggrandizing.

3. *Conversion disorders* refers to anxiety-based syndromes in which the patient shows "hysterical" bodily symptoms, such as paralysis, blindness, and eating disorders, which are presumed to be of psychological origin. The *borderline personality disorder* is characterized by identity confusion, self-destructive behavior, compulsive sexual behavior, and the tendency to create scenes in interpersonal life and to have shallow relations with others. The *histrionic personality disorder*, a cousin to the borderline disorder, is characterized by tendencies to overdramatize one's life and problems.

CHAPTER

2

Masculinity and Femininity: Gender Within Gender

I felt I had with an impious and secret finger traced a first wrinkle upon [my mother's] soul and made the first white hair shew upon her head. This thought redoubled my sobs, and then I saw that Mamma, who had never allowed herself to go to any length of tenderness with me, was suddenly overcome by my tears and had to struggle to keep back her own. Then, as she saw that I had noticed this, she said to me, with a smile: "Why, my little buttercup, my little canary-boy, he's going to make Mamma as silly as himself if this goes on. . . ."

—*Remembrance of Things Past*
Marcel Proust

One of the most revered novelists of the 20th century, Marcel Proust possessed great literary, artistic, and musical sensibility. He was introspective, emotionally sensitive, physically delicate, foppish, and averse to anything rough-and-tumble. Witty, verbal, and drawn to the mannered life of aristocratic salons, he was inordinately attached to his mother and sexually attracted to men. In short, it seems reasonable to describe Proust as "feminine."

Proust provides a concrete example of what common sense tells us—that some men are more masculine and some more feminine than others. But what do the words *masculine* and *feminine* mean? Proust's traits suggest some possibilities. Femininity (the opposite of masculinity?) consists of emotional sensitivity, artistic sensibility, a focus on manners, a tendency to timidity and nonaggressiveness, a nurturant, attached orientation to others, and sexual attraction to men. Admittedly, all these "feminine" characteristics are stereotypic. They reflect an essentialist view of femininity—that there are core qualities to femininity, a Platonic essence if you will, that exist despite cultural and historical variations.

To research psychologists, the concepts of masculinity and femininity have referred to individual differences (that is, variations) in people's gender-related traits and behaviors—*variations that exist within each sex*. Masculinity and femininity refer to *those aspects of gender that vary among men and among women*. Chapter 1 considered the question, how much do men and women differ? We turn now to the second key question related to gender: How do men vary in their masculinity, and how do women in their femininity?

Research on masculinity and femininity has a long, complex, and controversial history. This may be due in part to the questions addressed. Do masculinity and femininity really exist, and if so, how are they best defined and measured? What causes people to vary on masculinity and femininity—biological factors, parental rearing, or social and cultural learning? Are masculinity and femininity essential traits of the individual—fixed "things" that exist inside people? Or are they social constructions—arbitrary concepts foisted on us by sexist societies? A central question for us is, what molds and determines a person's degree of masculinity and femininity, nature or nurture?

Because the roles of men and women have been the subject of passionate debate in recent years, it's no wonder that research on masculinity and femininity has become embroiled in the debate. If masculinity and femininity are real traits—perhaps even genetically determined to a significant extent—then gender would seem to be partly "wired into us." On the other hand, if masculinity and femininity are social constructions—learned patterns of behavior that are culturally and historically variable—then existing gender roles may be malleable and subject to liberating alternatives.

What in fact *does* science tell us about masculinity and femininity? To understand research on masculinity and femininity, it helps to begin at the beginning—in Palo Alto, California, in the 1920s.

THE SEARCH COMMENCES: TERMAN AND MILES'S EARLY WORK AT STANFORD

In 1936, Lewis Terman and Catherine Cox Miles began the modern study of masculinity and femininity with the publication of a classic book, *Sex and Personality*. In their book, Terman and Miles presented both a method for measuring masculinity-femininity and a decade's worth of research investigating what masculinity-femininity was related to.

The Anology Between Masculinity-Femininity and Intelligence

Terman, a Stanford University psychologist, was famous for developing the Stanford-Binet intelligence test, which remains to this day (in revised form) a respected and much used test. Catherine Cox Miles, who had worked with Terman as a graduate student, was well known for her PhD dissertation estimating the IQs of eminent historical figures based on biographical information (Cox, 1926). In the late 1920s, after working for a time as a clinical psychologist in Cincinnati, Miles returned to Stanford to assist Terman with his burgeoning research on masculinity-femininity, which Terman described as "about the most interesting thing I have ever tackled" (Lewin, 1984a, p. 161).

During the 1920s Terman started a classic study of "gifted children," and it was this study that triggered his interest in the topic of masculinity and femininity. In his gifted children study, Terman identified 856 boys and 672 girls with high IQs to trace their social and intellectual development over time (Terman & Oden, 1947). Terman observed that, despite their shared high intelligence, the gifted boys displayed quite different patterns of interests from the gifted girls. Terman reasoned that such gender differences might serve as a means to measure variations in psychological masculinity and femininity *within each sex*.

Terman proposed that, like intelligence, masculinity-femininity was a trait that could be measured through an appropriately designed test. Just as IQ tests provided an "objective" means to assess intelligence, so Terman hoped that his masculinity-femininity test might "enable the clinician or other investigator to obtain a more exact and meaningful, as well as a more objective, rating of those aspects of personality in which the sexes tend to differ" (Terman & Miles, 1936, p. 6). The items in early IQ tests were selected based on age-related changes in children's performance. IQ researchers believed that children's intelligence increased with age and that the relation between age and performance provided a means to assess the "difficulty" of IQ test items. For example, an IQ question answered correctly by 50% of 10-year-olds and by 20% of 8-year-olds was viewed as more difficult than an item answered correctly by 80% of 10-year-olds and 50% of 8-year-olds.

What was the corresponding way to determine whether an item measured a person's masculinity-femininity? (Think of an item here as a question on a self-report questionnaire—e.g., "True or false: I like to watch football games.") Terman and Miles (1936) proposed that a given question could serve as a measure of masculinity-femininity if large groups of men and women (or boys and girls) answered the question differently on average. If many more men than women, for example, answered "true" to the question, "I like to watch football games," then Terman and Miles would consider this item to measure masculinity-femininity, with a "true" response indicating masculinity and a "false" response indicating femininity. In contrast, if about equal numbers of men and women answered "true" to a question (e.g., "I like to go to movies"), then they would consider that question to be unrelated to masculinity-femininity.

It is a well-demonstrated statistical principle in psychological testing that no single test item can provide a reliable measure of the thing we are trying to measure. To obtain a reliable (that is, a stable and repeatable) test score, researchers must use many test items. To obtain a reliable measure of masculinity-femininity, Terman and Miles (1936) created a huge (at least by modern standards) 456-item questionnaire, which they called the Attitude Interest Analysis Survey. The reason for their bland and uninformative title is that Terman and Miles did not want people who completed the test to realize that it was actually measuring their masculinity-femininity.

Terman and Miles's Attitude Interest Analysis Survey was quite varied, including subscales that measured general knowledge, emotions, occupational interests, reading preferences, personality traits, word and picture associations, and attitudes. (Table 2.1 lists some actual items; see if you can guess which responses are "masculine" and which are "feminine.") Some of Terman and Miles's masculinity-femininity subscales proved to be more reliable than others. In particular, the subtests on knowledge, emotions, occupational preferences, and interests had the highest reliabilities.

Terman and Miles (1936) acknowledged that their masculinity-femininity test was not based on any theory of masculinity or femininity. They also conceded that their test might be culturally limited, based as it was on gender differences "in the present historical period of the Occidental culture of our own country" (p. 6). Their goal, as they saw it, was to assess individuals' levels of masculinity-femininity accurately and reliably and to investigate whether these levels were related to other interesting physical and psychological characteristics, such as people's educational accomplishments, intelligence, personality traits, body types, and sexual orientation.

Terman and Miles (1936) remained open-minded about why men and women varied on masculinity-femininity: "[The] M-F test rests upon no assumption with reference to the causes operative in determining an individual's score. These may be either physiological and biochemical, or psychological and cultural; or they may be the combined result of both types of influence" (p. 6). Thus Terman and Miles acknowledged the possibility that individual differences in masculinity-femininity might be a function of both nature and nurture.

TABLE 2.1   Items from Terman and Mile's Masculinity-Femininity Test

Look at the word in capital letters, then look at each of the four words that follow it. Draw a line under the word that seems to you to go best or most naturally with the word in capitals.

TRAIN	engine +	gown −	travel −	whistle −
JACK	cards −	money +	tool +	toy −
JEALOUS	angry −	green −	lover +	women +
GARDEN	flower −	fruit +	vegetable +	weeds +

In each of the following sentences, draw a line under the word that makes the sentence true.

Marigold is a kind of:	fabric +	flower −	grain −	tone +
Things that are cooked in grease are:	boiled +	broiled +	fried −	roasted +
A loom is used for:	cooking +	embroidering +	sewing +	weaving −
The chief cause of tides is the attraction of the:	moon +	planets −	sun 0	stars 0

*Below is a list of acts of various **degrees of wickedness or badness**. After each thing mentioned, draw a circle around 3, 2, 1, or 0 to show how wicked or bad **you** think it is. 3 means "EXTREMELY WICKED"; 2 means "SOMEWHAT BAD"; 1 means "DECIDEDLY BAD", 0 means "NOT REALLY BAD."*

Picking flowers in a public park	3	2	1	0	(0 − + +)
Stealing a ride on a truck	3	2	1	0	(− − + +)
Telling a lie to avoid punishment	3	2	1	0	(− + + +)
Whispering in school	3	2	1	0	(+ 0 − 0)
Boys teasing girls	3	2	1	0	(− − + +)

*For each occupation below, ask yourself: Would I like that work or not? If you would **like** it, draw a circle around L. If you would **dislike** it, draw a circle around D. If you would **neither like nor dislike** it, draw a circle around N. In deciding on your answer, **think only of the kind of work**. Don't consider the pay. Imagine you have the ability to do the work, that you are the right age for it, and that it is equally open to men and women.*

Architect	L	N	D	(+ − −)
Chef or cook	L	N	D	(− 0 +)
Auto racer	L	N	D	(+ − +)
Librarian	L	N	D	(− + +)
Building contractor	L	N	D	(+ − 0)

Answer each question as truthfully as you can by drawing a line under YES or NO.

Are you extremely careful about your manner of dress?	YES −	NO +
Have you ever kept a diary?	YES −	NO +
Do you ever dream of robbers?	YES +	NO −
Were you ever expelled from school, or nearly expelled?	YES +	NO −
Can you stand as much pain as others can?	YES +	NO −

Note. According to Terman and Mile's scoring system, a response followed or indicated by a + sign count 1 point toward masculinity, a response followed by a − sign count 1 point toward femininity, and those followed by 0 are neutral. Adapted from Sex and Personality: Studies in Masculinity and Femininity (p. 482–554), by L.M. Terman and C.C. Miles, New York: McGraw-Hill. Copyright 1936. Reprinted with permission.

The Bipolar Assumption

Terman and Miles's (1936) test made an important assumption: Masculinity and femininity are opposites. This necessarily follows from the way they constructed and scored their test. If you answered a question the way women tend to, you necessarily were not answering the question the way men tend to, and vice versa. Raw scores on Terman and Miles's test ranged from negative scores (feminine) to positive scores (masculine). The scoring system therefore assumed a single dimension, ranging from feminine to masculine. The more masculine you were, the less feminine your were; and vice versa. Stated a bit more formally, Terman and Miles proposed a unidimensional (i.e., single dimension) bipolar (either-or) approach to masculinity and femininity. To paraphrase Rudyard Kipling, masculine is masculine, and feminine is feminine, and "never the twain shall meet." Notice that the hyphenated term *masculinity-femininity* embodies the bipolar assumption in its very structure.

Terman and Miles's notion of masculinity-femininity provided the conceptual framework for many subsequent researchers. One noteworthy example was Edward Strong—a colleague of Terman's at Stanford University—who developed one of the first occupational interest tests, the Strong Vocational Interest Blank (which, in updated forms, is still used today; Campbell, 1971; Strong, 1936, 1943). People taking this test are asked to rate how much they like or dislike various occupations and hobbies (e.g., "farming," "sewing") and how interested they are in taking various school subjects (e.g., "geometry," "English"). Based on his research, Strong came to believe that masculinity-femininity constituted a major dimension underlying occupational preferences. Accordingly, he developed a masculinity-femininity (M-F) scale for his test.

What determined if an occupational preference item was placed on Strong's M-F scale? Like Terman and Miles (1936), Strong (1936, 1943) selected items for his M-F scale that showed large and statistically significant (i.e., not due to chance) gender differences. If many more men than women expressed an interest in being farmers and race car drivers, for example, then these items would be placed on the M-F scale, keyed in the masculine direction. Conversely, if many more women than men expressed an interest in being elementary school teachers and librarians, then these items would be placed on the M-F scale, keyed in the feminine direction. When Strong gave his M-F scale and the Terman and Miles M-F test to the same group of people, he found only a weak correlation between people's scores on the two tests. This early piece of evidence hinted that various M-F scales were not always measuring the same things.

The 1940s and 1950s witnessed the development of a number of well-known omnibus (that is, broad, multitrait) personality inventories, including the Guilford-Zimmerman Temperament Inventory (Guilford & Zimmerman, 1956), the California Psychological Inventory (Gough, 1957), and the Minnesota Multiphasic Personality Inventory (Hathaway and McKinley, 1951). Many of these inventories took the Terman and Miles approach to masculinity-femininity. That is, they assumed that gender differences in response could be used to select and validate items intended to assess masculinity-femininity.

Because various personality inventories included somewhat different questions, their portraits of masculinity-femininity varied accordingly. The Guilford-Zimmerman (1956) scale of masculinity (which, by the bipolar assumption, is the opposite of femininity) assessed inhibited emotional expression, male-typical vocational interests, and a cluster of "masculine" emotional traits (e.g., not being easily disgusted, fearlessness, and a lack of sympathy). The California Psychological Inventory (CPI; Gough, 1957) was developed to embody "folk concepts" of personality—that is, dimensions of personality that make sense to lay people. The CPI M-F scale—labeled the Fe (femininity) scale—assessed sensitivity, the ability to perceive the nuances of social interaction, acquiescence, compassion, niceness, female-typical work and interests, and lack of interest in politics and social issues. According to this conceptualization, the "feminine" individual is portrayed as nice but rather passive, unengaged, and dependent, whereas the "masculine" individual is somewhat disagreeable but active, engaged, and independent.

The Minnesota Multiphasic Personality Inventory (MMPI; Hathaway & McKinley, 1951) is perhaps the best known *clinical* personality inventory in use. Since its inception in the 1930s and 1940s, the MMPI has been used to diagnose mental illness. Indeed, many of the scales of the MMPI are labeled by the kind of mental illness they are meant to measure and predict (e.g., depression, paranoia, hypochondriasis). As a result, the developers of the MMPI approached the measurement of masculinity-femininity from the vantage point of psychopathology. In particular, they were interested in masculinity-femininity as a means of diagnosing gender identity disturbances and sexual "inversion" (i.e., the kind of homosexuality shown by men who act like women or by women who act like men).

Terman and Miles (1936) had also been interested in the relationship between masculinity-femininity and homosexuality. Several chapters of their book were devoted to this topic. In one study, they collected data from 134 gay men (many of whom were prison inmates), which indicated that gay men scored considerably higher in the feminine direction on their M-F test than did heterosexual men. Influenced by these findings, the developers of the original MMPI, Starke Hathaway and J. C. McKinley, made a rather unusual decision in developing their masculinity-femininity scale—which they named the MMPI Mf scale (Hathaway, 1956). Rather than initially choosing a set of items that distinguished men from women, they chose instead items that distinguished gay men from heterosexual men. The groups they used to test their first items were quite small—13 gay men contrasted with 54 "normal" heterosexual men (who were all soldiers). It is not surprising that a number of the items on the original MMPI Mf scale directly addressed sexual orientation, same-sex attraction, and "unusual" sexual behavior—for example, "I am very strongly attracted to members of my own sex" and "I have never indulged in any unusual sex practices."

Once Hathaway and McKinley (1951) identified their initial set of Mf items, they used Terman and Miles's (1936) strategy to further validate the items. That is, they demonstrated that their Mf items distinguished men from women, and they also gathered data to show that their scale distinguished "feminine" men identified by Terman and Miles's test from "normal" men. In other words, the MMPI Mf scale was in part validated against Terman and Miles's earlier test.

In addition to including items that asked explicitly about same-sex attraction, the original MMPI Mf scale contained items that assessed narcissism and hypersensitivity, stereotypic feminine and masculine interests, heterosexual "discomfort" and "passivity," and introspectiveness and social reticence (Greene, 1991). Research shows that the MMPI Mf scale distinguishes gay men from heterosexual men fairly well (Haslam, 1997). However, this is not terribly surprising, given that a number of items in the original MMPI Mf scale asked directly about same-sex attraction. The MMPI was revised and renormed (i.e., administered and calibrated against large contemporary samples of men and women) in the 1980s (Butcher, Dahlstrom, Graham, Tellegen, & Kaemmer, 1989). The revised MMPI Mf scale omits items that directly ask about same-sex attraction, but the other content remains much the same.

What Is Masculinity-Femininity Related To?

Most of the bipolar masculinity-femininity tests developed in the 1930s through 1950s showed acceptable levels of reliability. That is, they measured *something* consistently. But did they also show validity—that is, did they predict real-life behaviors and criteria in a way that made both theoretical and practical sense?

In their early research, Terman and Miles (1936) found that school children's M-F scores *did not* correlate much with their teachers' ratings of how masculine or feminine they were. Similarly, college students' M-F scores did not correlate much with their self-ratings of how masculine or feminine they believed themselves to be. These results were puzzling, for they seemed to raise questions about the validity of the M-F scale. Terman and Miles speculated that these results were due in part to the unreliability of lay people's ratings of their own and other people's masculinity-femininity. They proposed (perhaps self-servingly) that their carefully developed M-F test was considerably more reliable than lay judgments and therefore a sounder measure of people's "real" masculinity-femininity.

Terman and Miles (1936) investigated additional factors that were linked to masculinity-femininity. They found, for example, that masculinity-femininity was somewhat age-related, with individuals—particularly males—showing their highest levels of masculinity in their late teens and early twenties. Not surprisingly, masculinity-femininity was related to people's interests and academic pursuits. Masculine men tended to be more interested in science and mechanical things, and feminine men in cultural pursuits and the arts. Among high school and college-aged women, masculinity was found to be associated with broad interests, high levels of education, and "intellectuality." In other words, for women, masculinity was associated with intellectual and educational accomplishment, and if one wanted to place a value judgment on these findings, one might conclude that in this regard, masculinity is "good" for women.

Later research extended and replicated these early results, indicating that feminine boys and masculine girls tend to show higher levels of creativity, scholastic achievement, and giftedness than more sex-typed children do (Lippa, 1998a; Maccoby, 1966) Lubinski & Humphreys, 1990. (Sex-typed children are those whose traits and behaviors are stereotypic for their sex.) Thus, in terms of creativity and intellectual achievement, femininity can be considered good for boys and masculinity good for girls.

Terman and Miles (1936) observed a significant relationship between masculinity-femininity and sexual orientation. Many subsequent researchers have replicated this finding (see Lippa, 2000; Pillard, 1991): Gay men tend to be more feminine than heterosexual men on M-F scales, and lesbian women tend to be more masculine than hetereosexual women. Is this good or bad? In Terman and Miles's time, the psychological establishment—as well as society at large—tended to view homosexuality as a kind of mental illness. Thus Terman and Miles's findings were taken as evidence that femininity was bad for men and masculinity was bad for women, for they upped one's odds for "sexual deviance." (It is important to note that since the early 1970s, both the American Psychological Association and the American Psychiatric Association have declared that homosexuality is *not* a mental illness.)

Research on masculinity-femininity and sexual orientation points to an unstated, if implicit, value judgment that permeated early research on masculinity-femininity: It is good for people to score in "gender-appropriate" ways. If you are a man, it's good to be masculine; and if you are a woman, it's good to be feminine. This assumption reflected psychological dogma common throughout the middle part of the 20th century. Developmental psychologists of that period earnestly studied gender socialization and sex typing—the ways in which children learn "appropriate" gender roles and behaviors from their parents and from society (see Huston, 1983).

But you may recall one set of findings (Maccoby, 1966) that challenged this assumption—namely, the data that linked boys' femininity and girls' masculinity to creativity and scholastic achievement. In the 1950s and 1960s, other evidence raised additional questions about whether extreme masculinity is necessarily ideal for males or extreme femininity ideal for females. For example, some studies showed that femininity in women was often associated with anxiety, depression, low self-esteem, and meekness, and that masculinity in boys and men was associated with aggressiveness and "acting out." Eleanor Maccoby (1966), a respected Stanford University developmental psychologist, hypothesized that highly masculine boys might be overly impulsive, whereas highly feminine girls might by overcontrolled, meek, and unassertive. In other words, masculinity in boys and femininity in girls may not be highly desirable after all.

MASCULINITY AND FEMININITY AS SEPARATE DIMENSIONS

By the early 1970s, the concept of bipolar masculinity-femininity was beginning to show its age, and attitudes toward gender were changing dramatically. In the era of women's liberation, psychologists began to rethink what they meant by *masculinity* and *femininity*.

Cracks in Terman and Miles's Edifice

A 1973 article by Vassar psychologist Anne Constantinople marked a sea change in attitude toward the M-F tradition begun by Terman and Miles (1936). Mincing no words, Constantinople wrote that "both theoretically and empirically [masculinity and femininity] seem to be among the muddiest concepts in the psychologist's vocabulary" (p. 390). Her words unintentionally echoed Sigmund Freud (1905/1953) who 70 years earlier had written: "the concepts of 'masculine' and 'feminine' whose meaning seem unambiguous to ordinary people are among the most confused that occur in science" (p. 219).

Unlike Freud, however, Constantinople (1973) based her conclusions on hard research evidence. Some of her criticisms were directed at the haphazard content of M-F scales. By selecting items solely based on gender differences in response, Constantinople argued, the creators of M-F scales had created a grab bag of M-F items. To illustrate, consider the following, which are all similar to items from actual M-F scales:

"I would like to be a truck driver."

"Uncouth and vulgar language disgusts me."

"I think a lot about my motives and feelings."

"I prefer a bath to a shower."

"Thunder and lightning storms terrify me."

"I like to attend theater and dance performances."

"The sight of a bug crawling on the wall fills me with disgust."

"I like to hang out with people who play lots of practical jokes on one
    another."

What do such items have in common at a conceptual level? Constantinople's answer was, Not much!

Because of their diffuse content, M-F scales often don't "hang together" statistically. A statistical technique called factor analysis is often used to analyze people's test answers to determine whether the items measure a single dimension (i.e., a single factor) or many different things (i.e., multiple factors). A factor analysis could be conducted on people's responses to IQ test questions to determine whether the test measures a single dimension (general intelligence) or several different dimensions (e.g., verbal ability, math ability, visual-spatial ability). Constantinople (1973) reviewed factor analytic studies of M-F scale items and concluded that they showed multiple factors, not the single bipolar M-F dimension claimed by early researchers like Terman and Miles (1936). In other words, masculinity-femininity seems not to be a single "either-or" dimension but rather a number of loosely related, and sometimes even unrelated, dimensions.

Constantinople (1973) criticized M-F research in still other ways. Various M-F scales did not correlate strongly with one another, she charged, and this raised questions about the coherence of M-F measures. Again, think of the analogy to intelligence. If people's scores on a number of different intelligence tests failed to correlate with one another, wouldn't you question whether all the tests were measuring the same thing (i.e, general intelligence)? Constantinople argued that M-F scales were often based on cultural stereotypes rather than on real differences between men and women. Empirically, M-F scores proved to be linked to people's social class and education levels. Typically, higher class and educational levels were associated with less extreme levels of masculinity in men and femininity in women. Thus, M-F scales may reflect demographic factors more than personality. Finally, Constantinople noted that M-F scores were often linked to age, becoming less extreme as people get older. After assembling all the evidence, Constantinople asked, in essence, is a "trait" that is diffuse, multidimensional, and linked to a host of demographic factors truly a coherent personality trait? Or is it really just a conceptual mess that should be abandoned by psychologists?

The Rise of Androgyny: Masculine Instrumentality and Feminine Expressiveness

The late 1960s and early 1970s marked the beginning of the modern women's movement. In this turbulent time of civil rights demonstrations and antiwar protests, feminist scholars offered devastating critiques of society's gender roles and began a process—that continues to this day—of identifying pervasive biases against girls and women in the worlds of education, government, and work. With the changing times came new views of masculinity and femininity.

Drawing on the work of Constantinople (1973) and others, Stanford psychologist Sandra Bem (now at Cornell University), combined feminist values with empirical research to create a dramatically new approach to masculinity and femininity. Whereas the old bipolar approach had viewed masculinity and femininity as *opposites*, Bem argued that they were instead *separate and independent dimensions*. And whereas the older M-F scales included motley collections of items that men and women answered differently, Bem focused her attention on a more limited domain—items that assessed *gender-stereotypic personality traits*.

Bem's conception of masculinity and femininity did not arise in a vacuum. Beginning in the 1950s, sociologists and social psychologists had noted that one set of personality traits—often labeled *instrumental* or *agentic* traits—is more associated with men, whereas another set—labeled *expressive* or *communal* traits—is more associated with women (Bakan, 1966; Parsons & Bales, 1955). Instrumental traits are goal oriented and focused on the external world of work and getting the job done. Examples of such traits are *independence, assertiveness, dominance*, and *leadership ability*. Expressive traits, on the other hand, are people oriented and focused on the private worlds of family and personal relationships; they are related to people's desire to nurture others and establish intimacy. Examples are *warmth, sympathy, compassion*, and *sensitivity to others*.

Bem (1974) drew on this existing distinction between instrumental and expressive traits when she developed a new test—the Bem Sex-Role Inventory (BSRI)—which measured masculinity (M) and femininity (F) as two separate dimensions. People who take the BSRI are asked to rate how self-descriptive various instrumental and expressive traits are. They are then assigned separate M and F scores based on their mean self-ratings on sets of instrumental and expressive personality traits.

To identify traits for inclusion in her M and F scales, Bem initially asked large groups of Stanford students to rate how socially desirable it was for a man and for a woman to possess various traits (e.g., to be warm, aggressive, dominant, etc.) If students rated a trait to be significantly more desirable for a man than for a woman, then it was classified as a masculine trait. Conversely, if students rated a trait to be significantly more desirable for a woman than for a man, it was classified as a feminine trait. Unlike the developers of earlier M-F scales, who chose items because they were answered differently by men and women, Bem selected trait items that were stereotypically judged to be relatively more desirable for men or for women. Bem's resulting M and F scales closely approximated the instrumental and expressive dimensions of personality described before.

At about the time that Bem (1974) developed her inventory at Stanford, a group of researchers at the University of Texas at Austin—Janet Spence, Bob Helmreich, and Joy Stapp (1974)—developed a similar test called the Personal Attributes Questionnaire (PAQ). The PAQ masculinity items comprise socially desirable personality traits stereotypically judged to be *more true* of men than women (e.g., self-confident, independent, competitive, never gives up easily), and the femininity items comprise socially desirable personality traits judged to be *more true* of women than men (e.g., emotional, gentle, kind, very understanding of others). Like Bem's scales, the M and F scales of the PAQ primarily tap instrumental and expressive traits, and indeed, many studies suggest that the M and F scales of the BSRI (particularly its short version; Bem, 1981a) and PAQ are quite similar in content (Lenney, 1991).

What was gained by measuring masculinity and femininity as two separate dimensions? Bem (1974) argued that the two-dimensional approach permitted a new way of conceptualizing sex roles and of classifying people on gender-related traits. Bem's research indicated that masculinity and femininity were indeed relatively independent of one another. In other words, a person's level of masculinity is unrelated to his or her level of femininity. After a period of debate with the Texas group, Bem applied a four-way classification scheme to people, based on whether they had low or high M scores, and low or high F scores. (See Table 2.2; in this context, think of *low* and *high* as meaning below or above the median, or the middle value for a given group of people).

People with high M scores but low F scores were considered to be stereotypically masculine. These people report that they are "independent" and "dominant," for example, but not "kind" or "compassionate." People with high F but low M scores were considered to be stereotypically feminine (e.g., "kind" and "compassionate" but not "independent"

TABLE 2.2
Bipolar Masculinity-Femininity Versus the Two-Dimensional Conception

From the 1920s to the early 1970s, masculinity-feminity was conceived as a single bipolar dimension. Thus, you could be either feminine or masculine, but not both. Traditional scales often implied the unstated value that it is good for women to be feminine and for men to be masculine.

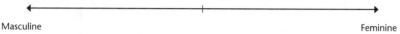

Masculine   Feminine

Traditional bipolar tests, like Terman and Miles's

In the 1970s, psychologists conceptualized masculinity and feminity as two independent dimensions. Masculinity scales measure the degree to which individuals report possessing positive instrumental traits, and femininity scales measure the degree to which individuals report possessing positive expressive traits. Individuals who have high degrees of both masculinity and femininity are termed "androgynous."

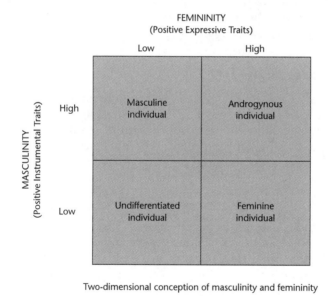

Two-dimensional conception of masculinity and femininity

Unidimensional and two-dimensional conceptions of masculinity and femininity.

or "dominant"). However, there are additional possibilities: People can have both high M and high F scores (e.g., "independent" and "dominant," *and* "kind" and "compassionate"). Bem (1974) labeled such people *androgynous* (i.e., having both male and female characteristics; from the Greek roots *andro* [male] and *gyn* [female]). Finally, people could have both low M and low F scores. In the research literature, such low-low individuals are referred to as *undifferentiated.*

Taking an explicitly feminist perspective, Bem (1974) argued that androgynous individuals might serve to define a new standard of mental health and adjustment. According to her, traditionally masculine people (high-M, low-F individuals, usually men) and stereotypically feminine people (high-F, low-M individuals, usually women) are restricted by their gender roles. Masculine men may do well at instrumental tasks (e.g., they are assertive); however, they may fail at expressive tasks (e.g., being nurturant). Conversely, feminine women may do well at expressive tasks but fail at instrumental tasks. Androgynous individuals, however, can be flexibly masculine or feminine, depending on the situation. Thus the androgynous person can be an assertive and forceful boss at work but a tender and supportive parent at home. The androgynous person has the best of both worlds.

By focusing attention on the androgynous individual, Bem (1974) broke radically with the values underlying older M-F scales, which held that it's good for men to be masculine and for women to be feminine. For Bem, it was best to be androgynous.

Putting Androgyny to the Test

In a series of early studies, Bem attempted to demonstrate that sex-typed individuals are restricted in their gender-related behaviors, whereas androgynous individuals are more flexible. In one study, Bem (1975) measured whether college men and women would stand up against group pressures to conform. Participants were asked to make judgments about how funny cartoons were in the face of peers who strongly disagreed with them. Bem found that stereotypically feminine people showed relatively high levels of conformity, whereas stereotypically masculine and androgynous people showed lower levels. Bem concluded that masculine and androgynous people showed "good" behavior (they stood up for what they believed in), whereas feminine people showed less admirable behavior (they "caved in" to group pressure).

In other studies, Bem, Martyna, and Watson (1976) investigated stereotypically feminine behaviors, such as nurturing others. In one of these, college men and women were individually placed in a waiting room with a baby. Researchers watched through a one-way mirror and observed how the students interacted with the baby. Feminine and androgynous individuals tended to interact more warmly and playfully with the baby, whereas masculine individuals tended to be more distant and offish. In a conceptually similar study, researchers observed college men and women in conversation with another student (who was actually a confederate). During the course of the conversation, the confederate shared some personal problems ("I'm having difficulty making new friends"), and the researchers observed how warm and supportive the students were to this troubled peer. The findings: Feminine and androgynous individuals tended to be more warm and supportive than masculine individuals were. Bem and her colleagues concluded from these studies that feminine and androgynous people can show "good" feminine behaviors when the situation calls for it. But masculine people often cannot; they are constrained by their masculine gender roles to be relatively cold and distant.

Bem and Lenney (1976) tested the sex-role flexibility of androgynous individuals more directly in a study in which college students had their pictures taken while they performed everyday activities, some of which were stereotypically masculine (e.g., "nail two boards together"), while others were feminine (e.g., "iron cloth napkins") or gender neutral (e.g., "play with a yo-yo"). Participants received a small amount of pay for each photo taken, and at times they were allowed to choose which photographed activities they would perform. The results suggested that sex-typed individuals were more likely to choose activities that matched their gender, even if this meant giving up pay. Androgynous individuals, on the other hand, were more comfortable being photographed performing both masculine and feminine activities. Bem and Lenney argued that, the sex-typed man says to himself, "If it's masculine I'll do it, but if it's feminine, forget it! I'd rather lose money than do that 'sissy' stuff!" The androgynous person, on the other hand, says, "Who cares whether it's masculine or feminine? I'll do whatever makes me the most money!" In other words, the sex-typed individual is constrained by traditional gender roles; the androgynous person is not.

A number of attempts to replicate Bem's early findings on androgyny and behavioral flexibility yielded inconsistent results (see Cook, 1985). In a review of many early studies, Marylee Taylor and Judith Hall (1982) concluded that M scales predict instrumental behaviors reasonably well (e.g., being assertive and resisting pressures to conform), and F scales predict expressive behaviors reasonably well (e.g., being nurturant to lonely peers). However, this might be expected simply based on the content of the tests. After all, M scales measure instrumental traits (e.g., assertiveness), and F scales measure expressive traits (e.g., nurturance). Despite Bem's early research and advocacy for the ideal of androgyny, the jury is still out on whether androgynous individuals—people who score high on both masculinity and femininity—truly show greater sex-role flexibility than other kinds of people.

Masculinity, Femininity and Psychological Adjustment

As a passionate feminist, Sandra Bem believed that androgyny defined a new standard of psychological adjustment, a standard that was liberated from gender. Some early research tried to test this directly by examining androgyny's relation to various self-report measures of adjustment (such as measures of self-esteem, depression, and anxiety). This research did in fact show that androgynous people tend to be more highly adjusted (i.e., high in self-esteem and low in depression and anxiety).

However, because androgyny was defined by two separate traits (masculinity and femininity), it was not always clear *why* androgynous people reported being more adjusted. Was it because of their instrumental (high-M) traits, their expressive (high-F) traits, or a combination of the two? The possibility that there is some emergent property of high-M and high-F traits, *in combination*, that fosters psychological adjustment and flexibility seems closest to Bem's original conception that "androgyny is best."

However, research didn't offer much support for the combination theory of androgyny. Many studies on the relationship between androgyny and adjustment suggested that M traits contribute to psychological adjustment more than F traits do (see Bassoff & Glass, 1982; Whitley, 1983, 1984). This means that *all* high-M individuals (high-M, low-F as well as androgynous individuals) tend to score high on self-esteem and low on anxiety and depression. The real difference then is between high-M (androgynous and masculine) individuals and low-M (feminine and undifferentiated) individuals. Masculinity's greater power than femininity's to predict adjustment has sometimes been referred to as the "masculine superiority effect" (Cook, 1985).

Why do M traits correlate with measures of adjustment better than F traits do? One hypothesis is that Americans live in an individualistic society, which values instrumental traits more than expressive traits. (Most early androgyny research was conducted in North America.) Wouldn't you agree that, in a dog-eat-dog, free enterprise society, assertiveness, independence, competitiveness, and leadership ability are all traits that foster success? Another and perhaps more fundamental explanation for the linkage between masculinity and adjustment is that the content of M scales overlaps significantly with the content of many adjustment scales. This can be seen most clearly for measures of self-esteem, which show some of the strongest correlations with masculinity (Whitley, 1983). The PAQ M scale includes items such as "self-confident" and "feels very superior." It makes sense that people's scores on such a scale would correlate with their scores on a self-esteem scale, which after all is simply a measure of the person's general sense of self-worth and self-confidence.

If you're feeling at this point that femininity seems to have been neglected in research on adjustment, you can take heart from a number of studies showing that F traits are linked to certain kinds of positive adjustment. Specifically, high F levels are related to being a good friend and marriage partner (Antill, 1983; Kurdek & Schmitt, 1986) and being empathetic (Spence & Helmreich, 1978). Again, perhaps this is to be expected, given the nature of F scales, which measure expressive traits (e.g., being nurturant, warm, sympathetic, and compassionate). Aren't those the kinds of traits you would want in a friend or romantic partner?

Whither Androgyny?

The two-dimensional model of masculinity and femininity (and the closely related concept of androgyny) was supposed to vanquish the older bipolar M-F model. Instead, it too was soon subject to a host of new criticisms. Janet Spence and Bob Helmreich (1980), two of the original developers of the PAQ, argued that M and F scales are really just instrumentality and expressiveness scales. While such scales predict instrumental behaviors (e.g., independence, assertiveness) and expressive behaviors (e.g., nurturance in close relationships) reasonably well, they do not necessarily predict other gender-related behaviors, such as stereotypically masculine or feminine activities, gender-role flexibility, gender ideologies, attitudes toward women, and so on. But these are exactly what we *would* want "masculinity" and "femininity" scales to predict! Many research studies have supported Spence and Helmreich's contention that M and F scales are at best weakly related to various gender-related attitudes and behaviors. In essence, Spence and Helmreich warned that labeling these scales "masculinity" and "femininity" may constitute a violation of truth in advertising. These scales should in fact be labeled I (for instrumentality) and E (for expressiveness).

There were additional criticisms of M and F scales. Usually, when psychologists develop new personality measures, they try to demonstrate that they don't simply measure what's already been measured by previous scales. This might be termed "the old wine in new bottles" problem. When M and F scales were first developed in the early 1970s, there was no consensus about what the fundamental dimensions of personality actually are. Today, however, there is growing consensus that there are five broad, fundamental dimensions to human personality, which are often referred to as the Big Five (Wiggins, 1996; see the discussion in Chapter 1). The Big Five dimensions are extraversion, agreeableness, conscientiousness, neuroticism, and openness to experience. Are masculinity and femininity independent of the Big Five? The answer from a number of studies is clearly no (Lippa, 1991, 1995b, in press). Masculinity overlaps strongly with extraversion and neuroticism, and femininity overlaps strongly with agreeableness and to a lesser degree with conscientiousness. In other words, M and F scales do not measure *new* personality traits.

Like Spence and Helmreich, Bem too revised her conception of masculinity and femininity. Bem's original notion was that the androgynous individual might come to define a new standard of mental health. However, on reflection, she came to believe that just as older conceptions of masculinity-femininity were unduly prescriptive ("it's good for men to be masculine and for women to be feminine"), so too was the newer notion of androgyny ("it's good for everybody to be androgynous"). With a touch of irony, she could note that in the bipolar tradition, people had one trait to worry about—men could feel inadequate for being insufficiently masculine, and women could feel inadequate for being insufficiently feminine. However, in the brave new world of androgyny, men and women could feel inadequate for *two* reasons—for being insufficiently masculine *and* for being insufficiently feminine. Paradoxically, sex role "liberation" brought with it a kind of double jeopardy.

Bem eventually came to believe that M-F, M, and F scales are *all* guilty of trying to make something real out of what are really just mental concepts. According to Bem's (1981b, 1985, 1993) gender schema theory, sex typing is not a matter of fixed, inner personality traits, but rather it results from a person's tendency to conceptualize the world too much in terms of "male" and "female," "masculine" and "feminine." Gender schematic people, according to Bem, promiscuously apply the category of gender to everything—to themselves, to their actions, to other people, and even to abstract concepts and objects (they see petunias as feminine, for example, and tigers as masculine). Gender schematic individuals are often aided and abetted by society at large, which makes gender gratuitously salient in all areas of life and socializes people to pay attention to gender and to believe that all behavior is "gendered." (Consider, for example, how in our society, the clothes you wear, the way you move your body, the occupations you choose, and the hobbies you engage in are often seen to have "gender.") Gender aschematic people, on the other hand, do not apply an imperialistic gender schema to everything they see and do. They do not organize and monitor their own and others' behaviors always in terms of gender.

Thus Bem came to see sex-typed individuals as being gender schematic, and androgynous individuals as being gender aschematic. In gender schema theory, Bem shifted her focus from the traits of individuals (masculinity and femininity) to society's tendency to make gender a central and salient category. The ideological conclusion was obvious to Bem: "The feminist prescription, then, is not that the individual be androgynous, but rather that the society be gender aschematic" (Bem, 1985, p. 222).

So Bem moved to a strong social contructionist position. "Masculinity" and "femininity" are not psychological realities at all. They are not real traits of the individual. Rather, they are cultural fictions, by which an arbitrary hodgepodge of traits, behaviors, and social roles are labeled "masculine" and "feminine," respectively. In Bem's (1987) words, "masculinity and femininity do not exist 'out there' in the world of objective realities. . . . [they] exist only in the mind of the perceiver" (p. 309).

BUT DON'T MASCULINITY AND FEMININITY MAKE SENSE TO MOST OF US?

Bem's social constructionist view raises an interesting paradox, spelled out clearly by Janet Spence and Camille Buckner in 1995. To some extent, masculinity and femininity *are* just concepts, whether originating in the fertile minds of research psychologists or in the collective mind of society at large. But—and here's the paradox—they are concepts that make sense to an awful lot of lay people. Why do research psychologists have such a hard time defining and measuring these traits, when they seem so obvious to the rest of humanity?

To illustrate this point, stop right now and forget everything you've read so far. Answer the following question based on your own experience: Do *you* believe that some men are more masculine than others and that some women are more feminine than others? If you answered yes to this question, then try to answer a second, perhaps more difficult question. What is it that makes some men seem more masculine than others and some women seem more feminine than others? Is it their appearance? The way they dress and move? The way they talk? Their hobbies and interests? Is it their sexuality? The way they relate to friends and lovers? Or what? This is the central question posed by research on *lay conceptions* of masculinity and femininity—what defines the vague but intuitively appealing concepts of masculinity and femininity?

Components of Masculinity and Femininity

A number of studies have suggested that there are at least several different components to lay people's conceptions of masculinity and femininity. For example, Anita Myers and Gale Gonda (1982) asked over 700 visitors to a science museum in Toronto, Canada, to provide their commonsense definitions of masculinity and femininity. Interestingly, their subjects *did not* emphasize the instrumental and expressive traits so commonly measured by recent M and F scales. Rather they listed physical appearance and traits (e.g., "muscular," "wears makeup," "deep voice"), traits other than instrumentality and expressiveness (e.g., "soft and fragile," "macho," "tough"), biological characteristics (e.g., bears children, has certain hormone levels), sexuality (e.g., "not gay," "virile," "seductive"), and social roles (acting the way society expects men and women to act). Similarly, in a series of studies conducted at Purdue University, Kay Deaux and Laurie Lewis (1983, 1984) found evidence that lay people's conceptions of gender, masculinity, and femininity have many components, including roles (e.g., "mother"), occupations (e.g., "truck driver," "nurse"), physical appearance (e.g., "muscular," "dainty"), and sexuality (heterosexual, homosexual). Again, these components are *in addition to* personality traits such as instrumentality and expressiveness.

Carnegie Mellon psychologist Vicki Helgeson (1994a) recently found still further evidence that lay people's conceptions of masculinity and femininity are multifaceted. Helgeson observed that a group of college students and their parents defined masculinity and femininity in terms of interests (e.g., feminine women are seen to be interested in family affairs, music, and art, whereas masculine men are seen to be interested in sports, work, and cars), and also in terms of personality traits and physical appearance. Interestingly, Helgeson also found that "masculinity" has more negative meanings when applied to women, and "femininity" has more negative meanings when applied to men. For example, masculine women were seen as aggressive, alcohol consuming, ugly, fat, and not very caring, and feminine men were seen as thin, insecure, shy, delicate, and weak.

Yet another noteworthy finding from studies on lay judgments of masculinity and femininity is that women are judged more than men based on their physical attractiveness. Attractive women are judged to be more feminine, whereas unattractive women are judged to be more masculine (Lippa, 1997, 1998c). Another noteworthy finding is that lay people tend to see masculinity and femininity as opposites (Deaux, 1987). That is, the more we judge a person to be masculine, the less we judge him or her to be feminine, and vice versa. Thus, people's everyday conceptions of masculinity and femininity (which are not necessarily true, but they are what people *think* are true) are more like the bipolar either-or approach to masculinity-femininity than like the two-dimensional approach.

Masculinity and Femininity as "Fuzzy Concepts"

In recent years, psychologists have proposed that masculinity and femininity are "fuzzy concepts" (see Deaux, 1987; Helgeson, 1994a; Maccoby, 1987, 1998). This means that masculinity and femininity are defined by multiple attributes, and the categories defined by these concepts (e.g., "feminine" people and "masculine" people) don't have clear-cut boundaries.

Consider another fuzzy category—fruits. What defines a fruit? A fruit is a part of a plant with multiple attributes (develops from a flower, has seeds, has sweet flesh, grows above ground, hangs on a stem). Not all fruits have all attributes, however. An avocado is a fruit, for example, even though it's not sweet. Sometimes there are ambiguous cases, which are hard to classify, that exist near the boundaries of fuzzy categories. Are tomatoes fruits? Are peanuts? Finally, fuzzy categories may be characterized by *prototypes*—that is, ideal examples of the category, which possess virtually all of the defining characteristics of the concept. An apple, for example, is a prototypic fruit.

We can apply these concepts from cognitive psychology (which studies human thought processes) to the study of masculinity and femininity. If masculinity and femininity are fuzzy concepts defining fuzzy categories, then it seems reasonable to ask, what *are* the defining attributes of masculinity and femininity? The studies described before help answer this question. Masculinity and femininity are defined by people's appearances and nonverbal mannerisms, and by their social roles, occupations, hobbies, interests, sexual behaviors, biological characteristics, and personality traits. The notion of a "prototype" would suggest that some people provide better examples of masculinity and femininity than others. For example, Marcel Proust (to me, at least) provides a good prototype of a "feminine man."

The concept of fuzzy categories raises another interesting question. Are some of the attributes that define masculinity (or femininity) more central than others. What do you think? What would most influence *your* judgment of whether a man was masculine? Would it be his personality traits (he is "dominant" and "aggressive"), his occupational preferences (he wants to be a jet pilot), his hobbies (he plays football and fixes cars in his spare time), his social roles (he is president of the Chamber of Commerce; a father of four), his appearance (he often wears jeans and flannel shirts; he is muscular), his sexuality (he is heterosexual and chases after women), his social relationships (he has a wife; he spends a lot of time with male friends playing sports), or what? Just because masculinity and femininity are multifaceted, does not mean they don't exist or that they are meaningless. It simply means they are complex.

Is there in fact a "core" to masculinity and femininity? My hunch is that there is and that it is to be found in gender-related interests (occupational preferences, hobbies, and everyday activities), gender-related appearances (nonverbal mannerisms, dress, grooming), and perhaps sexuality (sexual orientation). As a psychologist long interested in measuring people's masculinity and femininity, I know that the first component (interests) is easier to measure via questionnaires than the last two (appearances and sexuality), so I frequently focus on interests in my research.

There are two additional reasons why I focus on gender-related interests as a route to measuring masculinity and femininity. First, considerable research indicates that gender-related interests develop very early in life—certainly by the time children are toddlers, and often before children's gender self-concepts and stereotypes have much of a chance to develop (see Huston, 1983; Ruble & Martin, 1998). Second, gender-related interests develop well before adult sexual orientation becomes apparent. However, children's gender-related interests are strongly related to their adult sexual orientation (see Chapter 4). Boys who grow up to become gay men have more feminine interests than boys who become heterosexual men, and girls who grow up to become lesbian women have more masculine interests than girls who become heterosexual women (Bailey & Zucker, 1995).

So, do gender-related interests provide the royal road to measuring masculinity and femininity? Perhaps. This leads us to a third, more recent approach to measuring masculinity and femininity. It is my own approach, and so I got to choose its name—*gender diagnosticity*.

DECONSTRUCTING AND RECONSTRUCTING MASCULINITY-FEMININITY

Before describing my approach to masculinity and femininity in more detail, let's first pause and take stock of where we have been, and let's consider the state of the field in recent years.

Recapitulation

By the 1980s and 1990s, scholarly respect for the concepts of masculinity and femininity was clearly in decline. These traits were regarded as stereotypes "in people's heads" more than as real characteristics of people. Feminist psychologists ridiculed Terman and Miles's bipolar approach, and many seriously questioned androgyny research as well (Bem, 1993; Lewin, 1984a, 1984b; Morawski, 1987). A consensus was emerging that gender does not comprise core traits of the individual; rather, it is a "social construction" manufactured and sustained by stereotypic beliefs and social settings (Deaux & LaFrance, 1998). This position proposes that differences in the behavior of men and women result largely from people's beliefs about gender (for example, "men are better at math"), which then become self-fulfilling prophecies (see Chapters 3 and 6). Gender differences are further enforced by patriarchal (i.e., male dominated and male-favoring) social structures, which give men more power than women. Social roles also serve to create and reinforce gender differences—when they encourage instrumental behaviors in men (e.g., in the role of worker) and expressive behaviors in women (e.g., in the roles of mother and homemaker). Stated simply, gender is something that's "done to us" by society, not something we're born with.

What was the evidence for the social constructionist position? Many studies have suggested that gender-related traits and behaviors—nonverbal mannerisms, dress, interests, abilities, and personality traits such as assertiveness and nurturance—are only weakly interrelated and quite variable across situations. Richard Ashmore (1990) offered a "loose glue" metaphor: The different components of gender—interests, attitudes, abilities, sexuality—don't really hang together very well. Janet Spence (1993) echoed this in her "multifactorial theory" of gender: "knowing that a person . . . enjoys cooking tells us little about how much the person likes or dislikes studying math" (Spence & Buckner, 1995, p 120).

If the various "parts" of gender don't hang together very well, then the scientific case for masculinity and femininity seems to be in trouble, for the defining feature of masculinity and femininity—indeed, of any personality trait—is that people show cohesive patterns of behavior that are consistent over time and across settings. Many recent gender researchers have argued that people do not behave in consistently "masculine" or "feminine" ways. Theorists like Sandra Bem (1987, 1993) have asserted the radical constructionist position that masculinity and femininity are "all in our heads." Spence and Buckner (1995) went so far as to suggest that the terms *masculinity* and *femininity* should be abolished from the scientific vocabulary.

Resurrecting Masculinity-Femininity: Gender Diagnosticity

By the late 1980s I too was dissatisfied with existing approaches to masculinity and femininity. On the one hand, I was sympathetic to arguments that masculinity and femininity are social and cultural constructs. These traits do seem to possess a kind of fluidity that's hard to pin down. What's "masculine" in one historical era (e.g., long hair on men) may be "feminine" in another. And what's "feminine" in one culture (e.g., being a doctor) may be "masculine" in another.

On the other hand, masculinity and femininity still made sense to me as a lay person. As I observed people about me, I had the clear impression that some men were indeed more masculine than others, and that some women were more feminine than others. For me, the paradox then became, how can these traits be real and consequential but at the same time culturally and historically variable? In nitty-gritty research terms, the question became, how can research psychologists *measure* these traits, which seem so apparent to the untrained eye yet so hard to pin down scientifically?

To answer these questions, I devised a new approach to measuring masculinity and femininity—an approach I termed gender diagnosticity (GD). This approach was a kind of compromise between essentialist and social constructionist views of masculinity-femininity. The GD approach holds that masculinity-femininity exists and can be measured, but at the same time, it varies somewhat over time and across groups and cultures.

What exactly is gender diagnosticity? It refers to the estimated probability that a person is male or female, based on some piece of gender-related information about the person. Examples of gender-related pieces of information are "this person wants to be a kindergarten teacher" or "this person has short hair." The gender diagnostic probability serves as a measure of masculinity or femininity within the sexes. The GD approach harks back to the bipolar M-F approach in that it assumes that "information" that distinguishes the sexes can serve to measure masculinity and femininity within the sexes. However, it differs from the older bipolar approach in that it allows the "information" that defines masculinity and femininity to change over historical time and across different groups. The reason this is possible is that the GD approach always calibrates masculinity and femininity against a particular group of men and women (or boys and girls) at a particular time in history. In other words, it establishes "local standards" of masculinity and femininity.

An example will make this clearer. Suppose I place before you a person wrapped in a burlap bag to ensure that you don't know whether the person is male or female. I give you just one piece of information: "This individual is aggressive." I then pose the question, "What is the probability that this person is male?" Your estimate is to be based on actual data. For example, you conduct a survey in which you ask a group of 100 men and 100 women in your neighborhood to rate whether they are aggressive or not. You are then in a position to compute the likelihood that the "aggressive" person in burlap is male or female. Suppose your study shows that 60 men and 40 women in your neighborhood labeled themselves "aggressive." If the "aggressive" person wrapped in burlap is from your neighborhood, then the probability is 60% that he is a man and 40% that she is a woman.

This is the essence of gender diagnosticity. Clearly, GD probabilities vary depending on the piece of information used to diagnose gender and on the group of people studied. For example, if I told you that the person in the burlap bag is a Michigan State University student (the group being studied) who wants to be an electrical engineer (the piece of information), what would you estimate the probability to be that this person is male? To answer this question empirically, you would have to know the relative proportions of Michigan State men and women who actually want to be electrical engineers. (Even without knowing this information, though, what would you guess is the probability that this person is male?)

Once again, gender diagnosticity is the computed probability that a person is predicted ("diagnosed") to be male or female based on some kind of gender-related information. In my research, I typically compute GD probabilities (which I'll call GD scores) based on peoples' occupational and hobby preferences, using a statistical procedure called discriminant analysis (for the technical details, see Lippa & Connelly, 1990). I compute these probabilities based on *multiple* pieces of information—for example, individuals' rated preferences for 70 different occupations. This allows me to compute reliable GD scores. Recall from our earlier discussion that good tests include many items so they will yield reliable scores. Still, the basic concept remains the same: gender diagnosticity is the computed probability that a person is male or female based on some set (rather than a single piece) of gender-related information.

Unlike M-F scores, GD scores are always computed anew for a particular group of men and women. For example, the GD score of a college student at Michigan State University would be computed in comparison to a group of Michigan State men and women. Because GD scores are computed for particular groups of people, the way masculinity-femininity is defined may vary from group to group. This is so because pieces of information that distinguish men and women in one group may not do so in another group.

Again, a concrete example will help illustrate this point. When Terman and Miles (1936) conducted their classic research over 60 years ago, college men and women showed a large difference in their desire to be lawyers, with men expressing greater interest in law than women. However, today this same piece of information is often *not* gender diagnostic. Contemporary college men and women do not differ much in their expressed interest in law as a profession. The moral of the story? We cannot necessarily use items that were gender diagnostic in the 1930s to measure "masculinity" and "femininity" at the start of the 21st century.

Consider another example. The behavior of wearing pants was undoubtedly more gender diagnostic 100 years ago than it is today. Many women wear pants today; however, few did in the late 1800s and early

1900s. Because wearing pants was more gender diagnostic then than now, it was probably a better indicator of masculinity (at least for women) then than it is today. A woman who wore pants in the 1800s was probably viewed as extremely masculine. Today, a woman who wears pants may be seen as quite feminine—in the United States at least. This qualification ("in the United States") suggests another interesting point. The behavior of wearing pants is probably more gender diagnostic in some countries and cultures (e.g., in Egypt) than in others (e.g., in the United States). Thus wearing pants may signal a woman's masculinity more in some cultures than in others.

Once again, the GD approach computes the probability that a person is male or female, based on pieces of information that distinguish men and women *in a particular group, in a particular culture, during a particular historical period.* Another way of saying this is that the GD approach computes how "malelike" or "femalelike" an individual is, compared to some local reference group of men and women, using some pieces of information that distinguish these men and women. The advantage of the GD approach is that it acknowledges that masculinity and femininity are *to some extent* historically and culturally relative.

Despite the fact that masculinity and femininity sometimes display themselves differently in different groups and cultures, the GD approach nonetheless asserts that individual differences in masculinity and femininity *can be measured.* In virtually all cultures and in all historical eras, there are some behaviors that are more typical of men and others that are more typical of women. If we measure individuals on those behaviors, we can compute the likelihood that a person is male or female based on these behaviors. That is, we can measure how male-typical or female-typical that person's behavior is for people in that culture.

Although it is true that some indicators of masculinity and femininity vary substantially over time and across cultures, it is also likely that some indicators do not. For example, the question, "How interested are you in being an electrical engineer?" was highly gender diagnostic in the 1930s in the United States, and it remains so today. Of course, this does not mean that men's and women's relative interests in being electrical engineers will never change in the future. However, it does suggest that some pieces of information may diagnose gender more consistently over time and place than others. Although the content of "masculinity" and "femininity" may fluctuate (as proposed by social constructionists), it may also have some consistency (as proposed by essentialists).

As a matter of convention, gender diagnostic probabilities are computed to be the individual's probability of being male (which is simply one minus the probability of being female). Thus, by convention, high probabilities mean that the individual is more malelike and low probabilities mean the individual is more femalelike. Let's bring back our person in the burlap bag one last time. This individual has expressed on a questionnaire a strong interest in being a Secret Service agent, a police officer, an auto mechanic, a truck driver, and an Army officer but a strong dislike for being a florist, a nurse, an elementary school teacher, a professional dancer, and a librarian. What's your best estimate of the probability that this individual is male?

By comparing this person's occupational preference ratings with the ratings of a particular group of men and women, I can actually compute this probability. I have no doubt that, if computed for most groups of men and women in our society today, this person's GD score would be high (say .90). That is, this individual is very likely to be male. If a person's GD score is around .50, then the person's occupational preferences are neither strongly male- nor female-typical. In other words, we're not sure about the individual's gender based on the occupational preference information. Finally, if a person's GD score is low, say .20, then the person is likely to be a female. A person receiving a low GD score is very female-typical; in short, he or she is feminine.

Now note, a man can receive a low GD score. A low score simply means that the man's occupational preferences are more femalelike than they are malelike, when compared to some larger group of men and women. Similarly, a woman can receive a high GD score—that is, she can be relatively malelike in her occupational preferences when compared to some larger group of men and women. Indeed, the whole purpose of computing GD scores is not to actually diagnose who is male and female. Real people, after all, are not wrapped in burlap bags. We usually know immediately whether they are male or female. The purpose of computing GD scores is to assess how malelike or femalelike a particular man or woman is—that is, to *measure individual differences in masculinity-femininity*.

What Is GD Related To?

Does the GD approach "buy" us anything more than previous approaches to masculinity and femininity have? I believe that the answer to this question is yes. Many studies have shown that GD scores are reliable (Lippa, 1991, 1995b, 1998b; Lippa & Connelly, 1990), and furthermore, that gender diagnosticity does not correlate much with instrumentality, expressiveness, or the Big Five personality traits. Thus the GD approach does not suffer from "the old wine in new bottles" problem. GD scores correlate moderately with bipolar M-F scales (Lippa & Hershberger, 1999; Lippa, Martin, & Friedman, 2000). However, GD scores often show superior validity to these scales (Lippa, 1991, 1998b, 2001).

To demonstrate the validity of a measure, researchers must show that it's related to traits, behaviors, and ratings that make theoretical sense. The most obvious way to show that a new measure of masculinity and femininity is valid is to demonstrate that it's related to lay people's judgments of their own and others' masculinity and femininity. Recall that Terman and Miles (1936) failed to demonstrate this with their early M-F test. In contrast, several studies have shown that gender diagnosticity is related to lay judgments of masculinity and femininity. In one of these studies, I asked 119 college men and 145 college women to rate how masculine and feminine they considered themselves to be. These ratings were then correlated with their M, F, and GD scores. The results showed that the men's and women's GD scores predicted their self-rated masculinity-femininity better than M or F scores did (Lippa, 1991).

Another study investigated the relation between men's and women's GD scores and their nonverbal masculinity-femininity as judged by others (Lippa, 1998c). Thirty-four college men and 33 college women were briefly videotaped as they gave talks. Research assistants then viewed these videotapes and rated how masculine and feminine the college students appeared to be, based on their appearance, movements, and vocal style. The results showed that the videotaped students' GD scores significantly predicted how masculine and feminine they were judged to be, again better than their M or F scores did.

A third study asked 37 college men and 57 college women to create autobiographical photo essays (Lippa, 1997). Each student took 12 photographs that showed "who they are" and assembled them into a booklet with captions. Research assistants then read the photo essays and rated how masculine and feminine the students seemed to be, based on the information in their photo essays. The results showed that college men's GD scores strongly predicted how masculine and feminine they were judged to be—again, much more strongly than their M or F scores did. However, women's GD (and M) scores only modestly predicted their rated masculinity and femininity. These different results for women seemed to reflect the fact that women's masculinity-femininity was assessed on the basis of their physical attractiveness. Women were judged to be feminine based more on how pretty they were than on the degree to which they displayed feminine behaviors and interests in their photo essays.

Additional validity studies have addressed whether gender diagnosticity is related to psychological adjustment, physical health, sexual orientation, scholastic ability, and intelligence. Let's start with gender diagnosticity and adjustment. In two separate studies, I measured large groups of college students on GD, M, and F traits and examined whether these traits were related to various measures of psychological adjustment (Lippa, 1995b). Recall that previous research often focused on self-esteem, anxiety, and depression as indices of "psychological adjustment." Many recent studies have shown that all these seemingly different measures in fact tap one broad, underlying personality factor—neuroticism or "negative affectivity" (*negative affectivity* means negative emotionality; see Watson & Clark, 1984, 1997). Like earlier studies, my study included various measures of negative affectivity. However, I also included measures of aggressiveness, meanness, overbearingness, vindictiveness, and unassertiveness. And in one study, I included a measure of authoritarianism—a trait linked to rigid, conventional thought patterns and prejudice against minority groups (see chapter 1).

What were the results? Measures of masculinity and femininity (M, F, and GD) were in fact related to various kinds of adjustment; however, each measure related to different kinds of adjustment. People who were high-M tended to be aggressive and overbearing (showing negative adjustment), but they also tended to be appropriately assertive and low on Neuroticism (positive adjustment). People who were high-F tended to be overly involved with others and too easily taken advantage of (negative adjustment), but they also tended to be agreeable (positive adjustment). Thus instrumentality and expressiveness (i.e., masculinity and femininity) prove to be two-edged swords in the sense that they are linked to both positive adjustment *and* negative traits. In contrast, high GD scores were related to only one kind of maladjustment, and this finding was true for men only. High-GD (i.e., masculine) men tended to be authoritarian. This result was bolstered by data showing that high-GD men showed increased prejudice against gay people and negative attitudes toward women's rights (see also, Lippa & Arad, 1999).

Following Terman and Miles's lead, I conducted research on whether masculinity and femininity—this time, as assessed by gender diagnosticity—are related to sexual orientation. In a series of studies, I found that GD scores are in fact strongly related to sexual orientation in both men and women (Lippa, 2000; Lippa & Tan, 2001). One study assessed gender diagnosticity, masculinity, femininity and sexual orientation in an unselected sample of over 700 college students. Two additional studies solicited participation from large groups of gay and lesbian volunteers and compared their GD, M, and F scores with heterosexual men and women. All these studies showed that gay men have considerably more feminine GD scores than heterosexual men do, and lesbian women have considerably more masculine GD scores than heterosexual women do. Furthermore, gender diagnosticity proved to be much more strongly linked to sexual orientation than masculinity or femininity is.

Pursuing a new line of M-F research, I have recently investigated possible links between masculinity and mortality. Could it be the case that masculinity is linked to physical illness as well as to psychological maladjustment? Is it possible that masculine men and women die younger than their more feminine counterparts, just as men on average die younger than women? Some recent evidence suggests that certain "masculine" traits (e.g., negative instrumental traits such as arrogance and egotism) are related to health risks such as smoking, hostility, and poor social relations (Helgeson, 1994b). But is masculinity actually related to a person's likelihood of *dying*?

A study I conducted with Leslie Martin of La Sierra University, Howard Friedman of the University of California at Riverside (2000) suggests that the answer to this question is, in fact, yes. To reach our conclusion, we analyzed data from Lewis Terman's classic study of "gifted children". That is, we returned to the data that had triggered masculinity-femininity research 80 years ago to uncover new facts about masculinity today. Although most of Terman's gifted children have died by now, the data collected from them lives on, safely stored in archives at Stanford University. In recent years, these data have been used to study psychological factors that influence health and longevity (see Friedman et al., 1995). My colleagues and I used these data to investigate the possible link between masculinity and mortality.

How did we measure masculinity? In 1940, Terman and his associates administered the Strong Vocational Interest Blank to many of his gifted children, who were by then about 30 years old. Using these archival data, we were able to compute GD scores for these subjects based on their occupational preference ratings. Because the Terman archives include records of participants' deaths, we were in a good position to investigate whether masculinity was related to mortality. Our results were quite clear: High GD scores were linked to higher mortality in both men and women.

Why was there a link between masculinity and mortality? We're not yet sure. Other studies suggest that a high GD score is related to high-risk activities in young men (e.g., reckless driving under the influence of alcohol; Arad, 1998). Additional possibilities are that masculinity is related to health risk factors, such as excessive alcohol consumption, cigarette smoking, poor diet, avoidance of needed medical care, high-risk hobbies, and poor social support. Future research will sort these possibilities out. For now, one thing is clear: Masculinity has implications for health and longevity.

What else is the GD score related to? Following the lead of earlier research, I investigated its relationship to scholastic aptitude and intelligence. Consistent with previous findings, I found that high school boys who are "feminine" and girls who are "masculine" tend to score higher than their more sex-typed peers on the National Merit Scholarship Qualifying Test (Lippa, 1998a).

Is There a "Deep Structure" to Masculinity-Femininity?

One strength of the GD approach is that it allows "masculinity" and "femininity" to vary over time and across groups of people. However, this flexibility carries with it a price—masculinity and femininity may seem to be shifting targets that have no stable core to them. Is there in fact a core to masculinity and femininity, as measured by gender diagnosticity? Recall that GD scores are typically computed from men's and women's occupational and hobby preferences (which I'll call "interests" for short). In recent years, there has been increased interest in how people's interests relate to other broad personality dimensions (Ackerman, 1997).

One model has dominated research on occupational preferences and interests over the past 30 years—John Holland's (1992) hexagon or RIASEC model. Holland argues that there are six basic kinds of occupations: realistic, investigative, artistic, social, enterprising, and conventional. (The RIASEC acronym is constructed from the first letters of each of these six occupational types.) See Fig. 2.1 for a brief description of each type of occupation.

Holland's model proposes that people's patterns of occupational likes and dislikes can be schematically summarized by a hexagon. If two RIASEC occupational types are next to each other on the hexagon (e.g., artistic and social occupations, for example) then people's preference

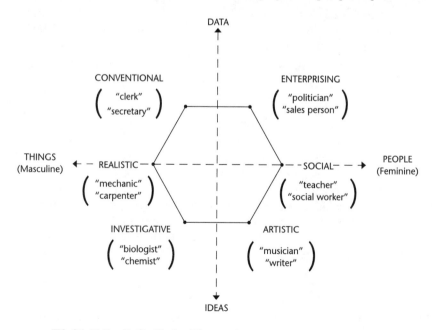

FIG. 2.1 Holland's Six Kinds of Occupations

for these kinds of occupations are likely to be similar. On the other hand, if two RIASEC categories are opposite each other on the hexagon (e.g., realistic and social occupations), then people's preferences for these kinds of occupations are likely to be unrelated or even opposite. Many studies have confirmed that people's occupational preferences do in fact follow the pattern suggested by Holland's model.

In 1982, Dale Prediger proposed two fundamental dimensions underlying Holland's hexagon, which he labeled the People-Things dimension and the Ideas-Data dimension (see Fig. 2.1). The People-Things dimension taps how much people like occupations that deal with people (e.g., managing, teaching, or counseling) versus occupations that deal with inanimate things (dealing with machines; the kind of work done by scientists, computer programmers, mechanics, and farmers). The Ideas-Data dimension taps how much people like occupations that deal with creative thinking (e.g., scientist, researcher, artist) versus occupations that deal with record keeping and data management (e.g., clerk, bookkeeper, secretary, accountant). In a sense, Prediger proposed a two-dimensional "deep structure" to people's occupational preferences.

Given that GD is often computed from occupational preferences, it seemed reasonable to ask, What is the relationship between GD measures and Prediger's two dimensions? In three separate studies, I sought answers to this question (Lippa, 1998b). I found that GD correlates strongly with the People-Things dimension but not at all with the Ideas-Data dimension. Thus my current working hypothesis is that gender diagnosticity is fundamentally related to the People-Things dimension of occupational preferences and interests.

It's important to emphasize what the People-Things dimension *is not*. It is not extraversion or sociability (part of what is measured by M scales). Nor is it agreeableness or expressiveness (measured by F scales). Rather it is some basic mental and attitudinal stance toward activities that involve people versus activities that involve mechanical things. By implication, I think it taps a person's desire to deal with and think about the fuzzy, messy, and ambiguous world of human motives, thoughts, and feelings versus the more clear-cut, precise, and deterministic world of mechanical and physical phenomena. The first is feminine, the latter masculine. And on this dimension, I have no doubt where Marcel Proust would fall!

SUMMARY

Research on masculinity and femininity took many twists and turns over the course of the 20th century. Terman and Miles (1936) conceived masculinity-femininity (M-F) to be a bipolar, unidimensional trait, and they measured the M-F trait with questionnaire items that showed sex differences. An implicit assumption of early M-F research was that it's good for men to be masculine and for women to be feminine. In the 1970s, a two-dimensional approach defined masculinity (M) in terms of instrumental traits and femininity (F) in terms of expressive traits. This approach held that the androgynous individual—high on both M and F traits—defined a new standard of mental health.

Lay conceptions hold that masculinity and femininity comprise many components including physical appearance, social roles, occupations, interests, sexuality, and personality traits such as instrumentality and expressiveness. The gender diagnosticity (GD) approach offers a compromise between essentialist and constructionist views of masculinity and femininity. It assesses how "malelike" or "femalelike" a person is based on interests that are gender-related in a particular group at a certain time in history.

All approaches to masculinity and femininity confirm one central point: Gender is not simply a matter of *sex differences*. Gender is also a matter of *variations within each sex*. Regardless of how they are conceptualized, masculinity and femininity are linked to consequential outcomes and traits in people's lives, including psychological adjustment, physical health, scholastic aptitude, intelligence, and sexual orientation. This adds significance to a fundamental question, What causes people to vary on masculinity and femininity—nature or nurture?

3

Theories of Gender

It's not just what we inherit from our mothers and fathers that haunts us. It's all kinds of old defunct theories, all sorts of old defunct beliefs. . . . It's not that they actually live on in us; they are simply lodged there, and we cannot get rid of them.

—*Ghosts*
Henrik Ibsen

It is time to turn to theories of gender. But before examining specific theories, let's first consider the general sorts of explanations that the most common theories of gender use to explain the behavior of men and women.

LEVELS OF EXPLANATION APPLIED TO GENDER

Theories of gender generally focus on four different levels of explanation: (a) group-level factors, (b) past biological and social-environmental factors, (c) current biological and social-environmental factors, and (d) traits residing within the individual (see Fig. 3.1). The group level (Level 1) of analysis considers you as a member of a group—either a biological group (e.g., people with XX chromosomes) or a cultural group (e.g., Latinas, members of the middle class, Southern Baptists, the social categories of "female" and "male"). Group-level processes include biological and cultural evolution, which respectively shape the characteristics of biological groups (such as species and the two biological sexes) and cultural groups (religious groups, ethnic groups, the socially defined categories of "male" and "female").

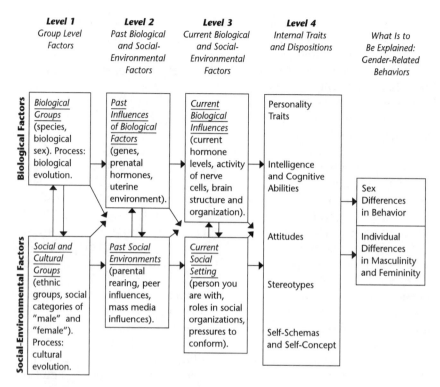

FIG. 3.1 Levels of Explanation Applied to Gender

Level 2 attempts to explain your gender-related behaviors in terms of the *past events* that affect you. These include both biological and social factors. For example, the genes you were born with, the chemicals you were exposed to as a fetus, and the way your parents treated you when you were young may influence your current behavior as a man or a woman. As analyzed at Level 2, you exist as an individual distinct from other individuals.

Level 3 moves forward in time and focuses on *current events* that influence your gender-related behavior. For example, the way your brain cells are organized right now, your current level of testosterone (a male hormone), and the setting you are now in may affect your current gender-related behavior. Level 3 again analyzes you as an individual, but the factors influencing your behavior are in the here-and-now, not in the past.

Level 4 analyzes your behavior in terms of your traits, abilities, and dispositions—factors that reside within you. Level 4 slips inside your skin and examines your makeup—characteristics that may be seen as resulting from both your biological inheritance and the experiences of your life.

At the far right side of Fig. 3.1 is what all theories of gender try to explain—gender-related behaviors. More specifically, theories of gender try to explain (a) behaviors that show average differences between males and females, and (b) individual differences in masculine and feminine behaviors within each sex.

At each of the four levels of analysis shown in Fig. 3.1 (group-level factors, past factors, current factors, and internal traits), both biological and social-environmental processes are present. Biological factors include evolutionary processes (Level 1); the past influences of genes, physiology, and biological environments (Level 2); the current influences of genes, physiology, and biological environments (Level 3); and all the residual effects these factors have on your individual traits (Level 4).

Biological influences may be both genetic and environmental (in the sense of biologically active environmental influences, such as uterine environments, exposure to chemicals, exposure to infectious agents, and so on). Social-environmental factors include influences from the cultures and social groups we belong to (Level 1), influences from events in our past, such as parental rearing (Level 2), influences from our current social setting (Level 3), and all the residual effects these factors have on our individual traits (Level 4).

Let's use a concrete example to illustrate social "causes." The behavior of men and women may vary depending on whether they grew up in the United States or in Saudi Arabia (Level 1—the influence of cultural groups). Your behavior as a particular man or woman may depend partly on how your mother and father reared you (Level 2—your past environment) and also on the people you are with right now—for example, a boyfriend or girlfriend (Level 3—the current environment). Finally, your behavior as a man or a woman may depend on your personality traits, abilities, attitudes, and stereotypes (Level 4—internal dispositions).

The arrows pointing from left to right in Fig. 3.1 indicate cause-effect relationships. All the levels of explanation are interconnected. Thus the biological evolution of males and females (Level 1) can influence the individual genes you were born with (Level 2), which may then influence the current structure of your brain and your level of sex hormones (Level 3), which ultimately influence your personality traits and abilities (Level 4). Biological causes thus flow from the distant past of our species, to your individual past, to the present. Ultimately, all these interconnected causes influence your behavior. The same is true for environmental factors. The culture you were born into (Level 1) can influence the way your parents reared you (Level 2), which influences your current friends and settings (Level 3), which in turn influence your traits and attitudes (Level 4) and your behavior.

Note that causality does not simply flow from past to present (from left to right in Fig. 3.1). Factors at a given level may interact with one another. This in indicated by the arrows that point up and down. Biological and cultural evolution can mutually influence one another. As human groups learned to domesticate milk-producing animals, for example, they simultaneously underwent biological evolution that increased the number of adults who could digest milk. Thus biological evolution was influenced by cultural changes, and cultural evolution depended on biological evolution. In the case of sex differences, a biological trait (e.g., greater upper body strength in males, female gestation and lactation) could influence cultural evolution (e.g., greater male involvement in warfare, women foraging and staying closer to home to care for biologically dependent infants). Similarly, cultural changes (e.g., the shift from hunter-gatherer to agricultural civilizations) could influence biological evolution.

Level 2 factors may similarly influence one another. Your genetic heritage can influence how your parents treat you. To give an obvious example, beautiful children are often treated differently from homely children. Your physical attractiveness, a substantially genetic trait, influences your past social environments. Past chemical environments (e.g., exposure to hormones or to drugs as a fetus) can influence which genes "turn on" and which did not "turn on" in your DNA. At Level 3, factors also interact. Your current social environment (being with an attractive romantic partner) can affect your current body chemistry (sex hormone levels), which can in turn activate some genes and deactivate others.

When viewed in terms of interactions (the up and down arrows in Fig. 3.1) and the simultaneous flow a causality from past to present causes (left to right arrows), you can see how difficult it can sometimes be to disentangle biological and social-environmental influences from one another. Rather than a system of clearly partitioned causes (nature vs. nurture; biological vs. nonbiological; genetic vs. nongenetic; environmental vs. nonenvironmental), we have a spaghetti-like network of interacting factors. The famous Swedish theologian Emanuel Swedenborg once noted that each instant "of a person's life entails a chain of consequences extending into eternity" (1987). Fig. 3.1 makes a converse point: Each behavior has a series of intertwined causes extending indefinitely into the past. Disentangling those causes is not always an easy task. However, it is the task we set for ourselves—to disentangle some of the causes of gender-related behaviors, based on the best evidence available.

Now it is time to consider specific theories of gender. Keep in mind that these theories are not necessarily mutually exclusive, and each theory may contain elements of truth.

BIOLOGICAL THEORIES

Biological theories of gender suggest that there are some innate differences between males and females, and that we may—to some extent—

be born masculine or feminine. The biological basis of sex differences is obvious for physical traits. Women produce ova, and men produce sperm. Women menstruate and have cyclic menstrual cycles that men do not. Women give birth and lactate (produce milk); men do not. Women's bodies produce more estrogens (female hormones), and men's bodies produce more androgens (male hormones). On average, women have bigger hips and breasts and more body fat than men do; men have broader shoulders and more muscle mass than women do. Women typically have less body hair than men do.

Though few would disagree that the two sexes are physically different and that these differences are largely caused by biological factors, scholars disagree continually over the related question, do biological factors lead to sex differences in human *behavior*? At Level 1, biological theories of gender focus on evolutionary processes and how they mold men's and women's genes, hormones, and nervous systems—and ultimately their behaviors.

Evolutionary Theory

The basic assumptions of Darwin's (1859) original theory of evolution are simple: (a) The traits of all living things show variation; (b) traits can be passed from generation to generation (principle of inheritance or heredity); and (c) natural selection is the "filter" that determines which traits are passed from generation to generation. The principle of natural selection—perhaps the core assumption of Darwin's theory—proposes that it is the organism's environment that selects which traits are passed from one generation to the next. How? In essence, the environment selects those traits that "work," in that these traits help organisms to survive and reproduce in that environment. Survival and reproduction are not independent, of course, because to reproduce, an animal must survive—at least to a certain age.

Natural selection is not a conscious, purposeful process, although its products often give the uncanny appearance of having been designed (Dawkins, 1986). Rather, natural selection is a blind algorithm—an unthinking, deterministic process—that occurs when variable organisms vie for existence and struggle to reproduce in changing environments. Some organisms live, but many die before maturity. Some organisms reproduce, but many do not. Life is a competition in which organisms struggle to survive and reproduce, and any trait that gives the slightest advantage in this struggle will be "bred into" the species over many generations.

Traits that foster survival and reproduction in a given environment are said to be adaptive. Adaptations are organized systems of physical or behavioral traits that have evolved because they serve some function that helps the organism to survive and/or reproduce. For example, eyes are adaptations—organized, evolved structures that help animals to survive (e.g., to run away from attacking predators) and to reproduce (e.g., to detect and approach attractive, available mates). Similarly, the reflex to duck when a fast-moving object streaks toward your head is an adaptation, which likely helped many of your ancestors survive in the past and thus to live, reproduce, and ultimately produce you as one of their descendents. You would not be here today if many of your ancestors had not ducked at the right moment!

Classic Darwinian theory focused on individual survival and reproduction, and it described how organisms adapt to their environments and gradually develop new traits, even to the point of evolving into new species. Natural selection is the unthinking process that "decides" which traits pass from generation to generation. Modern evolutionary theory has refined some of Darwin's ideas. Recent views of evolution, for example, focus more on *genetic survival* as the central principle of natural selection (see Dawkins, 1989). According to this view, natural selection is a process that maximizes the *transmission of genes* to future generations. Genes are successful to the extent they increase and spread in future populations. Conversely, they are unsuccessful when they decrease in numbers. The ultimate failure of a gene (or of a set of genes) occurs when it ceases to exist altogether—when a species goes extinct, for example.

The "selfish gene" view of evolution holds that plants and animals are, in a sense, "gene machines" designed to carry and protect their genes for a while and then pass them on to new gene machines (i.e., offspring) to be carried into the future. This selfish-gene view may seem a bit disconcerting at first glance, for you probably view yourself as having your own goals and plans and not as a temporary physical container for a set of genes clamoring to be injected into some new bodies and passed on to future generations. You might think that the gene-centered versus individual-centered approach to natural selection is just a matter of semantics. However, it is not. Genetic survival is not the same as individual survival. For example, who is more successful according to the gene-centered view of natural selection: an 18-year-old boy who fathers 10 children and dies in a motorcycle crash before reaching 19, or a successful and rich businessman who lives to age 99 without fathering any children?

There is another important way in which genetic survival is not identical to individual reproduction. The way animals typically pass their genes on to future generations is through reproduction. However, this is not the only way. The theory of kin selection (also known as "inclusive fitness") proposes that animals can also ensure that their genes live on by helping those who share their genes (i.e., blood relatives) to survive and reproduce (Hamilton, 1964). Altruism toward kin can evolve because it fosters the transmission of our own genes (i.e., the ones we share by descent with our kin) to future generations. Thus being "altruistic" to kin is genetically "selfish" in the sense that we foster the propagation of our own genes whenever we help our kin to flourish and reproduce.

Evolutionary theories argue that, over the history of our species, men and women have been subject to somewhat different evolutionary pressures. Edward O. Wilson (1975, 1978), the father of modern sociobiology, proposed that because hominid women were responsible for bearing, nursing, and caring for children, they evolved to be more nurturing. And because men were responsible for hunting and fighting, they evolved more aggressiveness and better visual-spatial ability.

The evolution of sex differences extends well beyond the human species. One way to think of the difference between females and males, at least at a basic biological level, is that females produce relatively few and large germ cells (eggs), which often come supplied with nutrients and are internally fertilized. Fertilized eggs may sometimes be sheltered and protected by females (as birds' eggs often are) or carried within the female's body (as in mammals). In contrast, males produce many tiny gametes (sperm)—minimalist, mobile packages of genetic code that compete to fertilize as many eggs as possible. Contributing sperm does not require much investment in time, nutrients, or energy on the part of males. However, producing eggs and (for humans) gestating, breast feeding, and rearing the offspring that result from fertilized eggs, requires a huge amount of time, nutrition, energy, and wear and tear on the body (Trivers, 1972).

There is another fundamental difference between female and male reproduction. Compared to men, women are much more limited—both theoretically and practically—in the number of offspring they can produce. At birth, a woman has just a hundred or so ova (eggs), some of which get "used up" every month once menstruation starts. Because of the extended periods required for gestation and lactation, and because of the bodily demands of pregnancy and childrearing, a woman can have only so many offspring over the course of her lifetime. In contrast, a man produces millions of sperm every day. Evolutionary theorists suggest that all these differences between female and male reproduction have led men and women to evolve different reproductive strategies (see Buss, 1999).

Parental investment in offspring is particularly high in human mothers, who invest more in their offspring than do the mothers of virtually any other species. Not only do human mothers carry their offspring internally for nine months and breast-feed them for many months more, but they also carry around their helpless infants for many months more. Then they must rear their children into well-socialized adults who learn to speak language fluently and to understand cultural rules, rituals, and technologies. This process may take as long as two decades. Although men invest in childrearing too, women traditionally invest much more, both physically (gestation, childbirth, lactation) and in terms of time and energy (childrearing, care, and instruction).

According to evolutionary arguments, then, women must guarantee that the relatively few, high-investment offspring they bear will survive. In contrast, men (who may father an indefinite number of offspring and don't necessarily invest much in some individual offspring) are more likely to "sow their wild oats." Men have evolved to be more sexually aggressive, competitive, and promiscuous, whereas women have evolved to be more sexually selective and desirous of committed relationships, which provide them and their children with protection and stable resources.

It is important to note that when evolutionary theorists talk about men's and women's evolved "mating strategies," they are not necessarily describing conscious strategies. Rather, they are referring to dispositions, sometimes unconscious, that have evolved over thousands of generations. Men do not necessarily walk around in everyday life thinking, "How can I best maximize my transmission of genes to future generations? Oh, I know. I can impregnate as many women as possible!" They don't need to have such conscious thoughts if evolution has produced, on average, higher male sex drives and less-committed male attitudes toward sexual intimacy.

Modern technological advances may sometimes short-circuit the original evolutionary "purpose" of a behavior. Although some men may be promiscuous, for example, the use of contraception cancels the evolutionary advantage of their behavior. Nonetheless, the dispositions persist even though their fitness has changed. The human preference for fatty and sweet foods provides a similar example. It may have been adaptive in our prehistoric past to show such preferences, when fatty and sweet foods were rare and people required many calories to fuel their energetic hunter-gatherer lives. But in today's food-rich and sedentary world, human preferences for sugar and fat bring diabetes and cardiac arrests rather than increased survival.

Darwin (1871) distinguished between two kinds of natural selection, and these have implications for the evolution of sex differences. The first kind of natural selection produces traits adapted to animals' natural environments. Examples of such traits are the long necks of giraffes (which allow giraffes to eat succulent leaves on high branches), the thick fur of polar bears (which provides warmth in frigid environments), and the fibrous, prickly skins of cacti (which conserve water in arid settings and protect against animals that might want to eat juicy cactus flesh). Darwin described a second, more specialized, form of natural selection, which he termed *sexual selection*. Sexual selection occurs when traits evolve because they help animals attract mates and reproduce.

In a rough sense, the first kind of natural selection favors traits that are adaptive in natural environments. The second kind—sexual selection—favors traits that help animals to compete for mates with same-sex members of their own species and to attract mates from opposite-sex members of their own species. The environment in the first kind of natural selection is almost everything—food supplies, climate, radiation, predators, and so on. The environment in sexual selection, however, consists of members of your own species—the same-sex members with whom you must compete and opposite-sex members whom you must entice as mates.

The gaudy tail feathers of peacocks provide a textbook example of sexual selection (Hamilton & Zuk, 1982; Petrie, Halliday, & Sanders, 1991; Zahavi & Zahavi, 1997). Peacock tails are costly, requiring a lot of food and energy to grow. Furthermore, they are cumbersome, making peacocks less nimble and more vulnerable to predators. Why then did they evolve? The simple answer is, because they are alluring to peahens. Peacock tails are not simply a frivolous display, however. They provide an honest signal of fitness. Well-formed, beautiful tail feathers tell a peahen that the peacock displaying them has good genes, good health, and good nutrition—in short, that he would make a good mate. Such a signal cannot be easily faked. Peacocks with bad genes, infectious diseases, and poor nutrition tend to produce shabby, stunted, asymmetrical tail feathers.

Once a process of sexual selection gets started (and this may initially occur by chance), runaway sexual selection can begin. A positive feedback loop is created, causing the "sexy" trait to become more and more exaggerated. Peacocks evolve larger and larger tails, until the overwhelming costs of such tails (in terms of nutrition, vulnerability to predators, interference with flight) eventually stops the process.

Can sexual selection explain human sex differences? Evolutionary theorists have recently argued that some *physical* traits of male and female humans (men's large penis size compared with that of other primates, women's large protruding breasts and exaggerated hip-to-waist ratios) may result from sexual selection (Barber, 1995). These physical traits may be comparable to peacocks' tails—they are sexy, honest signs of fitness we display to one another to show our youth, fertility, and good prospects as mates.

"Do you sometimes feel like we're in a rut?"

*Sexual selection: According to evolutionary theory,
males compete for sexual access to females.*

Even more intriguing are recent speculations that human brain size, language development, psychological astuteness, and artistic creativity may have evolved through sexual selection (Miller, 2000). Perhaps humans evolved to entrance and seduce desirable mates through the use of language, storytelling, dance, and humor. Does this theory relate to sex differences? Miller proposes that men use language and artistic creativity more as a kind of status and sexual display than women do, and this may account for greater levels of male productivity in certain kinds of artistic and creative endeavors.

In general, evolutionary theories of gender focus on *sex differences* in human mate choices and sexual behavior. Men prefer youth and beauty in a mate more than women do (youth and beauty are presumed to be signals of health and high fertility), whereas women prefer status and monetary resources in a mate more than men do (because such resources ensure that their few offspring will flourish; see Chapter 1). Females are seen as the "choosier" of the two sexes. Because women produce relatively few offspring in which they invest considerable bodily resources and time, they must carefully choose mates who contribute good genes and sufficient resources to their offspring. Good genes ensure that a woman's offspring will survive and grow into successful, sexy adults who in turn survive and reproduce. Sufficient resources (food, money, status) ensure that a woman will be able to protect and rear her children successfully. Because males can produce many offspring, and because they may invest little in some of them, evolutionary theorists argue that men have evolved to be more promiscuous and indiscriminate—at least in their short-term mate choices—than have women (see Buss, 1999).

Although some men produce many offspring (e.g., Indian maharajas with large harems), others may fail altogether in the "mating game" and end up with no offspring. Consistent with this observation, evolutionary theorists propose that there is more variability in men's mating success than in women's. One implication of this asymmetry is that fertile women become the "limiting resource" for male reproduction. Women can be relatively picky and try to choose the best mate, in terms of his genes and resources. Women can also trade mating privileges (i.e., sex) for other goods (e.g., gifts, food, money, nice homes, and stocks and bonds) (Symons, 1979). Because women are a limited resource, men must actively court and compete with other men for mates. And because of their greater chances of failure, men often take greater risks to attract or acquire a mate. (Think of the swagger and risk taking of young males, who often put on a show of prowess for admiring young women—on the football field, in sports cars, or on the battlefield. Literally, young men are dying to impress attractive women.)

Male displays of money, power, status, and talent can be viewed—from an evolutionary perspective—as an evolved strategy for attracting mates. Evolutionary theories suggest that it is no accident that prominent athletes, rock stars, actors, and CEOs are desirable as mates. Through their creative and career successes, such men compete with other men and indirectly display their good genes and resources to the desirable women they hope to attract.

Evolutionary theories of gender do not focus exclusively on sex and mating. Other traits, such as dominance and physical aggression, may also have evolutionary origins. Dominant males have more power and resources, and therefore they are more attractive to women, more likely to mate, and more likely to pass their genes on to future generations. Aggression (or the threat of aggression) is part of male-male competition. Male-on-male homicides are more common than any other kind (see Chapters 1 and 4). Furthermore, evolutionary theory proposes that certain kinds of aggression—for example, that directed by jealous males at mates suspected of infidelity—serve an evolutionary purpose: to protect your reproductive "assets" and to ensure that your mate's offspring are in fact yours (Daly, Wilson, & Weghorst, 1982).

While evolutionary theories have had much to say about sex differences in mating strategies and in other social behaviors, they have generally had much less to say about individual differences in masculinity and femininity. In some species, males are known to take different forms (termed *morphs*) that specialize in different kinds of mating strategies. For example, in the bluegill sunfish, large dominant males take on a distinctive coloration and acquire a harem, which they dominate and inseminate. Smaller, nondominant males, in contrast, can maintain a coloration more like females, which allows them to raid dominant males' harems and inseminate at least some of the females (Gross, 1982). Thus, one way evolutionary theories may attempt to explain individual differences among men and among women is to argue that individual males and females differ so they can adapt to specialized "niches" in the mating game (Miller, 2000).

Another evolutionary view of individual differences is that they simply represent random noise in evolutionary processes (Markow, 1994; Moller & Swaddle, 1998). The development of individual males and females can be "jiggled" by innumerable biological and environmental factors: outside temperature, infectious agents, immunological reactions, maternal stress and its associated hormones, chemical exposure, and so on. Such factors may perturb the development of individual males and females and produce individual differences in masculinity and femininity (i.e., variations in how male-typical or female-typical any particular male or female turns out).

A final evolutionary view—and a complicating factor in the evolution of males and females—is that because males and females share most of their genes, genetic traits that greatly increase the fitness of one sex can sometimes show up in the other sex. (As an obvious example, think of nipples, which have a more obvious function in women than in men. Despite the fact that nipples foster women's but not men' s reproductive success, they exist in both sexes.) Whenever evolution produces differing traits in males and females, it must generate complex mechanisms that "turn on" genes in one sex but "turn off" corresponding genes in the other sex. Often these turn-on and turn-off mechanisms involve the action of sex hormones at various critical stages of development. Variations in the timing and strength of these hormonal events can lead to individual differences in masculinity-femininity.

Genetics and Prenatal Hormonal Factors

Ultimately, evolution influences our genes and our bodies. In terms of Fig. 3.1, causes at Level 1 (e.g., biological evolution) influence causes at Levels 2 and 3 (genes, hormones, physiology). Though Darwin assumed that traits could be passed from one generation to the next, he understood nothing of modern genetics. Gregor Mendel's classic experiments on the genetic transmission of traits in pea plants took place during

Darwin's lifetime. However, Darwin never read Mendel's paper, which was published in an obscure agricultural journal. Other biologists too ignored Mendel's work until the beginning of the 20th century.

Mendel's seminal discoveries showed that there are discrete packets of heredity—what we now call genes (Mendel, 1866). In the mid-20th century, the molecular basis of genetics was revealed. The exact chemical structure of DNA, the molecule of heredity, was deciphered. We now know that genes—segments of DNA—work by coding for the manufacture of various proteins, which are the building blocks of life. Some popular writers describe DNA as the "blueprint" of life. A more appropriate metaphor is that DNA provides the "recipe" for life (Dennett, 1995). DNA instructs a cell how to manufacture proteins needed to run the cell and to build additional cells. The chemicals (proteins, hormones, enzymes) produced under the guidance of DNA form the stuff of which cells are made, and they guide cell growth, division, and differentiation into various tissues and organs.

As proteins are produced under the direction of DNA, they feed back and further influence the action of DNA. For example, hormones (chemical messengers carried by blood from one part of the body to another) are manufactured according to the instructions of DNA. Once they come into existence, sex hormones can turn off some segments of DNA and turn on others segments within cells. The outside environment can also influence the action of DNA. A peculiar but fascinating example is provided by certain reptiles, whose eggs hatch into females when it is very hot or cold outside, but into males when temperatures are more moderate (Crews, 1994; Crews, et al., 1994). In other reptiles, only females are produced by low incubation temperatures, and in still other reptiles, only males are produced by low incubation temperatures. Therefore the genes that lead the reptiles to become male or female are turned on or turned off by environmental factors.

Think again of the metaphor of a recipe. A recipe for a cake tells you which ingredients go into the cake and in what order to add the ingredients. A recipe, however, does not provide a precise blueprint for a cake, and there definitely is no little "model cake" stored inside a recipe. Sometimes recipes require that the cook follow a precise sequence of actions: "Wait until the sauce has cooled before adding the beaten egg; otherwise, it will curdle." Recipes can be very sensitive to outside environments. "It's best not to make this pastry if it is too hot and humid outside," or, "If you bake this cake at high altitudes, you must alter the amount of baking soda." The outcomes of recipes can be jiggled by noise-like events affecting the cooking process: slamming the oven door, using jumbo rather than large eggs, not realizing that your oven thermostat is off a bit, and so on.

The analogy between DNA and a recipe should sensitize you to two important points: (a) Heredity is not destiny, a least in any fixed, precise, and deterministic sense; and (b) complex, multistage recipes—and the DNA instructions for building living organisms are as complex and multistage as recipes get—produce lots of noise-like variations in their outcomes. Some of these may be due to variations in the timing of events and variations in environments while the ingredients are assembled.

Other variations may be due to variations in the recipes themselves. Genetic recipes vary for two main reasons. First, some genes come in more than one variety (or *allele*), and therefore the recipes for human beings all differ to some degree. (There are lots of different recipes for apple pies, too.) Second, recipes can vary because mistakes occur when the recipe is passed from cook to cook. In genetic recipes, such mistakes are called mutations.

Biologists now know that the recipe of life—DNA—is arranged in 23 paired packages of genetic material called chromosomes, which consist of many genes strung together, along with "junk DNA" (sections of DNA that do not code for useful information, or that coded for useful information in the evolutionary past but not today). One pair of chromosomes is critical for determining sex, and these chromosomes are called (appropriately enough) the sex chromosomes. In humans, but not always in other animals, there are two kinds of sex chromosomes: X and Y. Most females are born with two X chromosomes (XX), and most males are born with an X and a Y chromosome (XY). It is the presence or absence of the Y chromosome that leads some embryos to develop into males and others into females. Because a female has two X chromosomes, a mother always passes her X chromosome on to her offspring, whether it be a son or a daughter. However, a father passes on his X chromosome only to his daughter and his Y chromosome only to his son.

The Y chromosome is much smaller than the X chromosome and carries much less genetic material. This helps explain why males suffer more from certain hereditary disorders (such as color blindness and hemophilia) than females do. Such conditions are caused by recessive genes on the X chromosome. Genes typically come in matched pairs, one on each of two matched chromosomes. Some genes come in alternative forms, or alleles. An allele is *dominant* when its effects win out over those of its matched partner, and an allele is *recessive* when its effects lose out against its paired gene. Thus, for example, genes for brown eyes are dominant over genes from blues. If you carried two genes, one for blue eyes and one for brown eyes, you would be brown-eyed.

Because the Y chromosome is small and doesn't carry many of the genes that are found on the X chromosome, a male must "make do" with the genes that are on his one X chromosome (which, remember, is always inherited from his mother). Thus if a male inherits a "bad" recessive gene from his mother—say for hemophilia—it will express itself, for there is no dominant matched gene on a second X chromosome to override its effects. If there is a deleterious mutation of a gene on the X chromosome, a female would tend to be more buffered against its effects than a male, because the female has another X chromosome that probably carries a normal version of the mutated gene. As noted before, a mutation is a change in the chemical structure of a gene, usually caused by copying errors when a cell divides or by environmental factors such as radiation or chemicals that alter DNA. Most mutations are deleterious. That is, they are maladaptive, often to the point of being lethal. The problems created by mutated genes on the X chromosome may help explain why more male than female fetuses are spontaneously aborted and why more males than females suffer from a variety of developmental problems such as childhood autism, attention deficit disorder, and speech disorders (Beal, 1994).

Though small, the Y chromosome carries one very important gene that makes all the difference in the world—because it determines the individual's sex. This sex-determining gene triggers the production of a substance called H-Y antigen, which signals the fetal sex glands (gonads) of males to develop into testes. Once testes come into existence, they produce testosterone (a male sex hormone), which is carried by the bloodstream and affects physical development. In the absence of this gene (in XX females), fetal sex glands develop into ovaries. It is the sex-determining gene that begins a cascade of events that leads XY embryos to develop into males.

It has been argued by some that the "default" sex of a human fetus is female. That is, unless acted on by the cascade of androgens (male hormones) triggered by the sex-determining factors on the Y chromosome, the fetus develops as a female. It takes a departure from this female norm for male development to occur. Androgens (male hormones) seem to be more important in causing male development than estrogens (female hormones) are in causing female development, although research on this topic is not settled (Collaer & Hines, 1995). Nonetheless, it appears that some minimum levels of sex hormones (typically estrogens) are necessary for normal female development.

In early male development (before puberty), there are two periods during which male hormones increase: (a) early in fetal development, starting at around the seventh week and peaking in the middle trimester (third) of pregnancy, and (b) for about half a year after birth (Wilson, 1999). The first androgen surge is better understood than the second. Biological theorists argue that androgens during the second trimester of pregnancy are critical both for the development of male internal and external genitals and for the development of a male-typical nervous system. Very early exposure to testosterone in fetal development may even influence gender identity (see Chapter 4). Research—both in animals and in humans—shows that fetal hormone levels guide the development of male or female reproductive organs and external genitals. Research further suggests that prenatal androgens may guide the development of parts of the nervous system and influence gender-related behaviors such as sexual orientation, aggressiveness, rough-and-tumble play, maternal/paternal behavior, and certain kinds of cognitive abilities (such as, visual-spatial abilities).

A distinction is often made between the "organizing" influence of sex hormones (which is thought mostly to take place prenatally in humans) and the "activating" effects of sex hormones (which may take place throughout life but especially after puberty) (Collaer & Hines, 1995; Cooke, Hegstrom, Villeneuve, & Breedlove, 1998). According to this distinction, prenatal sex hormones affect the organization of the central nervous system (for example, the growth of nerve cells and nerve connections, and the size of brain structures and other parts of the nervous system), whereas sex hormones after puberty activate neural systems and behavioral patterns that have been laid down earlier.

To give an example, prenatal hormones may influence sexual orientation early in life. However, hormonal surges at puberty may activate orientations set early in life and motivate adult sexual behaviors consistent with these orientations. Although some have challenged the distinction between organizational and activational effects, it remains useful as a way of thinking about the possible effects of hormones. This distinction should sensitize you to the fact that the effects of *prenatal* hormones may differ from the effects of hormone levels in adulthood. Prenatal exposure to testosterone may "masculinize" behavior and increase the odds that an individual will be sexually attracted to women, for example. In adulthood, however, high testosterone levels may not affect sexual orientation, but they may affect sex drive, increasing adults' interest in sex, whatever their sexual orientation.

No one doubts that sex hormones affect how we *physically* develop into males or females. During the first trimester of pregnancy, the human fetus has both male and female internal structures—Wolffian ducts, which are destined to become the vas deferens and seminal vesicles in males (i.e., the internal "plumbing" of the male reproductive system), and Müllerian ducts, destined to develop into the fallopian tubes and uterus in females (i.e., internal tubes and structures of the female reproductive system). In males, the sex-determining gene leads the testes to produce testosterone and a related male hormone called dihydrotestosterone. These hormones respectively trigger the development

of the Wolfferian ducts and the external male genitals (penis and scrotum). Another hormone—the Müllerian inhibiting factor—causes male
Müllerian ducts to disappear. In the absence of the sex-determining
gene and the male hormone production triggered by this gene, female
gonads develop into ovaries, and female external genitals develop into
the clitoris, labia, and vaginal opening. The penis and clitoris are ho-
mologous structures. That is, the same fetal "bud" of tissue is destined
to grow into one or the other, depending on prenatal hormones.

Structural Differences Between Male and Female Nervous Systems

The notion that prenatal sex hormones have organizational effects implies that hormones may lead to structural differences in male and female nervous systems. Do the brains and nervous systems of men and
women actually differ? This is a highly controversial and contentious
research topic. Although the debate continues (see additional evidence
presented in Chapter 4), recent research suggests that some significant
on-average differences probably exist between parts of male and female
brains. It's important to emphasize, however, that showing a sex difference in brain structure does not tell us why the difference exists
(Breedlove, 1994). Brain structures are molded by environmental influences as well as by genes and hormones. Furthermore, the fact that
men's and women's brains differ in some ways should not obscure the
fact that men's and women's brains are much more similar than they
are different.

On average, men have larger brains than women, but conversely,
women may have more densely packed neurons (nerve cells) in parts
of their brain (Janowsky, 1989). Whatever the difference in brain size,
most experts have concluded that men and women do not differ much
in their average general intelligence (see Chapter 1). However, men and
women do show on-average differences in certain specific mental abilities (such as mental rotation and verbal fluency) that may be related to
brain differences.

Some researchers have suggested that men have more *lateralized*
brains than women do (Annett, 1985; Hellige, 1993). Lateralization
refers to differences between the right and left hemispheres (or halves)
of the brain. Lateralization in human brains is linked to language and
visual-spatial abilities. For most people, the brain areas responsible for
producing and understanding language are located more on the left
side of the brain, whereas the brain areas responsible for certain kinds
of visual-spatial, geometric problem solving, and pattern recognition
tasks are found more on the right side of the brain. Men's brains seem
to be more lateralized than women's in two senses: (a) The respective

compartmentalization of language and visual-spatial processing in the left and right hemispheres seems to be more extreme in men than in women; and (b) certain size asymmetries between areas of the left and right hemispheres are more extreme in men than in women (Fitch, Miller, & Tallal, 1997; Geschwind & Levitsky, 1968).

The greater lateralization of men's brains suggests that men's right hemispheres may be more exclusively devoted to visual-spatial tasks and men's left hemispheres to linguistic tasks, whereas women may have more diffuse areas devoted to both kinds of tasks (e.g., parts of both the right and left hemispheres seem to be devoted to language tasks in women). Men's and women's brains may not only show different degrees of lateralization but may also be functionally organized somewhat differently within each hemisphere (Pugh et al., 1996). For example, the language functions of women seem to be located in the anterior (forward) portion of the left hemisphere, whereas those of men seem to be diffused over the entire left hemisphere (Kimura, 1987, 1999).

One theory holds that the greater lateralization of the male brain is due to the early effects of testosterone (Geschwind & Galaburda, 1987). Research suggests that the left hemisphere is slower to develop than the right hemisphere. Because it is slower to develop, the left hemisphere is more vulnerable to factors that could interfere with its development. Testosterone is one such factor; it has the effect of slowing the growth of neurons. The net result is that males—who have high levels of testosterone—may experience less development of the left hemisphere than women do. Recall that in most people, the left hemisphere is more responsible for language abilities. In contrast, females—who have low levels of testosterone—may experience a greater relative development of the left hemisphere. One prediction of Geschwind and Galaburda's theory is that left-handedness should be more common in men than in women. Left-handedness reflects a more dominant right hemisphere. Because the right hemisphere controls the muscles of the left side of the body, increased development of the right hemisphere produces more left-handedness. A number of studies have supported this prediction (for a review, see Halpern, 2000).

The two hemispheres of the brain are joined by a great "connecting cable"—a huge crescent-shaped band of nerve fibers called the corpus callosum. A number of recent studies suggest that the corpus callosum (after correcting for brain size) is larger in women than in men (Allen & Gorski, 1992; Bishop & Wahlsten, 1997; Holloway, 1998; Holloway, Anderson, Defendini, & Harper, 1993). If additional research supports the larger size of women's corpus callosum, it may suggest that the two sides of the brain have more fluent communication in women than in men. This might help explain research findings that women show more verbal fluency than men (see Chapter 1).

Another brain region that has received considerable research scrutiny is the hypothalamus—a little structure attached to the pituitary gland, buried deep in the brain—which is responsible for many essential motives such as hunger, thirst, aggression, and sex. Some regions of the preoptic area of the hypothalamus show sex differences—for example, they are larger in men than in women. Research in lower animals suggests that corresponding areas of the hypothalamus in animals are related to sexual behaviors, such as sexual mounting in male rats and assuming the sexually receiving posture (what's termed lordosis) in female rats. Some recent research has suggested that the size of certain preoptic structures in the hypothalamus may be related to sexual orientation in men (LeVay, 1991; see Chapter 4). Gay men seem to have preoptic areas more like women's than do heterosexual men. A recent study additionally found that another region of the hypothalamus (called the *bed nucleus of the stria terminalis*) showed a size difference between male-to-female transsexuals and normal (i.e., nontranssexual) men; the transsexuals' bed nuclei were more similar in size to women's than to men's (Zhou, Hofman, Gooren, & Swaab, 1995).

In short, a number of studies suggest that there are sex differences in some parts of the human brain. As brain studies continue and as their methods become ever more sophisticated, it seems likely that additional sex differences in brain structure and function will be identified. The more difficult task, however, will be to demonstrate how such brain differences come to be and how they are related to behavioral sex differences.

We have now briefly considered three interrelated biological perspectives that attempt to explain sex differences and variations in masculinity and femininity: evolutionary theory, research and theory on the effects of sex hormones, and research and theory on differences in the nervous systems of men and women. Biological theories of gender argue that men and women have evolved to differ on certain behavioral traits (e.g., mating strategies, aggressiveness).

How does evolution produce these sex differences? Biological theories propose that males and females follow different paths of fetal development, and they experience different levels of sex hormones at critical stages of development. These differences ultimately lead to different brain structures and patterns of brain functioning in the two sexes. Similarly, individual differences in masculinity and femininity may depend on variations in exposure to prenatal sex hormones and on variations in the ways in which male and female fetuses develop. These individual differences could be due in part to genetic variations among people and partly due to the noise-like variations that inevitably occur when complex DNA recipes produce living bodies.

FROM NATURE TO NURTURE

Evolutionary theory is an *environmental* theory in one important sense: It is the environment that does the "selecting" in natural selection. Furthermore, evolutionary theories often argue that evolved dispositions are sensitive to environmental conditions. Men may be especially aggressive when their sexual jealousy is aroused, for example. Nonetheless, biological theories do not focus predominantly on the social environment as a cause of sex differences in behavior or as a cause of individual differences in masculinity and femininity. We turn now to theories that do.

Social Learning Theories

Biological theories entertain the possibility that some differences between men and women may by innate. In contrast, social learning theories argue that the differences are learned. According to theorists such as Albert Bandura and Walter Mischel (Bussey & Bandura, 1999; Mischel, 1966) the differing behaviors of women and men can best be explained in terms of well-understood principles of learning, such as classical conditioning, operant conditioning, and modeling.

Classical conditioning is the kind of learning that occurs when a neutral conditioned stimulus, such as a bell, is paired with a second, unconditioned stimulus, such as food. The unconditioned stimulus (the food) automatically produces a response (salivation), whereas the conditioned stimulus (the bell before learning takes place) does not. Think of Pavlov's famous dogs. Classical conditioning occurs when the conditioned stimulus (the bell) acquires the power to trigger the response (salivation), which initially was triggered only by food. Such conditioning occurs readily for involuntary responses such as salivation, changes in heart rate, and reflexive eye blinks—responses that are not under conscious control.

How might classical conditioning apply to gender? According to Walter Mischel (1966), classical conditioning helps explain why "labels like 'sissy,' 'pansy,' 'tough,' or 'sweet' acquire differential value for the two sexes" (p. 61). The word sissy is usually used to ridicule a boy, and because it is associated with events that trigger shame and disgust, it becomes a very unpleasant label for most boys. A boy will not want to behave like a "sissy" if the very concept is conditioned to produce loathing in him. Boys often are unwilling to engage in "girlish" activities such as playing with dolls, playing house and "dress up." According to Mischel, this may be because boys are conditioned to have horrible feelings about such activities.

A second kind of conditioning—operant conditioning—occurs when voluntary (i.e., consciously controlled and chosen) behaviors are molded by rewards and punishments. Social learning theorists argue that boys and girls are systematically rewarded and punished for different kinds of behaviors throughout their lives. Imagine that little Joey dresses up in his mommy's stockings, dress, and high heels and "plays house." Is he likely to be rewarded or punished for this behavior? Imagine instead that Joey puts on a baseball uniform and cap and plays on the local Little League team. Will he be praised or ridiculed for these actions? Common sense tells us that boys and girls are rewarded to do quite different sorts of things throughout their lives.

Finally, children learn to behave as boys or girls by observing and imitating the behavior of others. Although children may not be directly rewarded or punished for "behaving like boys" or "behaving like girls," they nonetheless may follow a "monkey see, monkey do" path to gender. Children learn to be male or female by imitating same-sex parents, siblings, friends, and media figures. Considerable research suggests that children are most likely to imitate people who are powerful and nurturing and who control rewards in their lives (Bandura & Huston, 1961; Bandura, Ross, & Ross, 1963; Mischel & Grusec, 1966). Parents fit the bill on all these dimensions. This leads to the obvious prediction that boys are particularly likely to imitate their fathers and girls are particularly likely to imitate their mothers.

Note that modeling theory can help explain both gender differences in behavior and individual differences in masculinity and femininity. Because males on average behave differently from females, when boys imitate other males and when girls imitate other females, they learn sex differences. However, some boys may have more masculine models than others, and some girls may have more feminine models than others. To the extent that children imitate same-sex parents and siblings—who necessarily vary in their own levels of masculinity and femininity—they will vary somewhat in the degree of masculinity and femininity they learn and display.

Social learning theorists make a distinction between the *acquisition* and the *performance* of behaviors. Children can learn do something through observation, but they don't always do it. For example, most women know how to shave their faces, and most men know how to shave their legs and underarms, even though they don't usually do so. Similarly, many women could walk with a male swagger if they chose to do so, and many men could sit with one leg crossed tightly atop the other and their hands daintily folded on their laps, as some women do. And women could wear jockey shorts and suit jackets if they wanted to, and men could wear lace panties and dresses if they wanted to. Social learning theories argue that men and women "don't want to" because of past conditioning, rewards, punishments, and observational learning. In short, men and women behave differently because of all the many ways in which society teaches them to behave differently. According to this theory, change society (and the conditioning and modeling it provides for the two sexes) and you will change the behavior of boys and girls. Eliminate differences in the ways boys and girls are reared, and you will go a long way to eliminating sex differences in behavior.

Cognitive Theories of Gender

Social learning theories portray the learning of gender as a rather passive process. Girls and boys behave as conditioning, rewards, and social models dictate. For human beings, however, gender is "in the mind" as well as "in the environment." Becoming male or female is not just a matter of genes, hormones, and social conditioning. It also depends on how we view ourselves.

Kohlberg's Cognitive-Developmental Theory. Lawrence Kohlberg (1966) argued that children's conceptions of gender are critical in motivating them to behave in masculine and feminine ways. These conceptions develop in step with children's more general levels of mental development. For example, most children can correctly identify their sex by age 2 or 3 (Gesell, Halverson, & Amatruda, 1940). This requires that they acquire stable gender categories—that they understand that people come in two varieties, male and female. About the same time children understand the difference between male and female, they acquire other kinds of object constancy as well—knowledge that classes of objects (cats, tables) have stable, enduring qualities.

According to Kohlberg (1966), once children develop a stable gender identity ("I am a boy" or "I am a girl") and stable gender categories for others ("All people come in two varieties, either male or female; John's a boy and Mary's a girl"), they begin to identify with and prefer others of their own sex (e.g., "I am a girl; I like other girls, and girls are good"). Although young children are aware of gender as a social category, they do not think about gender as adults do. For instance, toddlers do not always realize that gender is defined most fundamentally by genital differences. Instead, they may define gender by its surface features, such as clothing, hair length, and kinds of play. Three- and 4-year-old children will often state that they could be the other sex if they wanted to—all they have to do is change their clothing, hairstyle, and toys!

By age 6 or 7, most children realize that sex and gender are constant (i.e., you can't readily change them) and linked to male and female genital differences. (Chapter 5 presents a more detailed account of research on children's conceptions of gender.) According to Kohlberg's (1966) theory, children older than age 7 nonetheless continue to develop their gender concepts. For example, they learn gender stereotypes (e.g., "Women are nicer and gentler than men," "Men are more violent than women"), and they learn that some cultural symbols (e.g., butterflies and flowers) are more associated with girls, whereas others (e.g., worms and frogs) are more associated with boys.

Kohlberg (1966) proposed that the act of categorizing themselves as male or female leads children to acquire stereotypically feminine or masculine behaviors. In Kohlberg's words, "cognitive theory assumes this sequence: 'I am a boy, therefore I want to do boy things, therefore the opportunity to do boy things ... is rewarding.'" According to Kohlberg, social learning theory argues for a different sequence: "I want rewards, I am rewarded for doing boy things, therefore I want to be a boy" (p. 89). It is not rewards that make the boy masculine, Kohlberg argued. Rather, it is identifying oneself as male that makes masculine activities rewarding. (Chapter 5 presents some evidence on the adequacy of Kohlberg's theory.)

In a sense, Kohlberg argued that sex differences are an inevitable consequence of identifying oneself as male or female. In a society in which men and women behave differently, once boys realize they are boys, they will want to act like other males. And once girls realize they are girls, they will want to act like other females. There is a "chicken and egg" issue here, however. Perhaps in a society without strong gender differences, self-identification as male and female would not lead so inexorably to sex differences in behavior. On the other hand, if there is a biological basis to some kinds of sex differences (for example, in physical aggression, rough-and-tumble play, nurturing doll play), then when children become mentally sophisticated enough to label themselves and others as male or female, self-identification may inevitably heighten these sex differences, for children will notice sex differences and try to act like members of their own sex. Indeed, modern research suggests that it is during middle childhood (say, 6 to 8 years of age) that children hold their most rigid and "sexist" views of gender (Ruble & Martin, 1998).

Kohlberg's (1966) theory does not speak directly to the issue of individual differences in masculinity and femininity. A related cognitive theory by Jerome Kagan (1964) does, however. According to Kagan, to decide how "masculine" or "feminine" they are, boys and girls compare their own behavior to that of other males and females. This process, like the one Kohlberg described, would seem to require that children first acquire stable gender categories. If a boy observes that his behavior is similar to that of most other males, he will infer that he is "masculine." If a girl observes that her behavior is similar to that of most other females, she will decide that she is "feminine."

Of course, Kagan's (1964) theory doesn't really explain why some boys behave more and some less like other boys in the first place, or why some girls behave more and some less like other girls. This, of course, brings us back to biological and environmental theories of sex-typed behaviors. Are such behaviors molded by genes, hormones, and brain structures, or by conditioning and social learning? Whatever their causes, Kohlberg's (1996) theory suggests that gender self-labeling will accentuate such differences, and Kagan's theory proposes that when children compare their own behaviors with those of other members of their sex, they infer how "masculine" or "feminine" they are. Once children develop such self-concepts, they may try to act in ways that are consistent with their self-concepts (see Swann, 1999). Thus gender labels and self-concepts may serve to accentuate sex differences and to perpetuate individual differences in masculinity and femininity.

Gender Schema Theories. Sandra Bem (1981b) extended Kohlberg's (1996) cognitive analysis of gender to adults. According to her gender schema theory, people learn a complex network of gender-related concepts and symbols from their culture. For example, "the moon" and "petunias" are feminine, and "the sun" and "jackhammers" are masculine. Once people have acquired gender schemas—organized knowledge and beliefs about gender—they perceive their own and others' behavior through the filter of those schemas. For example, if you have strong gender schemas, you may judge a new acquaintance in terms of her masculinity and femininity. On the other hand, I—a persnickety college professor—may judge the same woman more in terms of her intelligence and vocabulary. Bem's theory moves beyond Kohlberg's in that she argues that gender schemas don't simply motivate males and females to act like members of their own sex. They also affect the way we perceive our own and others' behaviors.

Bem's (1981b) theory proposes that people who are strongly gender-schematic tend to judge the world in terms of "male" and "female," and they try to keep their own behavior consistent with stereotypical standards for their own sex. Thus Bem would view highly masculine men as highly *gender-schematic* men. They hold strong gender stereotypes, and they strongly categorize their own and other people's behavior in terms of gender. Agreeing with Kohlberg's (1996) theory, Bem sees a motivational consequence to gender categorization. Gender-schematic men see masculine behavior to be desirable and feminine behavior to be undesirable, both in themselves and in other men. In contrast, gender aschematic people don't care whether their own or others' behavior is masculine or feminine. Gender-schematic men readily notice masculine and feminine behaviors in other men. Gender-aschematic men do not.

In a sense, gender aschematic people are *androgynous*—they may display both masculine and feminine behaviors. Indeed, Bem's (1981b) gender schema theory evolved from her earlier theorizing about the androgynous personality (see Chapter 2). The emphasis of gender schema theory is different, however. The androgynous person, according to Bem's original theory, possesses both masculine (instrumental) and feminine (expressive) traits. In gender schema theory, however, Bem focused not so much on the kind of person you are (masculine, feminine, or androgynous), but rather on the strength and organization of your beliefs about gender (gender schematic versus gender aschematic).

Where do gender schemas come from? Here Bem's (1981b) theory is only suggestive. Bem proposed that gender schemas come from one's culture, family, and peers. Thus, if you grow up in a strongly gender polarized culture that emphasizes differences between men's and women's roles, you will likely end up being highly gender schematic. On the other hand, if you grow up in settings that minimize the differences between men and women, you are more likely to end up being gender aschematic. Bem (1998) describes her attempt to raise her own two children in a totally nonsexist and gender-aschematic environment.

Other researchers have offered different gender schema theories (Markus, Crane, Bernstein, & Siladi, 1982; Martin, 2000; Martin & Halverson, 1981, 1987). Some of these have focused, more than Bem's (1981b) theory, on the cognitive consequences of gender schemas—for example, how gender schemas influence attention and memory. Arizona State University psychologist Carol Martin describes how her 4-year-old niece, Erin, concluded that girls have eyelashes but boys don't. Accordingly, when Erin drew stick-figure pictures of boys and girls, the girls had eyelashes and the boys did not. One suspects that Erin's developing gender schemas would lead her to focus more on certain aspects of girls' physical appearance and on somewhat different aspects of boys' physical appearance. Departing from Bem's contention that there is a unitary gender schema, some theorists have argued that people possess different schemas for the two sexes, and that same-sex schemas often are more complex and well-developed than other-sex schemas (see Martin, 2000).

In essence, both Kohlberg's (1996) cognitive-developmental theory of gender and gender schema theories assign a central importance to people's *beliefs about gender* and the ways in which people label themselves and their own behavior. Sex differences and individual differences in masculinity and femininity follow from the beliefs and identities we hold. The ultimate sources of gender schemas are cultures, families, teachers, and peers. In this regard, cognitive theories of gender emphasize nurture more than nature.

Social Psychological Theories of Gender

According to social psychology, the current social setting is a major cause of our behavior (Level 3 in Fig. 3.1). Gender stereotypes and beliefs also have an important role in many social psychological theories of gender. However, social psychological analyses tend to focus more on how stereotypes affect *other people's* behavior toward us and how stereotypes lead to self-fulfilling prophecies. Social psychological theories of gender emphasize nurture (environmental and social influences) over nature (biological influences).

Let's briefly examine four important social psychological theories: Alice Eagly's (1987) social role theory of gender, gender as a self-fulfilling prophecy; Claude Steele's (1997) stereotype threat theory; and self-presentational theories of gender. Because the concept of a *gender stereotype* is common to all these approaches, we begin by briefly examining the nature of gender stereotypes.

Gender Stereotypes. The word *stereotype* was coined by the journalist Walter Lippmann (1922), who wrote of the simplified "pictures" that we carry around in our heads about social groups. Contemporary social psychologists view stereotypes as probabilistic beliefs that we hold about groups of people. For example, Deaux and Lewis (1983) asked college students to estimate what percentages of men and women possessed various traits (see Table 3.1). Students' beliefs about men and women were not black and white. Nobody believed that all men are "aggressive," for example, or that all women are "kind." Nonetheless, most students did believe that *on average* more men than women are "aggressive" and more women than men are "kind."

Social psychologists have long wrestled with the question, are stereotypes wrong? Considerable research suggests that stereotypes are oversimplifications of reality. They may cause us to overestimate the differences between groups and to underestimate the variability within groups. This notion is captured by the bigoted statement, "They all look the same to me." Furthermore, stereotypes may distort our perceptions and memories, leading us to see what we expect to see and to remember only information that confirms our stereotypes (see Lippa, 1994, for a review). At the same time, it is important to note that many social psychologists recognize that there may be a "kernel of truth" to some stereotypes. Indeed, some recent research suggests that people's

TABLE 3.1
Gender Stereotypes—Judged Probabilities that Men and
Women Have Various Characteristics

Probability Judgments of Traits*			Probability Judgments of Role Behaviors*			Probability Judgments of Physical Characteristics*		
Charac-teristic	For Men	For Women	Charac-teristic	For Men	For Women	Charac-teristic	For Men	For Women
Independent	.78	.58	Financial provider	.83	.47	Muscular	.64	.36
Competitive	.82	.64	Takes initiative with opposite sex	.82	.54	Deep voice	.73	.30
Warm	.66	.77	Takes care of children	.50	.85	Graceful	.45	.68
Emotional	.56	.84	Cooks meals	.42	.83	Small-boned	.39	.62

Note: *The larger the difference in the estimates for men and women on a given item, the more that chracteristic was stereotypically perceived to differentiate the two sexes.*

Subjects' estimates of the probability that the average person of either sex would possess a characteristic. Subjects' stereotypes tended to be stronger for role behaviors and physical characteristics than for personality traits.

Components of stereotypes about men and women. Source: *Based on Deaux and Lewis (1983).*

social beliefs can at times be surprisingly accurate (see Eagly & Diekman, 1997; Lee, Jussim, & McCauley, 1995). We cannot settle these complex questions here; rather, we simply describe the content of common gender stereotypes.

People hold strong stereotypes about the personality traits possessed by men and women. In one early study, (Rosenkrantz, Vogel, Bee, Broverman, & Broverman, 1968) college students agreed that certain kinds of traits (e.g., "competitive," "logical," "skilled in business," and "self-confident") were more characteristic of men, whereas other kinds of traits (e.g., "gentle," "aware of the feelings of others," and "easily expresses tender feelings") were more characteristic of women. These stereotypes—that men possess instrumental traits and women possess expressive traits—have been documented in many later studies as well (Ashmore, Del Boca, & Wohlers, 1986; Deaux & LaFrance, 1998). These stereotypes are held by children, teens, and adults; by single and married people; and by educated and uneducated people. Furthermore, these stereotypes are fairly consistent across cultures (Williams & Best, 1982), and they are endorsed by both women and men. Despite dramatic changes in women's roles over the past half-century, these stereotypes about men's and women's personalities have remained relatively unchanged over time. You may recall from

Chapter 1 that research offers some support for these stereotypes: The two assessed personality dimensions that show the biggest sex differences are assertiveness (an instrumental trait) and tender-mindedness (an expressive trait).

Of course, gender stereotypes are not just about personality. People also hold stereotypes about men's and women's physical traits (e.g., "muscular," "soft," "hairy"), social roles (e.g., "provider," "does house work"), occupations (e.g., "engineer," "librarian"), and sexuality (e.g., "has a high sex drive," "sexually attracted to men"). One kind of gender stereotype that may have especially negative consequences for women is that there are differences between men's and women's abilities. Although research findings are complex and sometimes inconsistent, they suggest that, in some circumstances, women are judged to be less able and qualified than men are, even when they are evaluated on the basis identical information (Swim, Borgida, Maruyama, & Myers, 1989). Furthermore, there are certain kinds of abilities—such as math and mechanical skills—that people believe show sex differences favoring men.

Social Role Theory. How do gender stereotypes get established in the first place, and once they are in place, do they then constrain what men and women do? In most cultures, women and men occupy quite different roles (Barry, Bacon, & Child, 1957; D'Andrade, 1966). Women are more responsible for childrearing, foraging, and domestic duties; men are more responsible for hunting, fighting, and, in modern society, producing income. According to Alice Eagly's (1987; Eagly, Wood, & Diekman, 2000) social role theory, this sex-based division of labor leads necessarily to gender stereotypes and sex differences in behavior. Constrained by gender roles to rear children and take care of homes, women show more nurturing behaviors, and as a result, people perceive women to be more nurturing. Constrained by their roles to participate more in the competitive world of work, sports, and public service, men display more assertive behaviors, and as a result, people perceive men to be more assertive than women.

Eagly's (1987) theory does not focus on biologically determined differences between women and men, although it does not deny that some may exist. Nor does it devote much effort to explaining the origins of gender roles. However, it seems plausible that biology plays a role—or at least that it played a role in the past—in molding gender roles. For example, female gestation and lactation would lead women in preindustrial societies to be more responsible for child care, and male upper-body strength would lead men to be more responsible for hunting and fighting. Note, however, that the biological explanations offered here focus on *physical* differences between men and women, not on innate psychological differences.

Eagly's (1987) social role theory stresses the power of social roles and settings to mold men's and women's behaviors, which then determine people's stereotypes about men and women. Social role theory argues that gender stereotypes are valid, in the limited sense that they reflect real differences in the current behaviors of men and women. Where stereotypes err, however, is in attributing these differences to innate dispositions rather than to the powerful social roles that channel men's and women's behaviors.

Change the traditional roles of men and women (for example, place women in high management positions while encouraging men to stay home and take care of children), and you will dramatically change the behaviors of men and women, according to social role theory. And ultimately these new behaviors will alter people's stereotypes about men and women. Behavior and gender stereotypes are a function of roles rather than sex chromosomes, hormones, and brain physiology.

Although social role theory focuses more on *sex differences* in behavior than on individual differences in masculinity and femininity, it could easily be extended to explain such individual differences. To the extent that women occupy varied social roles (business manager, mother, teacher, U.S. senator), social role theory would predict that women's degrees of "masculine" and "feminine" behaviors would vary. Thus the source of individual differences in masculinity and femininity is seen to reside in variations among social roles and settings, not in genes, hormones, brains structures, or immutable personality traits.

One prediction of social role theory, then, would seem to be that societies that have more variations in their gender roles will produce men and women who vary more in their levels of masculinity and femininity. Conversely, societies that have more limiting and rigid gender roles will produce men and women who vary less in masculinity and femininity. Strong gender roles would serve to encourage sex differences, but they would discourage variations within each sex. On the other hand, weak and varied gender roles would do just the opposite. Social roles could also interact with genetic predispositions. Societies with varied gender roles would allow freer expression of genetically influenced variations in masculinity and femininity, whereas societies with rigid gender roles would restrict such expression. In this view, cultures and roles are "filters" that permit the expression of some genetic traits but not others (see Brown, 1965).

Gender Stereotypes as Self-Fulfilling Prophecies.   Once people believe something to be true, they often act to make it come true. The sociologist Robert Merton (1948) coined the phrase *self-fulfilling prophecy* to capture this idea. Many social psychology experiments have probed how social beliefs become social reality. The self-perpetuating nature of gender stereotypes was demonstrated in a clever experiment by Berna Skrypnek and Mark Snyder (1982). Pairs of University of Minnesota college students—one male and one female—were asked to divide stereotypically feminine tasks (e.g., decorating a cake) and stereotypically masculine tasks (e.g., fixing a light switch) between them. The man and woman could not directly see one another in this experiment. They sat in different rooms and communicated via switches that signaled their task preferences on a light panel before each student. This arrangement allowed the experimenters to play a trick on some of the male students, who were told that their partners were men, when "he" was in fact a "she."

Perhaps it would come as no surprise to you if this experiment found that in actual male-female pairs, men chose more of the "masculine" tasks and women chose more of the "feminine" tasks. But what do you think happened when a man and a woman were paired together, but the man falsely believed that his female partner was another man? The experiment showed that women "chose" more feminine tasks when they were labeled as women but fewer feminine tasks when their partners incorrectly believed they were men. In other words, women's choices of activities didn't depend solely on their own preferences but also on the expectations of their partners.

Research on self-fulfilling prophecies argues that once gender stereotypes exist, we all unknowingly behave in ways that make them come true. If a teacher, for example, believes that boys tend to do better at math, the teacher might then subtly behave in ways that encourage the boys to do better at math. For example, the teacher might smile more when boys answer math questions, and respond more to boys' questions about math and call on them more when they raise their hands in math classes.

Stereotype Threat. Stanford University psychologist Claude Steele (1997) has described another way in which gender stereotypes may lead to sex differences in behavior. When stereotypes describe women in a negative light (e.g., "Women aren't good at math"), they may then trigger in women anxiety, negative self-evaluations, and concerns about how well they will "come off" in front of others when working on math problems. Steele coined the term *stereotype threat* to refer to this process, which occurs when a negative stereotype about a group triggers thought processes and anxieties that serve to undermine the performance of someone who belongs to the group.

According to Steele (1997), the effects of stereotype threat occur particularly among people who possess the requisite ability to perform well and are highly identified with the ability in question. For example, stereotype threat experiments on the effects of stereotypes about women's math ability often study women who have taken many college-level math classes and who want to do well at math. Experiments find that when college students are given challenging math tests, women perform worse than men do when the test is described as related to math ability and to gender. However, women perform as well as men when the test is seen as unrelated to their ability or to gender.

Why is the performance of competent women undermined when ability and gender are made salient? According to Steele (1997), when women take a math test, the negative cultural stereotype about women's lack of math ability is always lurking in the background, ready to create worry and anxiety that will undermine test performance. Women worry most about negative gender stereotypes (about their math ability, for example) when they believe that a test measures their ability and when they are induced to think about gender stereotypes.

Self-Presentation Theory.   The various theories we've examined try to explain how people end up with something called gender. Gender shows itself in two ways—as differences between males and females and as individual differences in masculinity and femininity within each sex. According to the theories we've considered, gender is dictated by genes, hormones, and brain structures; or it's molded by early relations with parents, by conditioning and modeling, by cognitive labeling and schemas, by social roles, and by stereotypes. Whichever approach you prefer, gender is a real "thing" that people end up possessing, in one form or another.

More radical views—often proposed by feminist theorists—hold that gender is a cultural invention, a social construction, and a self-presentation we enact in certain settings, with certain people (Fausto-Sterling, 1992; Gergen & Davis, 1997; Kessler & McKenna, 1978). According to this perspective, gender is not something we *are* but something we *do*. Psychologists Kay Deaux and Brenda Major (1987) argue that we play our roles as men and women depending on our own conceptions of gender (self-schemas and self-concepts), others' gender expectations (gender stereotypes), and the setting we happen to be in. For example, a woman may be a no-nonsense, assertive executive at work but quite feminine when she's on a date. Furthermore, this woman may alter how she behaves on a date depending on the setting (going hiking versus going dancing) and depending on what she thinks her date expects of her.

One study found that college women performed worse on an intelligence test and described themselves in more stereotypically feminine terms when they anticipated meeting a very attractive man who said he preferred "traditional" women (Zanna & Pack, 1975). Another study found that women changed the amount of food they ate depending of the man they were with (Mori, Chaiken, & Pliner, 1987). Because people stereotypically judge women who eat small amounts to be more "feminine," if a woman wants to present a feminine image, she may eat less. Indeed, this study found that a woman who talked to a man she considered to be attractive tended to eat less snack mix (which just happened to be sitting on a table nearby) than did a woman who talked with a man she considered unattractive. Another study found that college women changed their style and tone of voice when they were talking with intimate versus casual male friends on the telephone (Montepare & Vega, 1988). When women spoke with boyfriends, their voices became more feminine, baby-like, and high pitched. All these studies suggest that femininity and masculinity may be "acts" that we go into or out of, depending on the situation.

Self-presentational theories propose that gender is socially constructed—that gender is defined, enforced, and created by cultural beliefs. Such theories are in opposition to essentialist views of gender, which hold that there are in fact real differences between the two sexes and that the traits of masculinity and femininity actually do exist. At their most extreme, social constructionist theories construe gender to be a social fiction, a chimera stitched together by cultural traditions, social roles, and gender stereotypes. In a utopian nonsexist society, the very concept of gender would cease to exist, according to this point of view. If boys and girls were treated the same and gender stereotypes were abolished, many behavioral sex differences would disappear, and though people would vary in the myriad ways that people inevitably do, masculinity and femininity would have no meaning. In short, there would be nothing for theories of gender to explain.

SUMMARY

Theories of gender focus on four kinds of explanations: (a) group-level factors, such as the biological and social groups we belong to, (b) past biological and social-environmental factors, such as fetal hormones and parental rearing, (c) current biological and social-environmental factors, such as current hormone levels and social settings, and (d) internal factors, such as personality traits, attitudes, stereotypes, and schemas. These levels of explanation are not independent of one another. Factors at each level influence factors at succeeding levels, and factors at each level may interact with one another.

Biological theories of gender use Darwin's theory of evolution as an organizing framework. Evolutionary theory describes how traits are selected based on their adaptiveness in particular environments. Traits that foster survival and reproduction tend to get passed on to the next generation; traits that do not die out. Modern evolutionary theory often takes a "gene-centered" rather than "individual-centered" view of natural selection. Sexual selection is a kind of natural selection whereby traits are selected because they help individuals to mate. Evolutionary theories of gender propose that, because of differences between male and female reproduction, men and women evolved to have somewhat different reproductive strategies and physical and behavioral traits.

Evolution shows its effects through genes and physiology. The physiological factors most studied in relation to gender are sex hormones and brain structures. Hormonal theories propose that prenatal hormones organize sex differences in the nervous system, whereas adult hormone levels activate gender-related behaviors.

Environmental theories of gender focus on rearing, social roles, gender beliefs, and social settings as causes of sex differences and of individual differences in masculinity and femininity. Social learning theories propose that sex differences are learned via classical conditioning, operant conditioning, and modeling. Cognitive-developmental theory suggests that when children label themselves as boys and girls, they try to act consistently with their gender labels. Gender schema theory argues that some people think more in terms of gender than others and this influences their behavior. The source of gender schemas is thought to be the social environment.

Social psychological theories of gender emphasize the power of the social setting to create sex differences. Such theories often focus on gender stereotypes, their causes and consequences. Alice Eagly's (1987) social role theory proposes that gender roles (e.g., women as mothers, men as workers) lead women and men to behave differently, and this leads people to form gender stereotypes. The theory of self-fulfilling prophecies suggests that once gender stereotypes exist, people act in ways that make them come true. Claude Steele's (1997) stereotype threat theory proposes that negative stereotypes about group performance (such as stereotypes about women's math abilities) lead group members to experience intrusive thoughts and anxieties about their performance, which undermine their performance. Self-presentation theories argue that gender is an "act" that varies depending on the situations we're in, the beliefs we hold about gender, and the expectations of others. According to such theories, gender is not something we *are* but something we *do*.

Social constructionists propose that gender is a cultural creation. They argue against essentialist views that hold that gender, masculinity, and femininity are stable characteristics of individuals, and they reject biological theories of gender.

4

The Case for Nature

Parents sometimes worry about restricting the masculinity of their sons. They shouldn't worry. With a million years of evolution behind them, most boys will be masculine no matter what their parents do. If they are not masculine, it is more likely because of physiology than parenting. General Douglas McArthur's mother wanted to guide him so carefully that she moved to West Point to watch over him when he was a cadet. MacArthur is not the only manly hero who had an "overprotective" mother.

—*Heroes, Rogues, and Lovers: Testosterone and Behavior*
James M. Dabbs

Do biological factors contribute to sex differences in human behavior? Do they also lead to individual differences in masculinity and femininity? How can we answer these questions? There are a number of possibilities. First, we can examine the results of experiments that probe the impact of sex hormones on animals' nervous systems and sex-linked behavior. Second, we can study people who were exposed to unusual levels of sex hormones early in life because of genetic or hormonal abnormalities. Third, we can examine evidence on whether people's levels of sex hormones are related to gender-related behaviors, such as aggression, visual-spatial ability, and sexual orientation. And finally, we can contemplate tragic real-life events that provide information about the power of nature and nurture to influence gender—such as when a baby boy loses his penis because of a botched circumcision procedure and is subsequently raised as a girl.

ANIMAL EXPERIMENTS

Because it is possible to do experiments on animals that would be un-
ethical to do on people, we have more detailed knowledge about the
effects of sex hormones on animals than on humans. Decades of research show that sex hormones affect animals' nerve cells, which are
the building blocks of their nervous system. Sex hormones influence
the growth of nerve cells, the selective death of nerve cells, the tissues
that nerve cells enter into, the density of nerve cells in various regions
of the brain and spinal cord, and the connections nerve cells make with
one another (Breedlove, 1994; MacLusky & Naftolin, 1981). All these effects may lead to sex differences in the nervous systems of people and
lower animals.

Consider the following example: Both lower animals (e.g., rats) and
humans have a collection of nerve cells in the lower spine called the
spinal nucleus of the bulbocavernosus. In humans, these cells control
(in men) a muscle that wraps around the base of the penis and con-
tracts during ejaculation and (in women) a muscle that wraps around
the opening of the vagina and controls vaginal contraction. In both rats
and people, males have more nerve cells in the spinal nucleus of the
bulbocavernosus than do females. Sex hormones—particularly prenatal or perinatal (around the time of birth) testosterone—affect the development and death rate of these nerve cells (Forger, Hodges, Roberts,
& Breedlove, 1992; Nordeen, Nordeen, Sengelaub, & Arnold, 1985).

Sex hormones affect animals' behaviors as well as their nervous systems. Indeed, the behavioral effects of hormones were shown before
their physiological effects were proven (Phoenix, Goy, Gerall, & Young,
1959). Experiments on rats and other rodents show that early exposure
to androgens masculinizes behavior. Females exposed to androgens (as
well as normal males, who are naturally exposed to androgens) show
male-typical behaviors, such as rough-and-tumble play and sexual
mounting. Males who have the effects of androgen stopped, either
through castration or through chemicals that block its action (as well
as normal females) show female-typical behaviors such as the female
sexual posture (called lordosis).

Experiments on primates also demonstrate that early exposure to
sex hormones influences later behaviors. Rhesus monkeys consistently
show sex differences in rough play and foot-clasp mounting (the sexual
posture that males use when mating). Exposing females to early androgens masculinizes their behaviors (Wallen, 1996). Other behaviors that
show sex differences in rhesus monkeys, such as sexual presentation of
the rump, aggression, and submissive postures, seem to depend more
on the social rearing of monkeys—whether monkeys are raised in

same-sex or mixed-sex environments, or whether they are reared by their mother or are separated from her. Nonetheless, these behaviors often show sex differences in natural settings, and they too are influenced by early exposure to testosterone.

A particularly fascinating example of the effects of hormones on brain structures and behavior comes from research on songbirds (Cook, Hegstrom, Villeneuve, & Breedlove, 1998). In a classic study, Nottebohm and Arnold (1976) showed that in zebra finches, the brain region that controls the production of song is more than five times larger in males than in females. Male finches sing much more and produce more complex and elaborate songs than females, and thus this brain difference is matched by a behavior difference.

The difference between the "song regions" of male and female finches' brains results from the effects of early exposure to sex hormones. In birds, testosterone often acts on brain cells by first being converted into estrogen (a process called aromatization). Experiments show that female finches exposed early in life to elevated levels of *estrogen* show masculinized brains and sing like male finches as adults, as long as they are given androgens as adults to activate their song production (Gurney & Konishi, 1979). Thus sex hormones show both organizational and activational effects in songbirds (see Chapter 3). The songs of male birds are molded by the environment as well as by hormones—male birds must be exposed to the songs of their species while growing up to show well-formed songs as adults. Thus biological factors work in concert with, not in opposition to, learning.

HUMANS WITH UNUSUAL EARLY EXPOSURE TO SEX HORMONES

Do animal results generalize to humans? For example, does early exposure to androgens masculinize human brains and behaviors? One way to answer this question is to examine evidence from people with unusual exposure to sex hormones.

CAH Females

Some girls suffer from a condition known as congenital adrenal hyperplasia (CAH). Because of a genetic defect, the adrenal glands of CAH girls enlarge prenatally and produce abnormally high amounts of androgens (male hormones). Though CAH girls are genetic XX females, they have nonetheless been exposed to unusually high levels of androgens prenatally (and sometimes postnatally as well, depending on how early their disorder is diagnosed and treated). CAH girls can experience varying degrees of genital masculinization, depending on the severity of their condition. In some cases (for example, where labia fuse to produce an empty scrotum or the clitoris enlarges to the point of appearing to be a penis) the genitals may be surgically altered to look more like those of a typical female.

CAH girls generally grow up to have a female gender identity. That is, they think of themselves as girls and women. However, a number of studies suggest that they are often less content with being female and more interested in being male than non-CAH girls (Ehrhardt & Baker, 1974; Slijper, 1984). Although most CAH girls grow up to be heterosexual, CAH women report an increased incidence of bisexual and lesbian attraction compared with non-CAH women (Dittmann, Kappes, & Kappes, 1992; Money & Schwartz, 1977). CAH girls tend to engage in more male-typical play than non-CAH girls. They like participating in rough-and-tumble activities and sports, dressing in clothing that appears more "masculine," and playing with boys and boys' toys (Berenbaum & Hines, 1992; Dittmann, Kappes, Kappes, Börger, Stegner, et al., 1990; Slijper, 1984). CAH girls often dislike girl-typical activities such as playing with dolls and wearing makeup, jewelry, and frilly clothes.

The degree of masculine behavior shown by CAH females does not seem to be related to their degree of genital masculinization, and this argues against the hypothesis that family reactions to genital masculinization produce the behavioral masculinization of CAH females (Berenbaum & Hines, 1992; Dittmann, Kappes, Kappes, Börger, Meyer-Bahlburg, et al., 1990, Slijper, 1984). On some personality measures, CAH girls score more like boys than non-CAH girls do. For example, they are higher on aggression scales. CAH girls also sometimes show more male-typical levels of visual-spatial abilities than non-CAH girls (Hampson, Rovet, & Altman, 1998; Resnick, Berenbaum, Gottesman, & Bouchard, 1986).

Overall, research on CAH girls suggests that early exposure to androgens masculinizes human females in a number of ways. It is important to note that although CAH girls have elevated levels of androgens, their prenatal androgen levels are not as high as those of boys. Presumably, if XX individuals were exposed to more typical male levels of prenatal androgens, they might show even more masculinization of their behaviors.

Androgen-Insensitive Males

There are a small number of genetic XY males who, because of a genetic error, do not have androgen receptors in their cells (Quigley et al., 1995). Androgen receptors are special proteins in cell membranes designed to "hook up" with testosterone, and unless they are present, testosterone cannot affect cells. Androgen receptors are present in many cells throughout the body, and this provides evidence for the pervasive impact of testosterone on bodily development and physiology.

The effects of complete androgen insensitivity are dramatic. Affected XY individuals develop as females, in the sense that their bodies look completely female (indeed, in some ways, ideally female), and they develop a female gender identity. In terms of their mental abilities, androgen-insensitive XY individuals are more like women than men. For example, they show female-typical performance on visual-spatial and verbal tests (Imperato-McGinley, Pichardo, Gautier, Boyer, & Bryden, 1991).

Such individuals are generally romantically and sexually attracted to males (Wisniewski et al., 2000). However, they have testes (male gonads) that produce normal amounts of testosterone. Their testes do not descend to an external position, though. Typically, androgen insensitivity syndrome is detected at puberty, when affected individuals fail to menstruate as normal women do. Because they have testes and no ovaries, androgen-insensitive XY individuals are infertile. Usually their undescended testes are surgically removed, because left inside the body, they have an elevated risk for cancer.

Studies of androgen-insensitive individuals show the importance of testosterone in promoting normal male development, and they demonstrate that even in XY humans, development will follow a "default" female pattern in the absence of successful action by testosterone. Is an androgen-insensitive XY individual a "man" or a "woman"? In virtually all external physical and behavioral characteristics, the individual is female. And certainly, the androgen-insensitive individual thinks of herself as female. As adults, androgen-insensitive XY individuals often marry men. However, *genetically* they are males.

Reductase-Deficient Males

Some XY individuals have a single-gene defect that creates problems with an enzyme (reductase) that converts testosterone to a related hormone called dihydrotestosterone (Imperato-McGinley, Peterson, Gautier, & Sturla, 1979; Wilson, 1999; Wilson, Griffin, & Russell, 1993). You may recall from Chapter 3 that testosterone masculinizes the brain; however, dihydrotestosterone is responsible for masculinizing the external genitalia. Reductase-deficient males experience male-typical levels of testosterone prenatally, and presumably they experience male-typical masculinization of their brains. But because of their lack of dihydrotestosterone, they are born with female or sometimes ambiguous-looking genitals. Such individuals are often reared as girls.

However, the androgen surge that occurs at puberty eventually masculinizes their genitals. The reductase-deficient individual's "clitoris" enlarges into a sexually functioning penis, and the formerly undescended testes lower into partially fused labia to form a scrotum. In the Dominican Republic, where isolated communities of people possess high frequencies of the genes that lead to reductase deficiency, the Spanish slang for the condition is *guevedoces,* which translates to "eggs (i.e., testicles) at twelve."

Individuals with reductase deficiency are fascinating to study because they have had normal male exposure to prenatal testosterone, but their female-appearing genitals often lead them to be reared as girls. Which wins out—prenatal hormones or rearing? The answer varies from individual to individual (Wilson, 1999). However, many of these people choose to change from "female" to "male" after puberty, and this suggests that prenatal exposure to androgens can have a potent impact on later gender identity and behavior, even in individuals who are reared as females and who have female-appearing genitals early in life.

Effects of Estrogen: DES Children and Turner's Syndrome Women

The studies just summarized address the early effects of *testosterone* (or of related androgens, such as dihydrotestosterone) on human behavior. What about estrogens (female hormones)? Do they also play a role in human sex differences and gender-related behaviors? There are two kinds of evidence relevant to this question: (a) data collected from people exposed prenatally to the artificial estrogen DES, and (b) data collected from women who suffer from a genetic condition known as Turner's syndrome.

Females Exposed to DES. In the 1950s and 1960s, hundreds of thousands of pregnant women received the synthetic estrogen DES to prevent miscarriages (Edelman, 1986). The use of DES was halted in the early 1970s when it was demonstrated that it was not effective in stopping miscarriages and that it increased the odds for certain kinds of cervical cancer in women exposed to DES prenatally. As noted before, estrogens can sometimes have paradoxical effects. In animal studies, they can masculinize rather than feminize brains and behaviors. The reason for this is that in many animals, testosterone is converted (aromatized) to estrogen inside of cells, and it is the estrogen that directly affects genes and tissue development.

You might wonder what keeps female fetuses' from being masculinized by their mothers' natural estrogen? The answer is that there are physical and chemical mechanisms that prevent the mothers' estrogen from entering fetal brains and from becoming chemically active in fe tuses. However, administration of DES may overwhelm female fetuses' natural defenses against too much estrogen. The net result may be that DES masculinizes female fetuses' brains and behavior in certain ways. Research shows that women prenatally exposed to DES are more likely to have homosexual or bisexual attractions than non-DES women (Ehrhardt et al., 1985; Meyer-Bahlburg et al., 1984; Meyer-Bahlberg et al., 1995). These findings are particularly interesting in combination with similar findings in CAH women. Because women exposed prenatally to DES do not have masculinized genitals, the effects of DES on sexual orientation cannot be due to this factor. Thus prenatal hormones, in and of themselves, can have effects on women's later sexual orientation.

DES exposure seems to have little or no effect on girls' patterns of childhood play or on adult women's sex-typed interests or cognitive abilities (Lish, Meyer-Bahlburg, Ehrhardt, Travis, & Veridiano, 1992; Wilcox, Maxey, & Herbst, 1992). Some studies suggest subtle brain differences between DES and non-DES women. For example, one study used a dichotic listening task (where participants are asked to recognize syllables in the right and left ears) and found that DES women appeared to have more lateralized brains, like men (Hines & Shipley, 1984). In animal research, exposure to DES also sometimes makes certain areas of females' brains more like males' (Hines, Alsum, Roy, Gorski, & Goy, 1987; Hines & Goy, 1985).

The effects of DES on men seem to be even weaker than its effects on women. There are hints that prenatal exposure to DES may slightly masculinize boys' childhood activities and reduce certain kinds of spatial abilities (Kester, Green, Finch, & Williams, 1980). In general, however, DES doesn't seem to have much effect on boys. More broadly, the effects of DES on human sex-typed behaviors are much weaker than the effects of androgens.

Turner's Syndrome.   Some human females lack estrogen completely because of a condition know as Turner's syndrome (Lippe, 1991; Rovet, 1993; White, 1994). Turner's syndrome females have only one X chromosome, whereas nonaffected women have two X chromosomes. (Turner's syndrome can come in varying degrees. Sometimes, not all the body cells in a Turner's syndrome woman lack an X chromosome. However, these variations need not concern us here. A corresponding syndrome does not exist for males, because a male embryo lacking an X chromosome would not survive.) Turner's syndrome females have gonads that degenerate during fetal development, and they are born without ovaries and uteri. Because of their lack of ovaries, they do not produce natural estrogens, and of course, they are infertile. Physically, Turner's syndrome women tend to be very short, and they often have somewhat abnormal physical traits (for example, thick necks, small breasts, childlike faces).

Despite their lack of estrogen, Turner's syndrome females develop a strong female gender identity, and their sexual orientation is generally heterosexual (Ehrhardt, Greenberg, & Money, 1970). If anything, Turner's syndrome girls often display highly feminine interests, dress, and play patterns (Downey, Ehrhardt, Morishima, Bell, & Gruen, 1987). They typically show normal performance on verbal tests but depressed performance on tests of visual-spatial and quantitative abilities (Bender, Linden, & Robinson, 1994; Pennington et al., 1985). They may also show a lack of social skills and difficulties in accurately judging people's facial expressions (Skuse et al., 1997), and in this regard, Turner's syndrome females are *not* like typical females. In studies of brain lateralization (such as dichotic listening tasks), Turner's syndrome women often show a kind of "hyperfeminine" pattern. That is, their brains seem to be even less lateralized than the average woman's, whose brain is in turn less lateralized than the average man's (Clark, Klonoff, & Hayden, 1990; Gordon & Galatzer, 1980).

In sum, Turner's syndrome women show enhanced femininity in certain ways (childhood play, brain lateralization) but cognitive deficiencies in other ways. Using evidence from these women to infer the effects of estrogen is complicated by the fact that the missing X chromosome can produce genetic effects above and beyond the effects of no estrogen—for example, Turner's syndrome females lack testosterone as well as estrogen. One hypothesis that is consistent with data from Turner's syndrome women is that some amount of estrogen is necessary for normal development in women, but estrogen doesn't have the powerful organizational and activational effects that androgens do. Despite the fact that Turner's syndrome individuals lack an X chromosome, ovaries, and estrogen, they are still women.

CORRELATIONAL STUDIES OF HORMONES AND BEHAVIOR IN HUMANS

We've just surveyed evidence collected from people with various kinds of genetic and hormonal abnormalities. We turn next to studies of normal human variations in sex hormones—particularly variations in testosterone—and how they are related to sex-typed behaviors.

Testosterone and Human Behavior

High levels of testosterone, in both humans and lower animals, are associated with aggressiveness (Archer, 1991; Benton, 1992). In one study of more than 700 prison inmates, psychologist James Dabbs and his

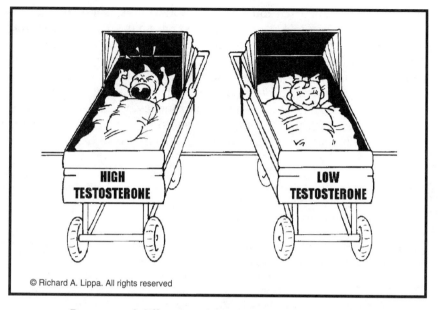

*Do prenatal differences in testosterone levels lead to
sex differences in behavior?*

colleagues found that high-testosterone inmates were more likely to
have committed violent crimes than low-testosterone inmates. They
were also more likely to have broken prison rules and to have acquired
the reputation of being tough and mean (Dabbs, Carr, Frady, & Riad,
1995). A U.S. government study provided additional information about
aggression and testosterone when it assessed more than four thousand
Vietnam veterans on a host of psychological and physiological measures, including serum (blood) testosterone levels. Analyses subsequently showed that veterans who were high in testosterone were considerably more likely to report delinquent behaviors as children. They
also reported higher adult rates of drug and alcohol use, greater numbers of sexual partners, and more participation in active combat during the Vietnam war (Dabbs & Morris, 1990). Yet another study showed
that college fraternities whose members had lower than average testosterone levels were more civilized and polite to female experimenters,
whereas fraternities whose members were high in testosterone were
more likely to live up to the *Animal House* caricature of being crude,
rude, and coarse (Dabbs, Hargrove, & Heusel, 1996).

Men who are high in testosterone are less likely to get married, and
when they do marry, they are more likely to have unhappy marriages
that end in divorce (Booth & Dabbs, 1993). They tend also to be less
successful in their jobs than men who are lower in testosterone, and

this may result from their impatience, impulsiveness, and aggressiveness. James Dabbs (2000), a psychologist who has spent years studying the effects of testosterone, notes that testosterone can have paradoxical effects on occupational success. On the one hand, it can foster dominance, risk taking, and bravado, which helps in some occupations—such as acting, professional athletics, trial law, and military combat. On the other hand, high testosterone levels can lead to imprudent, reckless, and just plain obnoxious behavior, which interferes with performance in more sedate occupations. Dabbs notes,

> High levels of testosterone evolved when the human race was young and people needed the skills of youth. High testosterone helped them compete, but it also led them to take risks, fight, get injured, and die young—and now it interferes with many modern activities. High-testosterone individuals are energetic but impatient; they do poorly in school and end up with fewer years of education; they can dominate others in face-to-face meetings, but they have trouble handling the complexities of business; they lean toward harsh and competitive activities and away from subdued and thoughtful ones. High testosterone is a drawback when careful planning, reliable work habits, and patience are needed, or when workers must attend to the needs of others. Except for a few of the top jobs in sports and acting, high testosterone, to my knowledge, does not contribute to financial success. (pp. 150–151)

Interestingly, high-testosterone men display different sorts of nonverbal behaviors than do low-testosterone men. They smile less in general and appear meaner, harder, and more threatening than low-testosterone individuals (Dabbs, 1997). When they do smile, high-testosterone men seem less warm and sincere, in part because they smile with their mouths but not with their eyes. One study found similar effects for women (Cashdan, 1995). The voice pitch of high-testosterone men tends to be lower than that of low-testosterone men, but this effect has not been observed in women (Dabbs & Malinger, 1999).

There is evidence that human testosterone levels are related to cognitive abilities as well as social behaviors. Some studies find that high-testosterone levels are linked to better visual spatial abilities (Silverman, Kastuk, Choi, & Phillips, 1999). According to other studies, however, the relationship between testosterone and spatial abilities follows an inverted U pattern, with both very low and high levels of testosterone associated with lower spatial ability and moderate levels associated with higher abilities (Nyborg, 1983; Tan & Tan, 1998). Because women have much lower average levels of testosterone than men, this would imply that testosterone may be positively associated with women's spatial abilities, but negatively associated with men's

(Gouchie & Kimura, 1991; Ostatnikova, Laznibatova, & Dohnanyiova, 1996; Petersen, 1976; Shute, Pellegrino, Hubert, & Reynolds, 1983). Doreen Kimura (1999), a prominent researcher on the effects of sex hormones on cognitive abilities, concludes that peak spatial abilities are shown by people whose testosterone levels are in the "low male range."

In one study, men with very low levels of testosterone showed impaired spatial abilities but normal verbal abilities (Hier & Crowley, 1982). In another study, when a group of men were given testosterone to improve their sexual functioning, they also showed improved performance on a block-design test as a side effect (Janowsky, Oviatt, & Orwoll, 1994). Female-to-male transsexuals who receive testosterone in preparation for sex reassignment surgery experience improved visual-spatial abilities, but they simultaneously suffer from decreased verbal fluency (Van Goozen, Cohen-Ketenis, Gooren, Frijda, & van De Poll, 1995). A Dutch female-to-male transsexual beginning testosterone therapy provided the following vivid account:

> I have problems expressing myself, I stumble over my words. Your use of language becomes less broad, more direct and concise. Your use of words changes, you become more concrete. . . .
> The visual is so strong . . . when walking in the streets I absorb the things around me. I am an artist, but this is so strong. It gives a euphoric feeling. I do miss, however, the overall picture. Now I have to do one thing at a time; I used to be able to do different things simultaneously.
> I can't make fine hand movement anymore; I let things fall out of my hands. (Van Goozen, 1994, p. 173)

You may have noticed that behaviors and traits that are linked to testosterone are often behaviors and traits that also show sex differences (see Chapter 1). For example, men and women show on-average differences in physical aggressiveness, sexual activity levels, dominance, nurturance, visual-spatial ability, and a number of nonverbal behaviors such as smiling. Testosterone research typically studies *within-sex* relationships between testosterone and behavior. It is an inferential leap to suggest that *sex differences* in aggression, dominance, nurturance, and nonverbal behaviors are due to sex differences in testosterone levels. Still, it is worth noting that, on average, men have testosterone levels 8 or more times those of women.

Although most research has focused on the correlates of men's testosterone levels, research has also demonstrated relationships for women. A study of 84 college women found that high-testosterone women reported being more enterprising, impulsive, and uninhibited but less anxious, kind, mature, and warm than low-testosterone women

(Baucom, Besch, & Callahan, 1985). And a study of 171 female inmates showed that, like men, women prisoners high in testosterone were more likely to have committed violent crimes and were more likely to be rated by prison staff as aggressive and dominant (Dabbs, Ruback, Frady, Hopper, & Sgoutas, 1988; Dabbs & Hargrove, 1997). In general, findings for women are similar to those for men. Women who are high in testosterone are characterized as aggressive, tough, competitive, dominant, and risk-taking. In both women and men, testosterone is linked to sensation seeking and lack of inhibition (Daitzman & Zuckerman, 1980; Daitzman, Zuckerman, Sammelwitz, & Ganjam, 1978).

Most studies on the relation between testosterone and human behavior have measured hormone levels in *adults*, usually from blood or saliva samples. You may recall, however, that biological theories propose that *prenatal* exposure to sex hormones is critically important in organizing later sex-typed behaviors (see chapter 3). Unfortunately, it's very difficult to measure prenatal hormones in humans. However, one recent study indirectly measured female fetuses' exposure to testosterone by measuring testosterone and other chemicals in their mothers' blood during pregnancy (Udry, 2000). The daughters' degree of feminine behavior was measured in adulthood. Daughters who had been fetally exposed to higher levels of testosterone in the second trimester of pregnancy were more behaviorally masculine as adults. That is, they were more interested in male-typical, high-status occupations, they were less interested in caring for children, and they were judged to be more masculine in their demeanor and nonverbal behaviors. They also were higher on personality scales of instrumentality (i.e., dominance) and lower on scales of expressiveness (nurturance).

Physical Characteristics Related to Prenatal Testosterone

Recent research has tried to infer people's exposure to prenatal testosterone levels indirectly, by measuring body characteristics thought to be related to prenatal testosterone. One such characteristic is the ratio of the lengths of the second and fourth digits of the hand (i.e., the index finger and the ring finger; Manning et al., 2000). Women tend to have shorter ring fingers relative to their index fingers, whereas men tend to have longer ring fingers relative to their index fingers. Index-to-ring-finger length ratios correlate with people's occupational choices, fertility levels, dominance, and sexual orientations (Manning, Scutt, Wilson, & Lewis-Jones, 1998; Williams et al., 2000). These findings suggest that prenatal testosterone levels are linked to adult gender-related behaviors.

Otoacoustic emissions provide another route to inferring prenatal testosterone exposure. Otoacoustic emissions are very faint sounds produced spontaneously by the inner ear or in response to faint clicks. Women tend to show more otoacoustic emissions than men, and this sex difference—like most physical sex differences that occur early in life—is thought to result from prenatal exposure to testosterone (McFadden, 1998). Otoacoustic emissions are related to adult sexual orientation (McFadden & Pasanen, 1998; McFadden & Pasanen, 1999). Once again, the implication is that prenatal testosterone levels influence adult gender-related behaviors. Both finger lengths and otoacoustic emissions seem to be fixed early in life—probably prenatally—and thus they are not likely to be influenced by socialization and cultural learning.

Other Hormones and Gender-Related Behaviors

Testosterone is only one of many sex hormones. Before leaving the topic of hormones and human behavior, let's briefly consider the effects of estrogen. Research on Turner's syndrome suggests that a certain minimum level of estrogen may be necessary for normal cognitive development in women. Are normal variations in estrogens related to other aspects of human behavior? Studying the effects of estrogen levels is complicated by the fact that the levels change dramatically over the course of women's menstrual cycles. Nonetheless, recent evidence suggests that estrogen, like testosterone, can influence behavior.

Some studies have investigated whether variations in women's estrogen levels are related to their performance on cognitive tasks. Several studies show that when estrogens are high (in midmenstrual cycle, around when ovulation occurs) women tend to show better speech articulation, verbal fluency, and manual dexterity. In contrast, when estrogens are low (around the time of menstruation), women tend to do better on visual-spatial tasks (Hampson, 1990a, 1990b; Hampson & Kimura, 1988; Phillips & Silverman, 1997). The relation between estrogen levels and cognitive performance is not necessarily large, particularly considering that women's estrogen levels can vary by a factor of 20 over the course of their menstrual cycle. Nonetheless, studies of changes in cognitive abilities over the course of women's menstrual cycles make the interesting theoretical point that estrogen levels in adults can display activating effects on specific cognitive abilities.

As noted before, some estrogen may be necessary for optimal mental performance. Postmenopausal women show improved performance on mental ability tests after taking estrogen supplements (Resnic, Metter, & Zonderman, 1997), and estrogen therapy may reduce symptoms of Alzheimer's disease in elderly women (Jacobs et al., 1998; Tierney & Luine, 1998).

"NATURAL EXPERIMENTS" AND SEX REASSIGNMENT

A small number of newborns suffer from a congenital disorder called pelvic field defect, which leads to gross abnormalities of the abdominal organs and, in a boy, a missing penis. In the past, doctors often recommended that these genetic boys be reared as girls and undergo surgical sex reassignment. The assumption was that a boy born without a penis could not live a normal life as a boy and would be better off reared as a girl. The sex reassignment entailed castration, for a boy with pelvic field defect is born with testicles even though he has no penis. Thus these XY boys were exposed to normal male amounts of testosterone prenatally but were castrated soon after birth and reared as females. What won out in this case—nature or nurture?

Johns Hopkins University psychiatrist William Reiner (2000) studied a group of pelvic defect children. He found that despite surgical reassignment and conscientious attempts by parents to rear them as girls, most of these XY children rejected their reassigned sex and insisted they were in fact boys. Thus, this natural experiment provides compelling evidence that normal prenatal exposure to androgens often leads to male-typical behaviors and a male gender identity, even in castrated boys reared as girls.

In the equally fascinating "John/Joan" case, one of two identical twin boys lost his penis due to a botched circumcision procedure. On the advice of doctors, the parents of the twin who lost his penis decided to surgically reassign him to be a girl and rear him as a girl. Bruce (the real name of the boy who lost his penis) became Brenda. Thus one of two identical XY twins was reared as a boy and the other as a girl. Although early reports suggested that the sex reassignment had been successful (Money, 1975), later evidence revealed that Brenda was never really comfortable as a girl (Diamond & Sigmundson, 1997). In early adulthood, Brenda became Bruce once again, and he now lives as a man with a wife and adopted children (for a gripping personal account, see Colapinto, 2000).

Several other cases have been reported of boys who lost their penises early in life and then were reared—with varying degrees of success—as girls. All these individuals were genetic XY males who had had prenatal exposure to typical male levels of testosterone but then were surgically castrated and reared as girls. Many but not all these XY children later chose to live as males, again suggesting that prenatal exposure to testosterone plays a powerful role in determining later male gender identity and masculine behaviors. Even when such an individual adopts the identity of a female, she may still be sexually attracted to women and show masculine interests (Bradley, Oliver, Chernick, & Zucker, 1998).

BIOLOGY AND HUMAN SEX DIFFERENCES

So far we have presented strong circumstantial evidence that biology plays a role in many behavioral phenomena related to gender. Animal research shows that early sex hormones lead to differences in the nervous systems of males and females, which in turn influence the behaviors of males and females. Data from humans with hormonal abnormalities and evidence from "natural experiments" suggest that early hormonal events in people are related to later gender-linked behaviors. And studies show that normal variations in sex hormones—particularly testosterone—are related to a number of socially significant human behaviors, many of which are sex-linked. Still, none of these studies directly confronts the question: Do biological factors cause human sex differences?

How can we assess the role of biology in human sex differences? There are four kinds of relevant evidence (see Maccoby & Jacklin, 1974): (a) the age at which sex differences emerge, (b) the consistency of sex differences across cultures and over historical time, (c) the consistency of sex differences across species, and (d) the relation of physiological factors (such as sex hormones and brain structures) to behaviors that show sex differences (e.g., aggression, visual-spatial ability).

Why are these four kinds of evidence relevant? Let's consider each in turn. The earlier a sex difference occurs in life, the less likely it is to be learned, and the more plausible it is that biology plays a role in producing the difference. The most clear-cut case would be if a sex difference appears immediately after birth. Some human sex differences do in fact appear at a very early age. For example, male infants are somewhat more irritable and active than female infants are (Eaton & Enns, 1986; Phillips, King, & DuBois, 1978). Unfortunately, newborn infants don't show many of the behaviors that gender researchers are most interested in studying—behaviors such as aggression, visual-spatial performance, and mating practices. If a sex difference does not occur until late in development, then the likelihood increases that social learning and cultural factors play a role. For example, boys begin to exceed girls in math performance in their teenage years, and this gender difference may reflect adolescent girls' acquired views about which behaviors are seen as "feminine" and which are not (Eccles & Jacobs, 1986).

Evidence on the developmental timetables of sex differences is at best suggestive about the roles of biology and socialization. You may recall from Chapter 1 that sex differences in aggression are largest in children, moderate in adolescents, and smallest in adults (Hyde, 1986). One interpretation of this pattern is that although boys are biologically predisposed to be more aggressive than girls, with increasing age, this sex difference is tempered by socialization, which often works to reduce everyone's aggressiveness. However, even when a sex difference does not emerge until late in development, it still may be strongly influenced by biological factors. Sex differences in many sexual behaviors don't emerge until after puberty. However, these differences cannot occur until boys and girls physically (i.e., biologically) mature into men and women. Pattern baldness is a largely genetic trait that does not show a sex difference until later in life. However, this does not imply that male pattern baldness is learned.

The consistency of sex differences across cultures constitutes a second kind of evidence about the contribution of biology to sex differences. The more consistent a sex difference is across cultures, the more likely it is influenced by biological factors. Conversely, the more a sex difference varies across cultures, the more likely it is culturally caused. If a sex difference occurs consistently, despite all the variations in learning and socialization practices that occur across cultures, then a biological "signal"—an innate predisposition—is probably showing through all the cultural "noise." If men are more physically aggressive than women in virtually all cultures, for example, there is probably a biological predisposition toward higher aggressiveness in men, which shows itself regardless of cultural learning. On the other hand, if sex differences come in all degrees and in all directions across cultures (men sometimes show the behavior more than women, men and women show the behavior equally, and women sometimes show the behavior more than men), then it would seem that there is no innate predisposition underlying the cultural variations. If men are more likely to be doctors in some countries but the reverse is true in other countries, then becoming a doctor would seem to be culturally, not biologically, determined.

Given the changes that have occurred in gender roles in recent years, another way to probe biological contributions to sex differences is to examine whether the sex differences have changed over time. Some sex differences—for example, in SAT math scores—seem to have narrowed somewhat in recent years (Feingold, 1988). Other sex differences—such as those in mental rotation test performance—have not (Masters & Sanders, 1993). If sex differences have decreased as gender roles have become less extreme, this would suggest the influence of cultural factors. On the other hand, if sex differences remain constant, despite changes in men and women's roles, then it becomes more plausible that biological factors underlie the differences.

By a similar sort of reasoning, the more consistency a sex difference shows across species—particularly species closely related to human beings—the more plausible it is that there are biological factors contributing to the sex difference. If young males engage in rougher play than young females—regardless of whether they are rhesus monkeys, orangutans, gorillas, chimpanzees, or human beings—then the case is strengthened that these sex differences are due in part to biological factors. Sex differences in rough-and-tumble play in nonhuman primates cannot be explained in terms of cultural learning. And similarities between primates and humans suggest some degree of evolutionary continuity between the two.

Perhaps the most direct evidence that biological factors contribute to sex differences is evidence that biological factors, such as sex hormones, are related to behaviors showing sex differences, such as aggression. (We've already described such evidence on links between hormones and behavior.) Most studies that investigate the relation between sex-linked biological factors and human behaviors are correlational. This means that they observe variables (e.g., testosterone levels, aggression) as they naturally occur in some populations and investigate whether they are related to one another. Unfortunately, correlational studies cannot provide clear-cut information about cause-effect relationships. For example, as described earlier, research shows that testosterone levels are correlated with aggressiveness. Does this mean that high testosterone "causes" increased aggression? Not necessarily. Why not? The cause-effect relationship could be in the opposite direction—aggressiveness could cause testosterone levels to increase. Or a third variable, such as having abusive parents, could lead both to elevated testosterone levels and to increased aggressiveness.

THE CASE FOR BIOLOGICAL INFLUENCES

Let's use the kinds of evidence just described to analyze sex differences in three kinds of human behavior: physical aggressiveness, visual-spatial ability, and sexual behaviors.

Physical Aggression

Sex differences in rough-and-tumble play (i.e., mock aggression) and actual aggression occur during children's third year of life—as early as groups of children can be observed in social settings (Maccoby & Jacklin, 1980; Parke & Slaby, 1983). Not only do boys and girls differ in actual aggression, they differ in fantasy aggression as well. One study collected some 500 stories made up by preschoolers. Aggressive and violent themes were present in 87 percent of the boys' stories but only in 17 percent of the girls' stories (Nicolopoulou, 1997), and this replicated findings from previous studies (Libby & Aries, 1989; Nicolopoulou, Scales, & Weintraub, 1994). Recall that meta-analyses have shown that sex differences in aggression are stronger in children than in adolescents or adults (Hyde, 1986). All these findings suggest there probably is a biological predisposition leading boys to be more physically aggressive than girls.

Across cultures, men are generally more aggressive than women (D'Andrade, 1966). Meta-analyses of sex differences in aggression have tended to focus on aggression in laboratory settings. However, more true-to-life evidence comes from social statistics. On virtually any measure of real-life aggression—rates of violent crimes, murders, assaults, participation in warfare, and suicide (which can be viewed as self-directed aggression)—men are much more aggressive than women (Kenrick, 1987). In the United States, men are about 6 times more likely to commit murders than women. The ratio of men's to women's same-sex homicides is remarkably consistent across cultures—about 9 or 10 to 1 (Daly & Wilson, 1988). In short, men murder much more than women do, and they mostly murder other men.

Although *absolute rates* of aggression vary considerably across cultures, *sex differences* in aggression appear to be relatively invariant across cultures (Archer & McDaniel, 1995). They are also relatively constant over historical time. European statistics for the past several centuries show consistently that men are up to 4 times more likely than women to commit violent crimes (Ellis & Coontz, 1990). Finally, despite dramatic changes in gender roles in recent years, sex differences in aggression seem not to have decreased as a result (Knight, Fabes, & Higgins, 1996).

Higher levels of male aggression occur not only in humans but in other primates as well. Male primates generally show more rough play, mock aggression, and actual aggression than female primates, and these sex differences appear at an early age (Lovejoy & Wallen, 1988; Meany, Stewart, & Beatty, 1985; Moyer, 1976). As is true for humans, aggression displayed by male primates is directed against other males more than females. Thus male primate aggression seems to be related to male-male competition, dominance, and access to mates—all of which are molded by biological evolution. Although sex differences in primate aggression can be influenced by rearing (for example, rearing in same-sex versus mixed-sex groups), the general finding remains that male primates are usually more aggressive than female primates.

Males are generally more aggressive than females in many other mammals as well. One interesting exception to this general pattern is the spotted hyena, whose females are more aggressive and dominant than males (Yalcinkaya et al., 1993). However, unlike females in most mammalian species, the female hyena has higher testosterone levels than the male does. Are testosterone levels in other species related to aggressiveness, and could typically higher levels of testosterone in males help explain sex differences in aggression? As described earlier, many experiments show that eliminating testosterone, either through physical or chemical castration, reduces aggressiveness and dominance in male animals. Conversely, providing or increasing testosterone increases dominance and aggressiveness, in both female and male animals (Moyer, 1976).

As noted before, correlational studies show significant links between human aggressiveness (as measured by personality scales or participation in violent crime) and testosterone levels (Dabbs, 2000; Olweus, 1986; Moyer, 1976). Some studies suggests that high testosterone levels lead human males to be aggressive, particularly when they are provoked—for example, by insults or physical attacks (Olweus, Mattsson, Schalling, & Low, 1980; Christianson & Knussman, 1987). The fact that there are situational triggers that work in concert with testosterone should not obscure the fact, however, that high levels of testosterone increase the likelihood of male aggression.

To summarize, sex differences in aggression (a) appear early in human development, (b) are consistent across cultures and over time, (c) are consistent across species, and (d) in humans, are related to testosterone levels, which are much higher in men than in women. All these pieces of evidence, taken together, suggest that biological factors play a role in producing sex differences in human aggression.

Visual-Spatial Ability

On average, men exceed women on certain kinds of visual-spatial ability (Silverman & Phillips, 1998; see Chapter 1), and some of these differences are large. Men perform particularly well on spatial tasks that require them to mentally transform three-dimensional objects, navigate three-dimensional space, or throw and target moving objects through space (Geary, 1998). Women perform particularly well at spatial tasks that require landmark learning or remembering where objects are located in complex arrays (Silverman & Eals, 1992).

Some studies have found sex differences in the spatial abilities of preschoolers (Levine, Huttenlocher, Taylor, & Langrock, 1999; Lunn, 1987; McGuiness & Morley, 1991) and those of older children as well (Kerns & Berenbaum, 1991; Merriman, Keating, & List, 1985). However, stable and substantial sex differences are typically not found until early adolescence, when puberty triggers dramatic hormonal changes in boys and girls (Burstein, Bank, & Jarvick, 1980; Johnson & Meade, 1987). After puberty, sex differences in spatial ability remain quite stable (Willis & Schaie, 1988), and these differences seem not to have diminished in recent years with changing gender roles (Masters & Sanders, 1993; Voyer, Voyer, & Bryden, 1995).

Sex differences in spatial abilities are quite consistent across cultures. They have been documented in England (Lynn, 1992), Scotland (Berry, 1966; Jahoda, 1980), Ghana (Jahoda, 1980), Sierra Leone (Berry, 1966), Japan (Mann, Sasanuma, Sakuma, & Masaki, 1990), Norway (Nordvik & Amponsah, 1998), and India, South Africa, and Australia (Porteus, 1965). In addition, they have consistently been reported in studies conducted throughout the United States (see Voyer, Voyer, & Bryden, 1995, for a review).

Nordvik and Amponsah (1998) assessed spatial abilities in Norwegian college students who were majoring either in science/technology or in social sciences. The science/technology students had much more experience with math classes than the social science students, and they generally performed better on all spatial tests. Nonetheless, sex differences in spatial abilities were equally strong for both groups of students. Thus, specialized training in spatial tasks did not reduce the observed sex differences. The Norwegian study is doubly interesting because Scandinavian countries promote egalitarian gender ideologies. This, however, had no effect on the sex differences in spatial ability reported in this study.

Sex differences in spatial abilities have been observed in a number of other species, including voles (a kind of rodent; Gaulin, 1992; Gaulin & Fitzgerald, 1989) and rats (Seymoure, Doue, Jauaska, 1996; Williams & Meck, 1991). Voles are typically studied in naturalistic settings as they navigate their home ranges, whereas rats are more likely to be studied in laboratory settings as they learn mazes. In animals, sex differences in spatial abilities are often explained in terms of evolutionary pressures. For example, male voles have better spatial abilities than female voles particularly, in polygynous species (species in which males have multiple mates). In such species, males have to roam over large ranges of territory to locate their mates. A possible evolutionary explanation for human sex differences in spatial abilities is that ancestral males were more involved in hunting and warfare, which required throwing projectiles and tracking prey and enemies across large territories, whereas ancestral females were more involved in foraging, which required good spatial location memory (Silverman & Phillips, 1998).

Brain structures have been identified that are related to sex differences in spatial ability. Recent research shows, for example, that the hippocampus—a region deep inside the brain—is the site of certain kinds of spatial abilities in both humans and animals (Maguire, Frackowiak, & Frith, 1997). The male meadow vole has a larger hippocampus than the female meadow vole has, and this may partly explain observed sex differences in meadow voles' spatial abilities (Jacobs, Gaulin, Sherry, & Hoffman, 1990). The ultimate cause of sex differences in the size and structure of the hippocampus seems to be prenatal or perinatal exposure to sex hormones, particularly testosterone.

Are sex hormones linked to human visual-spatial ability? The answer seems to be yes. As we described earlier, women exposed to high levels of prenatal testosterone because of CAH perform better on spatial tests. Other studies show that the absence of sex hormones (as in women with Turner's syndrome) or insensitivity to androgens (as in androgen-insensitive XY individuals) leads to decreased spatial abilities. And finally, normal variations in levels of sex hormones (testosterone and estrogen) are correlated with people's spatial performance.

In sum, a number of spatial abilities show sex differences in humans—particularly after puberty—and some of these sex differences are large. Sex differences in spatial ability are consistent across cultures, and despite changing gender roles, they have remained constant in recent times. Sex differences in spatial ability are often observed in other species, and they seem to be related to early exposure to sex hormones, which produce sexually dimorphic brain structures. Human spatial abilities are correlated with sex hormone levels, both in individuals who have experienced early hormonal abnormalities and in men and women with normal variations in sex hormone levels. In sum, a variety of evidence suggests that biological factors contribute to sex differences in spatial abilities.

Sexual Behavior

Men's and women's sexual behaviors differ in a number of ways (see Chapter 1). Men are more interested in casual sex than women, and they engage in various sexual activities more than women do. Men tend to rate youth and beauty in a mate more highly than women do, whereas women rate dominance, material resources, and status in a mate more highly than men do. Finally, men are sexually attracted to women on average, and women are sexually attracted to men on average.

There is considerable evidence that biological factors contribute to all three of these sex differences; however, we focus here mostly on the last difference (sexual orientation). Because sex differences in sexual behavior do not generally emerge until puberty, the age at which sex differences emerge will generally not be an important piece of evidence for this domain of behavior. However, the other three kinds of evidence remain relevant—cross-cultural consistencies, cross-species consistencies, and the relationship between biological factors (brain structures, sex hormones) and sexual behaviors.

Many sex differences in human mate preferences show substantial cross-cultural consistency, and this suggests that biological factors are at work. University of Texas psychologist David Buss (1989, 1994) conducted a landmark study in which he assessed over 10,000 people from 37 cultures scattered across six continents. Some of the cultures he studied were preindustrial; others were highly developed (countries like the United States and Canada). Some of the cultures had strong gender roles (e.g., in various Latin American countries); others had more egalitarian gender roles (e.g., in the Scandinavian countries). Participants from some cultures practiced polygyny (men allowed to have more than one legal mate); others practiced monogamy. Despite all these variations, however, sex differences in human mate preferences were often quite consistent across cultures. For example, women valued a marriage partner's financial prospects about twice as much as men did, regardless of culture. Men universally preferred mates younger than they, and they rated a mate's physical attractiveness to be more important than women did (Buss, 1989; Buss & Schmitt, 1993).

Greater male sexual activity has been documented repeatedly by sex surveys in modern industrialized countries (Oliver & Hyde, 1993; see Chapter 1). Cross-culturally, polygyny (males having multiple mates) is a much more common practice than polyandry (females having multiple mates) (Daly & Wilson, 1983; Symons, 1979). Men seek sexual stimulation through pornography much more than women do (Byrne & Osland, 2000), and men seek sex for pay (from prostitutes) much more than women do (Burley & Symanski, 1981; Kinsey, Pomeroy, & Martin, 1948, 1953). All these male tendencies seem to be true cross-culturally. Sex hormones—particularly testosterone—are related to sex drive and sexual activity levels, both in animals and in men and women (Sherwin, 1988). This evidence points to the conclusion that biological factors likely contribute to differences in men's and women's sexual interest and activity levels.

Because a person's degree of sexual attraction to men and to women shows such powerful sex differences in humans, it is worth analyzing in detail the evidence for biological influences on this aspect of human sexuality. Sexual object choice (i.e., attraction to men or to women) not only shows huge sex differences, but it is also linked to individual differences in masculinity and femininity within each sex (see Chapter 2). Thus sexual orientation is linked to each of the two faces of gender discussed in this book.

Although many sexual behaviors do not emerge until puberty, there are childhood behaviors that predict adult sexual orientation (Bailey & Zucker, 1995). On average, boys who grow up to be gay men are more likely to display feminine behaviors as children. They avoid rough-and-tumble activities, physical aggression, and competitive sports. They like playing with girls and they often possess the social reputation of being "sissies." In contrast, boys who grow up to be heterosexual show more male-typical interests: They like aggressive play and competitive team sports. They also show a more masculine demeanor and prefer to play in all-male groups.

Girls who grow up to be lesbian are more likely to display masculine behaviors as children. They tend to like the kinds of activities that pre-gay boys dislike, and they have the reputation of being tomboys. In contrast, girls who grow up to be heterosexual tend to show more female-typical behaviors with other girls; they often like to play with dolls, play house, and wear feminine clothes. The fact that early masculine and feminine behaviors are linked to later sexual orientation suggests that there may be common biological factors that underlie both child-hood sex-typed behavior and adult sexual orientation.

The presence of opposite-sex attraction is universal across cultures. Indeed, this consistency is so taken for granted that social scientists have not studied it much. The incidence of homosexuality (same-sex sexual and romantic attraction) is harder to assess across cultures. Tolerance for homosexual behaviors clearly varies across cultures, and studies of preindustrial cultures suggest that about two thirds have at least some form of accepted or institutionalized homosexual behavior (Ford & Beach, 1951). However, such behavior is usually shown only by a minority of individuals.

Recent sex surveys in North American and European countries provide relatively stable estimates of the percentage of men who identify themselves as gay (around 3 percent to 5 percent of the population) and of the percentage of women who identify themselves as lesbian (around 2 percent or 3 percent) (Diamond, 1993). Because homosexuality has been stigmatized in many countries and cultures, it seems likely that surveys may underreport gay and lesbian populations. Nonetheless, it seems almost certain that a very large majority of men and women have heterosexual orientations and a relatively small minority of men and women have bisexual or homosexual orientations. Both sex differences in sexual orientation and individual differences in sexual orientation within each sex show substantial cross-cultural consistency, and this would suggest that biological factors are operating (Bolton, 1994).

Heterosexuality seems to be a norm across species as well as across human cultures. At the same time, many examples of homosexual behavior can be found in lower animals (Bagemihl, 2000). Given that reproduction is the central engine of Darwinian natural selection, it seems obvious that biological evolution fostered opposite-sex sexual attraction and mating. From an evolutionary perspective, homosexuality is the puzzle in need of explanation. Various explanations have been proposed (e.g., see McKnight, 1997, and Miller, 2000). Among the most promising are: (a) homosexuality is maintained through kin selection—that is, it aids the survival of genetic relatives of homosexuals; (b) genes fostering homosexuality, while decreasing reproductive fitness in one sex, may produce offsetting increases in fitness in the other sex; and (c) genes that, in combination, lead infrequently to homosexuality in some individuals may at the same time foster traits that have offsetting reproductive value for most individuals. Regardless of which explanation is correct, few doubt that biological evolution has molded the heterosexual majority's sexual attractions and behavior (see Buss, 1999, for a comprehensive review).

As described earlier, animal experiments show that early exposure to androgens masculinizes sexual behavior, and deprivation of androgens feminizes sexual behavior. Critics have noted that "male" and "female" sexual behaviors in animals are not the same as human sexual orientations. In animals, early hormones affect stereotyped sexual behaviors and "reflexes" such as mounting and lordosis, but they do not necessarily determine the object (male or female) of sexual attraction (Breedlove, 1994). However, unless there is a complete discontinuity between humans and lower animals, it seems likely that the hormonal influences that are powerful in channeling animals' sexuality play a role in human sexuality as well.

Research shows that *adult* levels of sex hormones are not much related to human sexual orientation. Theoretical speculation has focused instead on the effects of prenatal hormones (Ellis & Ames, 1987; Meyer-Bahlburg, 1984). As we have seen, women exposed to unusual prenatal hormone environments (such as CAH and DES-exposed women) show higher levels of homosexual and bisexual attraction as adults. And studies of homosexual-heterosexual differences in physical traits such as finger length ratios, otoacoustic emissions, and hip-to-waist ratios also suggest that adult sexual orientation is linked to early androgen exposure (Singh, Vidaurri, Zambarano, & Dabbs, 1999).

Left-handedness is another trait that is related to sexual orientation (gay and lesbian individuals show a higher incidence; Lalumiere, Blanchard, & Zucker, 2000). Left-handedness also shows sex differences (more men than women are left-handed), and it is likely linked to early exposure to testosterone. Thus handedness research again implicates biological factors in sexual orientation. Recent research shows a relationship between birth order and male homosexuality, with gay men more likely to have older brothers than heterosexual men (Blanchard, 1997; Blanchard, Zucker, Siegelman, Dickey, & Klassen, 1998). The most likely explanation for this finding is again biological. Immunological reactions between mothers and their male fetuses are more likely with each succeeding male fetus, and these reactions probably affect prenatal hormone levels (Williams et al., 2000).

Behavior genetic studies show that homosexuality is partly herita-ble. One study found that when one identical twin was gay, there was a 52 percent chance that the other twin was also gay. For fraternal twins, however, there was only a 22 percent chance that the second twin was gay (Bailey & Pillard, 1991). Although the results of other studies vary, most find some degree of heritability for homosexuality (Bailey, Dunne, & Martin, 2000; Kendler, Thronton, Gilman, & Kessler, 2000; King & McDonald, 1992). Another study assessed lesbian and bisexual women with twins or adoptive sisters (Bailey, Pillard, Neale, & Agyei, 1993). When one identical twin was lesbian or bisexual, there was a 48 percent chance that the other twin was as well. However, concordance percent-ages went down to 16 percent for fraternal twins and to 6 percent for adoptive sisters.

Family pedigree studies show that homosexuality runs in families (Bailey & Bell, 1993; Bailey & Benishay, 1993; Bailey et al., 1999; Pat-tatucci & Hamer, 1995; Pillard & Weinrich, 1986). Some research sug-gests that the pattern of inheritance shows maternal linkage—that is, families with gay male children show an increased number of gay rela-tives on the mother's side but not on the father's side of the family. This suggests that the X chromosome may be involved, for this chromo-some is passed from mothers to sons but not from fathers to sons. Re-cent molecular genetic studies specify a locus on the X chromosome that may be related to sexual orientation (Hamer, Hu, Magnuson, Ju, & Pattatucci, 1993). However, this research awaits replication.

In a much publicized study, neuroscientist Simon LeVay (1991) found that regions of the preoptic area of the hypothalamus (a small structure deep in the brain, next to the pituitary gland) show significant size dif-ferences in gay and heterosexual men. These regions show sex differ-ences, and gay men have preoptic areas more like those of women. Ani-mal studies corroborate the human findings, showing that regions of the preoptic area show sex differences. In addition, these areas are influ-enced by prenatal hormones, and they are linked to sexual behaviors.

Taken together, the threads of evidence just summarized suggest that biological factors play a role in determining human sexual orientation.

DEMONSTRATING BIOLOGICAL INFLUENCES ON INDIVIDUAL DIFFERENCES IN MASCULINITY AND FEMININITY: BEHAVIOR GENETIC STUDIES

We have just argued that biology contributes to three kinds of human *sex differences*. But there is a second side to gender: individual differences in masculinity and femininity. Correlational research on sex hormones and human behavior provides information about biological influences on masculinity and femininity as well as offering hints about biological influences on sex differences. For example, when studies show that high-testosterone men are more aggressive, risk taking, and nonverbally dour than low-testosterone men, they indirectly suggest that testosterone is a biological factor that contributes to individual differences in men's masculinity.

Behavioral genetic studies provide another route to studying biological contributions to individual differences in masculinity and femininity. We briefly discussed such studies in relation to sexual orientation. But behavior genetic research studies many other kinds of individual differences as well, including traits such as masculinity and femininity. By examining the similarity of traits in twins, siblings, and members of adoptive families, behavior geneticists try to untangle genetic and environmental causes of individual differences.

The mathematical methods of behavior genetic studies are often quite complex. However, the basic ideas are easy to grasp if you consider simple examples. Imagine that a researcher studies 100 identical twins, for example, who were separated at birth and reared in unrelated families. Suppose further that the researcher measures these twins on various traits (aggressiveness, masculinity-femininity, intelligence) and determines how similar twins are in these traits. Because the twins are genetically identical but do not share their environments, you would probably agree that if twins are similar to one another, this similarity must be due to genetic factors.

Consider another equally extreme example: when families adopt babies at birth from genetic strangers. After the adopted children grow up, we can measure them and members of their adoptive families on various traits (aggressiveness, masculinity-femininity, intelligence), and we can see how similar family members are to one another. Because adopted children are genetically unrelated to members of their adoptive families, if they are similar to their family members, these similarities must be due to shared environments, not to shared genes.

Actual behavior genetic studies get more complicated because twins usually are not separated at birth. Thus they share both genes and environments. Furthermore, different kinds of blood relatives share different percentages of their genes by descent. For example, identical twins share 100 percent of their genes. Regular brothers and sisters (as well as fraternal twins) share on average 50 percent of their genes, as do parents and their biological offspring. Thus, behavior genetic studies must mathematically model varying degrees of genetic and environment similarity and investigate what degree of genetic and environmental influence best explains the observed patterns of similarity between various family members.

To make matters even more complicated—and also more interesting—behavior genetic studies often distinguish between two kinds of environments: shared and unique. Shared environments are shared by all the children in a given family, and thus they should have the same effect on all the children. Examples of shared environments are the socio-economic class of a family, the neighborhood in which the family lives, and general parenting styles that equally affect all children in the family (e.g., one mother is alcoholic and abusive, while another is loving and fair). A commonsense way to think of shared environmental factors is that they tend to make children in a given family *similar* to one another. If all the children in a given family grow up in a low socio-economic neighborhood, for example, then this environmental factor may depress the IQ scores of *all* the children in the family (that is, make the children more similar in IQ levels).

In contrast, unique environmental factors affect each child in a family differently. Each child may have different friends and teachers, for example. Parents may treat one child differently from another. Unique environmental effects tend to make children in a given family *different* from one another. Imagine for example that Moe and Joe grew up in the same family. However, mom always loved Moe better than Joe and treated him better. Moe had caring teachers, but Joe did not. Moe hung out with a good crowd in school, but Joe joined a street gang. As a result, Moe became a model citizen, whereas Joe became a juvenile delinquent and later a violent criminal.

Behavior genetic studies typically produce estimates of the proportion of variability in a given trait (such as aggressiveness or masculinity-femininity) that is due to genetic factors, shared environmental factors, and unique environmental factors. These proportions add up to one. For example, the behavior genetic research on intelligence suggests that among adults, 50 percent to 80 percent of variability in intelligence is due to genetic factors, and most of the rest is due to unique environmental factors (Jensen, 1998).

The percent of variability due to genetic factors is termed the *heritability* of a trait. Heritability estimates apply only to *populations* of people, not to individuals. A behavior genetic study may conclude that 50 percent of the variability of IQ scores in a given sample of people is due to genetic factors. It can never conclude, however, that 50 percent of Joan's IQ is due to genetic factors. Because the study of masculinity and femininity is the study of individual differences in personality, behavior genetic studies offer an important source of evidence about genetic and environmental factors that contribute to these individual differences.

Behavior genetic analyses of measures of masculinity and femininity—such as instrumental personality traits (e.g., dominance),

expressive personality traits (e.g., nurturance), and sex-typed occupational preferences and interests—indicate that all these traits show significant heritability (Lippa & Hershberger, 1999; Mitchell, Baker, & Jacklin, 1989; Rowe, 1982). A recent study of over 800 identical and fraternal
twin pairs found that 36 percent of the variability of nurturance, 38 percent of the variability of dominance, and 53 percent of the variability of
gender-related interests was due to genetic factors, and this was true for
both males and females (Lippa and Hershberger, 1999). In addition to
demonstrating potent genetic influences, this study also showed that
unique environmental factors contribute substantially to individual differences in masculinity and femininity, but common environmental factors do not. In commonsense terms, environmental influences tend to
make siblings dissimilar on masculinity and femininity, not similar.

Future research may help identify the unique environmental factors
that lead people to differ in their levels of masculinity and femininity.
Perhaps people seek out environments that amplify their genetic differences. Maybe Bret, who is somewhat feminine, joins the drama club in
high school and has a number of close female friends, whereas his
brother Bart, who is more masculine, joins the football team and hangs
out with the other high school "jocks." Bret's innate femininity may lead
him to gravitate to settings and friends that encourage his feminine interests, whereas Bart's masculinity leads him down a more macho path.

Of course, biology does not operate in a vacuum. Nature may interact
with nurture. Richard Udry's (2000) research on links between prenatal
hormones and adult women's femininity provides a good example. As
described earlier, Udry found that women exposed to high testosterone
during the second trimester of their fetal development tended to be
more masculine as adults than women exposed to lower levels. However, Udry also measured how much women's mothers encouraged
them to be masculine or feminine as children. Interestingly, he found
that women with low prenatal exposure to testosterone were more influenced by their mothers; they became more feminine when their mothers encouraged femininity, but they became more masculine when their
mothers encouraged more masculine behaviors. In contrast, women
with high prenatal testosterone exposure were less responsive to their
mothers; they were simply more behaviorally masculine in general, regardless of whether their mothers encouraged them to be feminine or
masculine. Thus some people may be more consistently influenced by
biological factors, and others may be more molded by rearing.

A similar study has yet to be reported for men. When it is, we will be
better able to judge if James Dabbs (2000) is right when he asserts that
"most boys will be masculine no matter what their parents do. If they are
not masculine, it is more likely because of physiology than parenting."

SUMMARY

Many kinds of evidence suggest that biology contributes to human sex differences and to individual differences in masculinity and femininity. Animal experiments show that prenatal hormones create differences in the nervous systems and behaviors of males and females. Studies of people with genetic and hormonal abnormalities—CAH females, androgen-insensitive XY individuals, reductase-deficient males, individuals exposed to DES, and Turner's syndrome females—suggest that early exposure to hormones, particularly androgens, has consequences for later sex-typed behaviors and abilities. Numerous studies show that people's testosterone levels are correlated with socially significant behaviors, such as aggression, criminality, sexual activity levels, dominance, occupational success, and spatial ability. Many of the behaviors and abilities linked to testosterone also show substantial sex differences. Natural experiments and accidents—when genetic males are castrated and reared as females—suggest that prenatal exposure to testosterone often produces male gender identities and male-typical behaviors, even in individuals reared as females.

To show that biological factors contribute to human sex differences, researchers seek four kinds of evidence: (a) early appearance of sex differences in development, (b) cross-cultural and temporal consistency of sex differences, (c) cross-species consistency of sex differences, and (d) empirical links between sex-linked biological factors (such as sex hormones and brain structures) and sex-linked behaviors. These kinds of evidence are generally present for sex differences in three behavioral domains: physical aggression, visual-spatial ability, and aspects of sexual behavior, including sexual orientation.

Several kinds of evidence suggest that biological factors contribute to individual differences in masculinity and femininity. Research on both prenatal and adult sex hormones, particularly androgens, shows that hormone levels are related to individual differences in masculinity and femininity. Behavior genetic studies show that individual differences in masculinity and femininity are heritable.

In short, a growing body of evidence suggests that biological factors contribute, sometimes strongly, to many of the phenomena described by the term *gender*.

5

The Case for Nurture

> *She wanted a son. He would be strong and dark, and his name would be Georges. This idea of giving birth to a male was like a hope of compensation for all her past frustrations. A man, at least, is free; he can explore the whole range of the passions, go wherever he likes, overcome obstacles, savor the most exotic pleasures. But a woman is constantly thwarted. Inert and pliable, she is restricted by her physical weakness and her legal subjection. Her will, like the veil tied to her hat with a cord, quivers with every wind; there is always some desire urging her forward, always some convention holding her back.*
>
> *The baby was born at six o'clock on a Sunday morning, at sunrise.*
> *"It's a girl!" said Charles.*
> *She turned her head away and fainted.*
>
> —*Madame Bovary*
> Gustave Flaubert

Like many great writers, Flaubert had the uncanny ability to get inside the heads of his characters. With a leap of empathy, he imagined the world from the viewpoint of a common, middle-class woman—Emma Bovary—and in so doing, he described how the life of a 19th century woman was constrained by a host of social conventions and legal restrictions. With a cynical irony, Flaubert understood too that sexism can be lodged in a woman's as well as in a man's mind, and that vanity, frailty, and self-delusion are *human* characteristics that know no gender. Flaubert helped us to understand the complexities of gender by portraying the myriad events that mold the lives of individual women and men.

Scientific research provides another, complementary route to understanding the ways in which society molds men and women. By collecting and analyzing empirical data, researchers have methodically dissected the social pressures that produce both sex differences in behavior and individual differences in masculinity and femininity.

This chapter summarizes research evidence on how various social factors influence gender. The central argument is as follows: Girls and boys are reared differently by parents, they are treated differently by teachers and peers, and they imitate different models in the mass media and in society at large. More broadly, the argument is that social roles and institutions channel the lives of boys and girls, and of men and women. In short, this chapter argues that social pressures enforce and reinforce many differences between the sexes.

Throughout much of the 20th century, social scientists believed that parental rearing and social learning held the key to understanding sex differences in behavior and individual differences in masculinity and femininity. A huge amount of research focused on how parents treat girls and boys differently and how society—in the form of teachers and the mass media—provides different models for girls and boys (see Huston, 1983; Mischel, 1966; Ruble & Martin, 1998; Sears, Maccoby, & Levin, 1957; Sears, Rau, & Alpert, 1965). This socialization perspective tended to portray children as "blank slates," ready to absorb the gender lessons provided by their surroundings.

Starting in the 1960s, psychologists increasingly realized that children engage in a kind of "self-socialization" as well (Kohlberg, 1966; Maccoby & Jacklin, 1974). Children don't simply respond to outside pressures when they act like girls and boys; they also actively try to understand gender—as best as their developing minds will allow (Martin, 2000). According to this *cognitive* perspective, children label themselves as female or male, they try to understand what these labels mean, and they often act in accordance with their developing knowledge of gender (see chapter 3). The cognitive perspective notes that human beings, unlike lower animals, are conscious creatures with self-concepts. Once children develop gender self-concepts, they try to act in accordance with them. The question then becomes: How do children acquire gender self-concepts and other sorts of knowledge about gender, and how do children's self-concepts and gender knowledge guide their behavior as boys and girls? Certainly, a central source of information about gender is the social environment—family role models, teachers, peers, and the mass media.

The 1980s witnessed another extension to socialization theory when psychologists realized that, even after including self-socialization in their theories of gender development, they still did not fully understand how girls and boys come to differ in their behaviors (Maccoby, 1990; Martin, 2000). Research increasingly suggested that *peer socialization* was also important. Researchers honed in on an important phenomenon of early and middle childhood: sex segregation—the strong tendency for children to interact and play mostly with members of their own sex. Childhood sex segregation is strictly enforced in some cultures, and thus it may result sometimes from parental rearing and social rules (Whiting & Edwards, 1988). However, sex segregation also occurs in cultures that do not directly encourage it, including much middle-class culture found in the United States.

Regardless of their rearing, children the world over segregate by sex, and this suggests that girls and boys respond to one another in ways that are not always dictated by their parents or cultures. Children have their own cultures, which differ from adult cultures, and children may often be more influenced by peers than by adults (Harris, 1995). Obvious examples are when children learn obscenities, slang, games, fashions, and Internet skills from other children, sometimes to the despair of their parents.

Because parents and society start the process of gender socialization, we start by describing how parents sometimes treat their daughters and sons differently. Next we turn to how children learn "gender lessons" at school, from peers, and from the mass media. We next consider the "self-socialization" of gender—how children acquire knowledge about their own and others' gender. Such knowledge includes stereotypes about the two sexes—beliefs about how males and females differ—and attitudes about what's appropriate for the two sexes.

Once gender stereotypes come into being, they influence behavior in predictable ways. First, they act as standards that guide people's actions (e.g., when women try to act in "feminine" ways, at least in some settings). Second, they cause people to encourage gender-stereotypical behavior in others (e.g., when a manager reins in an "aggressive" female employee more than he reins in an equally "aggressive" male employee). Finally, negative stereotypes about the relative abilities of women and men sometimes serve to undermine individuals' performance (e.g., when a girl experiences doubts about her math ability because of the stereotype that "girls aren't really good at math").

We conclude this chapter with a discussion of broad social factors that lead men and women to behave differently. These factors include restrictive gender roles, status differences between women and men, and patriarchal social structures that empower men and devalue women. Overall, the evidence suggests that social and environmental forces have a potent impact on the various phenomena we label "gender."

LEARNING TO "DO GENDER"

Do parents' beliefs about gender influence their treatment of infant boys and girls? Both cursory observation and the research literature indicate that differential treatment by sex begins at birth. The newborn nursery is likely to be decked out in pink if the infant is a girl, and gifts to the new-comer are carefully selected by sex. Girls receive pastel outfits, often beruffled, whereas boys are given tiny jeans and bolder colors. . . . It is virtually automatic to present one's child, like oneself, as male or female, signaling to the world what the newcomer's gender role will be and how she or he is to be treated. Thus is the dance of gender begun. (Fagot, Rodgers, & Leinbach, 2000, pp. 272–273)

Boys' and Girls' Toy Preferences

Boys and girls show different toy preferences at a very early age, cer-tainly by the time they are toddlers (Caldera, Huston, & O'Brien, 1989; Carter & Levy, 1988; Eisenberg, Murray, & Hite, 1982; Martin, Eisenbud, & Rose, 1995). On average, boys prefer blocks, transportation toys (e.g., toy trucks and trains), construction toys (e.g., tool sets, erector sets), and action-oriented, mock aggression toys (e.g., guns, *Star Wars* light swords); on average, girls prefer dolls, sex-typed clothing (e.g., dress-up props, jewelry), and domestic toys (e.g., tea sets, play houses). Not only do boys and girls differ in their toy preferences, but they also differ in their play styles. For example, boys like rough-and-tumble play more than girls do. One study observed trios of boys or girls in nursery school as they jumped on a trampoline. Boys were 3 to 6 times more likely than girls to throw themselves on top of one another and engage in mock wrestling and fighting (DiPietro, 1981).

Some studies find that sex differences in toy preferences already ex-ist in 1-year-old children (Jacklin, Maccoby, & Dick, 1973; O'Brien & Huston, 1985; Snow, Jacklin, & Maccoby, 1983). How do such differ-ences come to be? Biological theories would argue that hormones and brain structures lead the two sexes to prefer different toys. But there is another plausible explanation. Perhaps boys and girls are offered differ-ent kinds of toys to play with from birth on, and they are reinforced (re-warded) when they play with "sex appropriate" toys and discouraged, and even punished, when they play with "opposite sex" toys.

Other factors may also influence sex-typed toy preferences. Once children label their own gender and understand basic gender stereo-types (typically, after 2 years of age), they become more motivated to behave like members of their own sex. In essence, they then want to act like "their own kind." Later still, after children learn to evaluate their behavior according to internal standards (typically, by age 4), they ac-quire powerful internal "rudders" that guide their further gender devel-opment. A boy will then deliver "self-rewards" (e.g., a strong feeling of pride) when he masters a masculine activity such as hitting a baseball, or he will deliver "self-punishment" (feelings of shame and embarrass-ment) when he's seen by his friends carrying his mother's purse. After age 4 or so, children carry a kind of "gender gyroscope" in their heads that exerts pressure for them to "stay on course" as boys or girls. This "gender gyroscope" may be particularly helpful (or harmful, depending on your point of view) in getting children to adopt the gender standards and practices of their local communities.

Parental Treatment and the Social Learning of Gender

Social learning theory proposes that rewards and punishments mold gender-related behaviors. Can this explain children's early sex-typed toy preferences? Parents do in fact encourage sex-typed toy play and activities in their children (Maccoby & Jacklin, 1974). At the same time, parents seem to treat their sons and daughters similarly in many other ways. University of Calgary psychologists Hugh Lytton and David Romney (1991) conducted a meta-analysis of 172 studies that measured parents' behavior toward their children, and they found little or no difference in the warmth, restrictiveness, or encouragement of achievement that parents directed at their sons versus daughters. However, parents did encourage girl-typical play (e.g., with dolls) more in girls and boy-typical play (e.g., with trucks) more in boys. Among North American parents, fathers encouraged sex-typed behaviors in their children more strongly than mothers did (effect sizes were $d = .49$ for fathers versus $d = .34$ for mothers). Other reviews confirm that fathers encourage sex-typed behaviors in their children more strongly than mothers do (Collins & Russell, 1991; Huston, 1983; Ruble & Martin, 1998; Russell & Saebel, 1997; Siegal, 1987).

Some research finds that baby boys are handled more roughly than baby girls are (e.g., Lewis & Weinraub, 1979) and that parents—particularly fathers—roughhouse more with sons than daughters (Jacklin, DiPietro, & Maccoby, 1984). As noted before, boys like to roughhouse more than girls do, and maybe fathers and sons together are like two boys together—their rough-and-tumble activities reflect male preferences rather than fathers' intentional attempts to encourage sex-typed behavior in their sons. Some parents talk and smile more with infant girls than with infant sons (Leaper, Anderson, & Saunders, 1998; Levine, Fishman, & Kagan, 1967; Tauber, 1979; Thomas, Leiderman, & Olson, 1972), and when children are older, parents may talk about life events and discuss emotions more with daughters than with sons (Fivush, Brotman, Buckner, & Goodman, 2000; Reese, Haden, & Fivush, 1996). Parents also encourage different kinds of emotions in boys and girls, tolerating anger more in boys and fear more in girls (Birnbaum & Croll, 1984). Finally, parents more often teach boys than girls to suppress emotional expression, as revealed in the common parental admonition, "Big boys don't cry" (Block, 1978).

"Wanna trade?"

Does biology or socialization lead to sex differences in children's toy preferences?

It's worth noting that even though parents do not necessarily treat sons and daughters differently, boys simply spend more time with men than girls do, and similarly, girls spend more time with women than boys do. This alone causes boys and girls to have different learning experiences with adults (Crouter, Manke, & McHale, 1995; Hoffman & Teyber, 1985). Research continues on how parents treat boys and girls differently, and it is possible that studies have yet to identify important differences in the rearing of sons and daughters. For now, however, the evidence is strongest that parents treat girls and boys most differently in their direct encouragement of sex-typed play.

A recent study by University of California, Santa Cruz, psychologist Campbell Leaper (2000) observed parent-child pairs as they played with either stereotypically masculine toys (cars and car tracks) or feminine toys (plate sets). The children were all of preschool age. All possible parent-child gender combinations were observed: mothers with sons, mothers with daughters, fathers with sons, and fathers with daughters. In general, parents treated their daughters and sons with equal warmth and directiveness. However, fathers tended to be more assertive than mothers, and mothers tended to be warmer than fathers, regardless of the sex of the child. In return, children were more assertive with their mothers than they were with their fathers. Thus this study found *sex differences* in mothers' and fathers' overall behaviors, and it also found differences in how children related to mothers versus fathers, but it did not find much evidence that parents *treat* their sons and daughters differently.

Leaper (2000) found that the most potent influence on parents' behavior was the assigned play activity itself. Parents were warmer and more directive during "plate play" than during "car play," regardless of the sex of the child. One implication is that once children show a preference for "boys activities" or "girls activities," they may—*as a result of their activities*—be treated differently by adults. Of course, there is a "chicken and egg" problem here: Do parents encourage and thereby create sex-typed play in their children in the first place, or do boys and girls naturally prefer sex-typed play? Whatever the cause-and-effect sequence, sex-typed play may lead to a consequential cascade of events, which includes differential parental treatment (see Eisenberg, Wolchik, Hernandez, & Pasternack, 1985). Sex-typed play activities may have other important consequences as well. Boys' toys and play may stimulate the development of visual-spatial abilities, problem-solving skills, and creativity more than girls' toys and play (Liss, 1983; Miller, 1987). Thus boys' and girls' play is not simply "kids' stuff."

Some studies show that parents physically punish boys more than girls (Lytton & Romney, 1991; Maccoby & Jacklin, 1974). Again, however, there is a "chicken and egg" question: Does differential parental punishment of boys and girls produce differences in boys' and girls' behaviors, or do boys' and girls' behaviors evoke different treatment from parents? In the case of punishment, there is evidence that boys are more mischievous and rambunctious than girls are; they "get into things" more and test limits more than girls do, and as a result, parents may on average need to control boys (e.g., discipline and sometimes physically punish them) more than girls (Bellinger & Berko-Gleason, 1982; Brooks & Lewis, 1974; Minton, Kagan, & Levine, 1971; Snow, Jacklin, & Maccoby, 1983).

One way to study whether parents' differing treatment of boys and girls is solely in response to gender is to present adults with young children mislabeled as the other sex. Most studies in this tradition have used infants as "stimuli," and they have studied parents' reactions to the mislabeled infants. For example, a researcher might dress a baby girl in boys' clothes, label her with a boy's name, and present her to an adult, who is asked to interact with the baby or rate the traits of the child. Psychologists Marilyn Stern and Katherine Karraker (1989) reviewed 23 such "Baby X" studies and they concluded that "knowledge of an infant's gender is not a consistent determinant of adults' reactions." Gender labeling showed a more substantial impact on *children's* perceptions of infants, though. Children tended to rate male-labeled infants to be "bigger," "stronger," "noisier," "faster," "meaner," and "harder" than female-labeled infants. (We'll return to this issue later—that young children's gender stereotypes may be stronger and more rigid than those of older children and adults).

For whatever reason, most children behave in more or less gender-appropriate ways. How do parents respond, however, when their children do not behave consistently with their gender? In one study, parents were considerably less than enthusiastic when asked to get their boys to play with baby dolls or their girls to play with trucks. After opening a box containing trucks for his daughter to play with, one perturbed father declared, "Oh, they must have boys in this study!" He then promptly closed the box and returned to doll play with his daughter (Caldera, Huston, & O'Brien, 1989). In another study, preschool children were instructed—without their parents' knowledge—to play with either same-sex or opposite-sex toys, and then their parents were brought in to watch (Langlois & Downs, 1980). Parents were pleased to observe their daughters play with girls' toys (a toy stove and pots and pans), and they were tolerant when their daughters played with boys' toys (a toy gas station, trucks). Mothers generally accepted their sons' play, regardless of whether it was masculine or feminine. However, fathers criticized sons who played with "girls' toys." One father even physically moved his son away from the cooking toys he was happily playing with.

One recent study found that many preschool boys reported that their fathers believed that playing with girls' toys is "bad," and furthermore, the boys who reported that their fathers frowned on girl-type play in fact showed more masculine play (Raag & Rackliff, 1998). A number of other studies document that fathers are more concerned than mothers about the "gender appropriateness" of their children's play (Bradley & Gobbart, 1989; Jacklin, DiPietro, & Maccoby, 1984; Margolin & Patterson, 1975). Furthermore, research suggests that both mothers and fathers are more disturbed by sons who play with "girls' toys" than by daughters who play with "boys' toys" (Tauber, 1979). In short, parents engage in "gender policing" when their children engage in cross-sex activities. Fathers tend to police more than mothers, and everyone polices boys more than girls.

Teacher Influences

Teachers as well as parents influence children's behavior. Outside the home, children spend most of their time at school. Some critics of the educational system have charged that classrooms are often unfriendly to boys and seek to "feminize" them (see Fagot, Rodgers, & Leinbach, 2000: Huston, 1983, and Wilkinson & Marrett, 1985). The argument is that boys are not allowed to be their rambunctious selves in many classroom settings, and that mostly female lower-grade teachers require boys to "tone down" and behave in compliant, orderly, self-controlled, and verbally interactive ways (i.e., more like girls). Others argue that classrooms are biased in favor of boys—that teachers pay more attention to boys, call on boys more, and encourage greater participation and achievement in boys than in girls (Hendrick & Stange, 1991; Sadker & Sadker, 1986; see Chapter 7). Setting aside the gender politics, researchers must answer an interesting empirical question: Do teachers in fact treat boys and girls differently? If so, why?

The existing research is unlikely to satisfy partisans on either side of the "biased against boys" versus "biased against girls" debate. Teachers may interact more with girls than with boys in preschool and early elementary school settings (Carpenter & Huston-Stein, 1980; Serbin, O'Leary, Kent & Tonick, 1973). Why? One answer is that girls often work more steadily than boys do, sit at their tables and desks more than boys do, and stay "on task" more than boys do. It makes sense that teachers would interact more with students who are "student-like," and such students are more likely to be girls.

In preschool and kindergarten classrooms, boys show more rough-and-tumble play; they crawl around on the floor more and engage in "transportation play" with trucks and cars. Unless teachers crawl, roll on the floor, and wrestle along with the boys, they are not going to participate in these sorts of activities (Fagot & Patterson, 1969). As a result, boys are often left more to their own devices, whereas girls are more clustered around teachers and supervised by adults. Again we are faced with a "chicken and egg" question: Do teachers' actions encourage sex-typed behaviors in boys and girls, or do children's sex-typed behaviors encourage teachers to treat boys and girls differently?

There is preliminary evidence that teachers may treat very young boys and girls differently, even when the children behave similarly. One study of 13- and 14-month-old children in a nursery-school-type setting found no sex differences in their assertiveness with other children or in their attempts to communicate with preschool teachers (Fagot, Hagan, Leinbach, & Kronsberg, 1985). However, teachers responded differently to girls' and boys' actions. Specifically, teachers responded more positively (by talking back) to girls' primitive attempts to communicate, whereas they responded more quickly and decisively to boys' attempts to push, kick, or grab toys from other children (usually by picking the boy up and moving him to another activity). A year later, in different classrooms and with different teachers, the same children showed substantial sex differences in their behaviors. Boys were more physically assertive with other children, and girls were more verbally engaged with teachers. Although the new teachers did not react differently to boys and girls, perhaps the previous year's teachers had already set the boys and girls on different paths. As Alexander Pope wrote, "as the twig is bent, the tree's inclined."

Despite the power that teachers and parents have over children's environments, there may be limits to how much they can influence children's sex-typed behaviors. Some experiments have asked teachers to intervene and encourage boys and girls to play together or to engage in "nonsexist" toy choices and activities. In general, such studies have produced only weak, short-term effects (Bigler, 1999; Lockheed & Harris, 1984). Furthermore, children quickly revert to their usual sex-typed behaviors as soon as the experiments are over. Similarly, studies that ask mothers to use non-gender-stereotyped playthings with their children don't seem to produce much change in children's behavior or attitudes (Roddy, Klein, Stericker, & Kurdek, 1981; Sedney, 1987). Many studies find only weak relations between parents' encouragement or discouragement of sex-typed play and their children's degree of sex-typed play when away from their parents (Eisenberg, Wolchik, Hernandez, & Pasternack, 1985; Katz & Boswell, 1986). It seems as though children often have "minds of their own" when it comes to choosing sex-typed toys and play activities.

Peer Influences

Children's play activities—especially boys' activities—may be molded more by peers than by adults, and perhaps this explains why interventions by parents and teachers don't have much effect. In one study, University of Oregon psychologist Beverly Fagot (1985) observed how teachers and peers influenced the sex-typed behaviors of 3- and 4-year-old children. She found that boys actively encouraged "masculine" behaviors in other boys and discouraged "feminine" behaviors such as playing with girls or with girls' toys. In contrast, girls didn't consistently influence other girls to behave in masculine or feminine ways. Most interesting of all was the finding that boys responded to pressures from other boys; however, they largely ignored girls and teachers.

In an earlier study, Fagot (1977) observed similar phenomena. Preschool girls were relatively tolerant of other girls who engaged in masculine activities. However, preschool boys policed other boys' activities. Boys who played with girls or who played girls' games were taunted with labels such as "sissy" and "baby boy." Fagot's studies suggest that peer pressures—particularly pressures from other boys—are especially powerful in making boys "tow the line" when it comes to gender (see Langlois & Downs, 1980; Zucker, Wilson-Smith, Kurita, & Stern, 1995, for further evidence of boys' disapproval of cross-sex behavior in other boys). Studies of older children also indicate that peer influences may be stronger than parent and teacher influences in predicting children's degree of sex-typed behavior (Katz & Ksansnak, 1994).

One factor that may intensify peer influences is childhood sex segregation. Starting as early as the 3rd year of life, boys and girls increasingly interact only with members of their own sex (Maccoby, 1998). Although sex segregation starts at about the time that children are first able to label gender, the evidence for a cause-effect relationship between gender labeling and sex segregation is mixed (Fagot, 1985; Fagot, Leinbach, & Hagan, 1986; Serbin, Moller, Gulko, Powlishta, & Colburne, 1994; Smetana & Letourneau, 1984). The ability to label gender, however, may intensify sex segregation, because it allows boys and girls to form a kind of "us versus them" mentality about the two sexes.

Why do children show sex segregation? One hypothesis is that it results from boys' and girls' differing play styles (LaFreniere, Strayer, & Gauthier, 1984). Boys' play is more rough-and-tumble, group oriented, and competitive than girls' play. A boy finds other boys more fun to play with because they like to engage in the same rough-and-tumble, active, arousing play he does. In contrast, a girl finds boys not so fun to play with because they are impulsive, domineering, and unresponsive to her verbal requests and negotiations. Although play incompatibility contributes to childhood sex segregation, it is unlikely to be a complete explanation, for even boys who don't particularly like rough games play mostly with other boys, and girls who like rough games usually play mostly with girls (Maccoby, 1998).

Learning Gender After Early Childhood

Although many studies have focused on early childhood, gender learning continues throughout life (Bussey & Bandura, 1999). Research on older children suggests that parents restrict school-aged girls more than school-aged boys (Huston, 1983; Newson & Newson, 1986). Perhaps this is because parents view girls to be more vulnerable than boys to violence and sexual assault. Across cultures, boys and girls are often assigned different kinds of chores and tasks when growing up (Whiting & Edwards, 1988). Boys' tasks often require more independence and physical activity (e.g., herding sheep, mowing the lawn, delivering newspapers), whereas girls' tasks involve repetitive domestic activities (e.g., cleaning, food preparation, care of younger siblings). Whatever their motivations, parents may end up giving their daughters a kind of "dependence training" and their sons a kind of "independence training" (Ruble, Greulich, Pomerantz, & Gochberg, 1993). Parents sometimes offer more help to daughters than to sons when they work on school problems and intellectual tasks (Fagot, 1978; Gold, Crombie, Brender, & Mate, 1984). Although this seems to favor girls on the surface, it may inadvertently train girls to be more passive and dependent than boys. At least one study has found that parents praise boys more than girls when assisting them with school problems (Allesandri & Lewis, 1993).

Although today's parents encourage both daughters and sons to achieve academically and to pursue good jobs, parents may still hold different expectations for their daughters and sons. In a carefully conducted longitudinal study of the academic performance and occupational choices of some 2,000 Michigan school children, University of Michigan psychologist Jacqueline Eccles and her colleagues (1993) found that, on average, parents believed girls to be better at English and boys to be better at math. Furthermore, these gender stereotypes were related to parents' expectations for their own sons and daughters. That is, parents who believed girls to have less math ability than boys tended to have lower expectations for their own daughters' math performance. Finally, parents' expectations for their children were linked to their children's self-rated ability and academic performance, even after statistically controlling for the children's actual ability levels. The implication is that parents' gender stereotypes influence their expectations for their sons and daughters, which in turn influence their children's self-concepts and ultimately their academic performance and career choices.

Modeling Gender

According to social learning theory, children don't learn to behave as boys and girls simply by responding to rewards and punishments. Children also model (i.e., observe and imitate) others. What is the evidence that children in fact model gender-related behaviors? The most obvious models for children are their same-sex parents. Surprisingly, research has not consistently shown that young boys prefer to imitate their fathers over their mothers or that young girls prefer to imitate their mothers over their fathers, nor do children strongly prefer to spend more time with their same-sex parent (Maccoby, 1998; Maccoby and Jacklin, 1974; Smith & Daglish, 1977). Children's personalities tend to resemble the personality of their most dominant or attractive parent, not necessarily that of their same-sex parent (Hetherington, 1967). This finding is consistent with other research indicating that children are most likely to imitate people who they perceive to be powerful, warm, and of high status (Bandura, 1977).

Is there a relationship between parents' sex-typed attitudes and behaviors and those of their children? Some studies show that the children of working mothers show less sex typing and more flexible attitudes about gender than the children of stay-at-home mothers (Levy, 1989; Marantz & Mansfield, 1977; Urberg, 1982; Weinraub et al., 1984), and this would seem to support the imitation hypothesis. However, when demographic variables such as socioeconomic status are statistically controlled for, there may in fact be little relation between a mother's employment status and her children's sex-typed behaviors or gender knowledge (Serbin, Powlishta, & Gulko, 1993). As we will see later, lower social class tends to be associated with higher sex typing.

Other studies have investigated the possible effects of fathers' absence on boys' masculinity. Psychologists Michael Stevenson and Kathryn Black (1988) conducted a meta-analysis of 67 studies that investigated this topic, and overall, they concluded that the results were weak and inconsistent. There was some tendency for preschool boys in father-absent homes to show less sex-typed toy preferences. Paradoxically, though, older boys from father-absent homes tended to be more masculine and, particularly, more aggressive. Stevenson and Black speculate that the effects of father absence depend on contextual factors such as the reasons for the fathers' absence (e.g., death, divorce, desertion, military service), socioeconomic status, and the presence of other male figures at home. In sum, a number of studies indicate that children do not imitate their same-sex parents' gender-related behaviors in any simple way.

Of course, parents are not the only role models boys and girls look to. Siblings are also important. Research suggests that same-sex siblings interacting together engage in more sex-typed behaviors than do only children (Rust, Golombok, Hines, Johnston, & Golding, 2000; Stoneman, Brody, & MacKinnon, 1986). Indeed, same-sex siblings may influence children's gender attitudes more than their parents do (Abramovitch, Corter, & Pepler, 1980; Barry, 1980; Katz & Ksansnak, 1994).

Findings about the effects of opposite-sex siblings are inconsistent and seem to depend on the spacing of siblings and the sex-ratios in particular families (Crouter, Manke, & McHale, 1995; Lawrie & Brown, 1992). Imagine, for example, a family with four older sisters and a "baby brother." Some research suggests that such a young solo male may become especially masculine, perhaps in reaction against all the female influences in his family (Katz & Boswell, 1984).

Finally, boys and girls may model the behavior of same-sex peers and same-sex adults outside their immediate families. Girls and boys may not be strongly influenced by any single same-sex model, but when they gain a sense that most males or most females engage in a particular kind of behavior, they are likely to "follow the crowd" and imitate that behavior (Bussey & Bandura, 1984; Bussey & Perry, 1982). Boys and girls are astute observers of their social world. They size up consistencies in the behavior of other males and females, and they generally behave like the majority of their own sex. It is through such imitation that boys and girls absorb the gender lessons provided by their communities and cultures.

Learning Gender from the Mass Media

In modern societies, children learn a lot about gender from the mass media—from TV in particular. Starting in the 1970s, studies examined the gender-stereotyped content of TV shows, commercials, and cartoons. In general, they found that the two sexes are portrayed very differently. TV shows often have more male than female characters— sometimes 3 to 4 times as many (Signorielli, 1993). Men on TV are portrayed having diverse occupations, and they are often portrayed as heroes and problem solvers. In contrast, female characters occupy a more limited range of roles—housewife, secretary, nurse, and witch. Female characters are often sexualized, even when they are portrayed in "serious" roles (e.g., as police officers, nurses, doctors, and lawyers). More than men, women in TV are portrayed as a few "types"—either as young, sexy, and attractive or as older, asexual, and comical.

Although the content of TV shows and advertisements has grown less stereotyped over the past 20 years, gender bias still remains. One recent study summarized 25 years of research on gender stereotyping in TV commercials, including studies from America, Australia, Denmark, France, Hong Kong, Indonesia, Kenya, Mexico, and Portugal (Furnham & Mak, 1999). Despite variations across cultures, authority figures in commercials were more often male than female, and product users were more often female than male. Men were more likely to be portrayed in professional roles or as interviewers, whereas women were more likely to be shown in dependent and domestic roles. There was a clear relation between the sex of salespeople in TV commercials and product types—women were more likely to sell home and body products, whereas men were more likely to sell automobile and sports products. Women tended to populate commercials for "at home" products (e.g., cleaning products, home furnishings, food and food preparation products), whereas men populated commercials for "out of home" products (e.g., cars, sports equipment, outdoor tools). Perhaps not surprisingly, TV commercials from traditional cultures (e.g., Hong Kong, Indonesia) showed more gender stereotyping than those from less traditional cultures (e.g., the United States, Denmark).

TV cartoons have been subjected to close research scrutiny, in part because they are targeted specifically at young children. University of Dayton communications researchers Teresa Thompson and Eugenia

"Do you think they're trying to tell us something?"

Do the mass media create and reinforce gender steretypes?

Zerbinos (1995) analyzed 175 episodes of 41 different children's cartoon shows, and they found gender stereotypes to be commonplace. Male cartoon characters were portrayed as much more ingenious, courageous, and aggressive than female characters. Male characters excelled in leadership—they often rescued other characters, particularly "damsels in distress." In contrast, female characters were portrayed to be more sensitive, emotional, warm, mature, and romantic than male characters. Female characters were often less technically competent than male characters. Thompson and Zerbinos found evidence that children's cartoons in the United Stated have become less gender stereotyped over time. Since 1980, female characters have been presented as more independent, assertive, intelligent, and competent than they had been. Nonetheless, many gender stereotypes remain.

Does this stereotyping register with the children who watch the cartoons? The answer seems to be yes. In one study, Thompson and Zerbinos (1997) interviewed 89 children, ranging in age from 4 to 9, who reported that male cartoon characters are more active and violent, whereas female cartoon characters are more domestic, interested in romance, and concerned with appearance. Furthermore, children who perceived more gender stereotypic behavior in cartoon characters tended also to estimate more gender stereotyped job possibilities for adults of their own sex. Although the cause-effect relationship is not clear here, one possibility is that the occupational stereotypes that children learn from TV cartoons influence the occupational options they envision for themselves.

Consistent with this view, a number of studies have found that heavy TV viewing in children is associated with stronger gender stereotypes (Eisenstock, 1984; McGhee & Frueh, 1980; Zuckerman, Singer, & Singer, 1980). Longitudinal studies suggest also that extended TV viewing fosters gender stereotypes, particularly in children who didn't hold strong stereotypes to start with (Morgan, 1982). In a study that comes closest to demonstrating a cause-effect relationship between TV viewing and gender stereotypes (Kimball, 1986), researchers studied a Canadian town that had not received TV transmissions because of its location in the Rocky Mountains (this town was nicknamed "Notel" by the researchers). When cable TV was introduced to Notel in the 1970s, children who lived there were studied and compared with children in two comparable Canadian towns that already received TV transmissions ("Unitel," which received transmissions from a single Canadian TV network, and "Multitel," which received transmissions from several Canadian and U.S. networks). Researchers found that before TV transmissions started, the children of Notel had weaker gender stereotypes than the children of Unitel or Multitel. However, after a couple of years of exposure to TV, the gender stereotypes displayed by Notel children grew significantly stronger, particularly among boys.

SELF-SOCIALIZATION OF GENDER

So far, we have marshaled considerable support for the basic contentions of social learning theories—that rewards, punishments, and role models influence children's gender-related behaviors and attitudes. The basic argument has been that parents, teachers, schools, and societies treat girls and boys differently, and as a result, children learn to "do gender." However, the social learning of gender is only part of the story. Children also actively construct mental categories of "male" and "female," and they apply these categories to themselves and to others. Throughout development, children infer "facts" about males and females, and as they grow older, they act more and more consistently with their gender labels and stereotypes. Children look to their social environments to learn about gender. Girls in Saudi Arabia undoubtedly learn very different lessons about what it means to be a woman than do girls in Sweden.

Researchers have posed some fundamental questions about the self-socialization of gender. Do children progress through definite stages of gender knowledge? Are children's gender-related self-concepts and gender knowledge related to their behavior as boys and girls? And most important from the vantage point of this chapter, does the social environment influence children's gender knowledge?

Gender Knowledge

Harvard psychologist Lawrence Kohlberg (1966) was the first to argue that children's self-labeling was critical in gender development. According to Kohlberg, once children label themselves as boys or girls, they start to act consistently with their gender labels (see chapter 3). How exactly do children come to understand the concepts of "male" and "female"? An enormous amount of research has focused on this question (for reviews, see Huston, 1983; Maccoby, 1990; Martin, 2000; Ruble & Martin, 1998; for a definitive early study, see Slaby & Frey, 1975).

The development of gender concepts in children turns out to be more complex than Kohlberg (1966) originally envisioned. Most children can correctly answer the question, "Are you a boy [or girl]?" by age 2½. A bit later, by age 3½, most children understand that gender (being male or female) is stable over time. Later still, between 4 and 7 years of age, children achieve "gender constancy"—the realization that being male or female is a stable attribute that does not change across situations or with superficial physical changes (such as cutting long hair short or wearing a dress rather than pants). Children throughout the world progress through these stages, probably because the stages are linked to children's broader intellectual development.

The development of gender knowledge does not stop at age 6 or 7. One longitudinal study followed 82 German children from ages 5 to 10 (Trautner, 1992). Over the five years of the study, children's gender stereotypes steadily increased. From 5 to 7 years of age, children held the most rigid, black-and-white beliefs about the two sexes (e.g., "only girls cry," "only boys play football"). From ages 8 to 10, in contrast, children developed more flexible and probabilistic beliefs about gender (e.g., "more girls cry than boys" or "both boys and girls cry"). Interestingly, although children's gender stereotypes grew more flexible with age, their play activities grew steadily more sex-typed, peaking by age 7. Thus children's sex-typed behavior did not closely track their gender beliefs.

Another study—this time of over 500 Canadian children in kindergarten through sixth grade (i.e., ages 6 through 12)—also found that children's knowledge of gender stereotypes, increased steadily with age (Serbin, Powlishta, & Gulko, 1993). To assess gender stereotypes, the researchers used the following sort of question: "What do you think that most people believe—that boys are more likely to be adventurous than girls or that girls are more likely to be adventurous than boys?" Children correctly answered increasing numbers of these questions as they grew older (*correctly* here means their answers were consistent with common social stereotypes). At the same time, their personal beliefs about gender grew more flexible. Whereas young children believed that only boys or only girls could have certain traits ("only girls are gentle," "only boys are adventurous"), older children increasingly believed that *both* boys and girls could have these traits.

Although the simultaneous increase in the accuracy and flexibility of gender stereotypes may seem paradoxical, it need not be. Children learn more about gender as they grow older, even though they see gender less in black-and-white terms. It is unlikely that a 3-year-old will be sophisticated enough to believe that "a man is more likely to be a nuclear physicist" and "a woman is more likely to be a nursing professor." However, adolescents may acquire these stereotypes as their knowledge of occupations and gender grows more elaborate. However, despite their increasingly elaborate gender stereotypes, adolescents may acknowledge that some nuclear physicists are women and that some nursing professors are men. In the Canadian study, children's percentage of correctly identified gender stereotypes considerably exceeded the percentage of traits they assigned flexibly to the two sexes. So perhaps we shouldn't overstate children's stereotype "flexibility."

Stereotypes develop in many ways as children grow older. In younger children, gender stereotypes tend to be concrete (e.g., "men are police," "women are nurses"). As children grow older, however, their gender knowledge expands to include metaphorical associations (e.g., "the moon is feminine," "the sun is masculine," "curved forms are feminine," "angular forms are masculine"). Thus gender stereotypes become more complex and elaborate with age, and for some people, everything under the sun—animals, artwork, occupations, clothing, automobiles, and hobbies—is viewed through the lens of gender (Bem, 1993; Fagot & Leinbach, 1993).

Gender Knowledge and Sex-Typed Behavior

Lawrence Kohlberg (1966) proposed that "gender constancy"—the mature understanding that sex is stable over time and place and despite superficial changes in appearance—is essential for sex typing to occur in boys and girls. Research, however, has proven him wrong on this point. As noted before, children show strongly sex-typed toy and activity preferences in their second year of life, well before they can label themselves accurately as male or female (Weinraub et al., 1984). Thus sex-typed behaviors can precede even basic kinds of gender knowledge.

Nonetheless, gender labeling has an impact on sex-typed behaviors. Boys who have learned to label their own and others' gender and who understand that gender is stable over time pay more attention to same-sex models (Slaby & Frey, 1975). In a similar vein, boys who have a higher degree of gender understanding watch more male characters and male-typical (e.g., sports) events on television (Luecke-Aleksa, Anderson, Collins, & Schmitt, 1995). Although sex-typed toy preferences exist before children can accurately label gender, when children achieve gender labeling, they may show more sex-typed toy choices as a result. For example, when presented with a choice between a highly attractive girl's toy and a not-so-attractive boy's toy, boys who can accurately label gender will choose the not-so-attractive boy's toy (Frey & Ruble, 1992). Thus gender understanding may tip the balance in favor of sex-typed choices in conflicted situations. Furthermore, older boys may avoid an attractive novel toy if it has been labeled as a "girl's toy"—a phenomenon called the "hot potato effect" (Martin, Eisenbud, & Rose, 1995).

The lowest level of gender understanding—the ability to label oneself and others as male or female—is sufficient to increase sex-typed toy choices in some settings (Bussey & Bandura, 1984; Fagot, 1985; Weinraub et al., 1984). In addition, it may sometimes increase preferences for same-sex playmates (Smetana & Letourneau, 1984). One study looked at three kinds of sex-typed behaviors in 2- to 3-year-old children: toy choices, same-sex playmate preferences, and aggression (Fagot, Leinbach, & Hagan, 1986). Children's ability to label the gender of pictured people was not related to their sex-typed toy choices. However, it was related to their playmate preferences and aggression. Children who could correctly label others' gender showed stronger preferences for same-sex peers, and girls who could correctly label gender were less aggressive than girls who could not. Another more recent study found that 4- to 6-year-old British school children who displayed higher levels of gender understanding were less willing to dress up in opposite-sex clothing when asked to do so by the researcher (Warin, 2000).

It seems reasonable that gender labeling *should* be related to certain kinds of sex-typed behaviors. To develop preferences for either male or female playmates, it would seem useful for children to be able to label accurately who is a boy and who is a girl. As noted earlier, children learn about "male" and "female" activities in part by observing what most males and most females do. Accurate gender labeling would seem to be a prerequisite to abstracting such information. And to follow the admonition that "big boys don't cry," a boy first needs to understand that he is a boy and that he belongs to the category of "boys in general." The admonition becomes even more powerful if he observes other boys and infers that many of them in fact don't cry as much as girls do.

The metaphor of a "booster rocket" is useful here. Children show sex-typed behaviors (e.g., toy preferences) before they are able to label gender accurately. But when they do acquire the ability to label gender, children ignite a kind of "second-stage booster" to the accelerating rocket of gender development. Accurate gender labeling amplifies already existing tendencies, and it provides a powerful conceptual schema for children to use in inferring additional gender-related information from their social world.

As noted before, increases in children's gender knowledge parallel more general kinds of cognitive development. The ability to label people as male or female coincides with the development of language in children and with the ability to form abstract concepts more generally. The development of gender constancy—the understanding that gender is a stable characteristic, impervious to surface alterations—coincides with children's developing ability to understand that other qualities (such as the amount of water in a container) also remain constant despite superficial changes (being poured from a low, wide container into a high, narrow one). Some researchers have suggested that in young children, stages of gender knowledge are related to children's general intelligence, with intelligent children achieving various stages of gender knowledge earlier (Bussey & Bandura, 1999).

If the ability to label gender provides a second-stage booster to the rocket of gender development, then the development of internal gender standards provides the "third-stage booster." Macquarie University psychologist Kay Bussey and Stanford University psychologist Albert Bandura (1992) found that this third stage typically occurs between 3 and 4 years of age. In a carefully conducted experiment, these researchers measured the gender knowledge and sex-typed behaviors of 40 nursery school children who ranged in age from 2½ to almost 5. Children were asked to rate how good or bad they would feel about playing with various toys, some of which were masculine (a dump truck) and some of which were feminine (a baby doll). Children were then given the opportunity to play with the toys, and their amount of play with masculine and feminine toys was measured. Finally, the children observed videotapes of individual 7-year-old boys and girls engaged in cross-sex play (e.g., the videotaped boy diapered a baby doll, and the videotaped girl played with a dump truck). The preschoolers were then asked to rate how good or bad the videotaped child's friends would feel about the portrayed play.

Not surprisingly, children's play was strongly sex-typed—boys played more with masculine toys, and girls played more with feminine toys. Children's level of gender knowledge (e.g., whether they accurately labeled gender, or understood that gender is consistent over time, or understood that gender is constant over time, situations, and superficial appearance changes) showed little relationship to their degree of sex-typed play, after controlling for age. The most interesting finding was a dramatic difference between older children (mean age of 4) and younger children (mean age of 3). The older children tended to evaluate cross-sex play much more negatively than the younger children did (see Fig. 5.1). Furthermore, older children's evaluations of playing with masculine (or feminine) toys predicted their actual amount of play with masculine and feminine toys, whereas younger children's evaluations did not.

At a conceptual level, Bussey and Bandura (1992) demonstrated that sometime between ages 3 and 4, children internalize gender standards. As a result, children evaluate their behavior in comparison with those standards, and they attach a kind of moral "right" or "wrong" to gender-related behaviors. Three-year-olds play with sex-typed toys because of social influences (reinforcement, modeling) and perhaps also because of innate preferences. But 4-year-olds play with sex-typed toys also because they have internalized standards of gender conduct and they feel

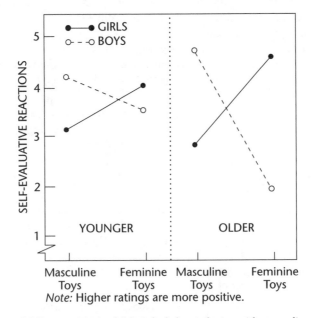

Figure 5.1 How positively children feel about playing with masculine and feminine toys.

Children are classified by age ("younger"= mean age of 3, and "older" = mean age of 4) and by sex.

Copyright 1992. Society for Research in Child Development. Adapted with permission.

bad (i.e., embarrassed, ashamed) when they violate these standards. Bussey and Bandura learned just how powerful such gender standards can be when they asked reluctant 7-year-old boys to serve as actors in the videotapes portraying cross-sex play. After diapering a baby doll in front of the researchers' video camera, one mortified 7-year-old boy declared, "It's the most awful thing I have ever done!"

Social Influences on Gender Knowledge

Where does gender-related knowledge come from? Two obvious answers are (a) people (i.e., parents, teachers, peers) teach children gender stereotypes; and (b) children infer "facts" about gender based on what they see around them. For example, if children observe only women as elementary school teachers and only men as police officers, they will infer that "elementary school teachers are women" and "police officers are men." Whether children learn from direct instruction or from indirect inference, social factors undoubtedly have a big influence on their developing knowledge.

A number of studies suggest that parents who possess strong gender stereotypes and traditional attitudes toward women are more likely to have children who similarly possess strong gender knowledge and stereotypes (Fagot & Leinbach, 1989; Fagot, Leinbach, & O'Boyle, 1992; Repetti, 1984; Serbin, Powlishta, & Gulko, 1993; Weinraub et al., 1984). One study assessed the gender knowledge of 376 children (in kindergarten and third grade) and found that the degree to which parents chose gender stereotypic toys and chores for their children predicted how gender-stereotyped versus flexible their children's gender beliefs and preferences were (Katz & Boswell, 1986). However, children's choices of media role models and their perceptions of peer attitudes predicted even more strongly their sex-typed preferences, and this was especially so for boys.

Lower- and working-class children tend to have more rigid stereotypes about gender than do middle- and upper-middle-class children (Lackey, 1989; Serbin, Powlishta, & Gulko, 1993). One reason may be that social class is correlated with education, and educated parents tend to have more liberal attitudes about gender roles. Furthermore, higher-class and more educated women are more likely to work in high-status occupations, and children learn that women can in fact be doctors, lawyers, and executives when they see their own mothers in such roles (Marantz & Mansfield, 1977). Finally, educated and higher-class fathers may be more likely to pitch in with child care. One study found that when fathers participated in child care, their 4-year-old daughters tend to have weaker gender stereotypes (Baruch & Barnett, 1981). Another study found that when their fathers engaged in feminine domestic tasks at home, their 2- to 3-year-old children were less likely to accurately classify people by gender (Weinraub et al., 1984).

CONSEQUENCES OF GENDER STEREOTYPES

We have focused on how gender and gender knowledge develop in childhood. And for good reason, for childhood sets the course for later years. Let's fast forward now and consider how gender is maintained in adolescence and adulthood. As adults, most of us have learned elaborate gender stereotypes, and these stereotypes influence our behavior in at least three different ways. First, we often try to live up to gender stereotypes. Second, we may influence others—both in subtle and not-so-subtle ways—to conform to our stereotypes. And finally, stereotypes about sex differences in ability (e.g., "women aren't good at math," "men can't handle infants properly") may serve to undermine individual women's and men's performance. In considering the ways in which stereotypes influence behavior, we shift our attention from past environments (e.g., childhood socialization) to current environments (how others influence us now and how we in turn influence them).

Enacting Stereotypes

Women and men often act in gender stereotypic ways, particularly in situations that make gender salient (Deaux & Major, 1987). One study showed that college women are more "cutesy" and "feminine" when interacting with their boyfriends than when interacting with men they are not interested in (Montepare & Vega, 1988). Other studies have found that women act more traditionally feminine—and even "dumb down" their performance on intelligence tests—when they anticipate interacting with an attractive college man who values "traditional women" (Zanna & Pack, 1975). In one experiment, interviewed women acted more femininely—both verbally and nonverbally (e.g., they prettied themselves up)—when they learned ahead of time that the man interviewing them for a job approved of "feminine" women (von Baeyer, Sherk, & Zanna, 1981).

Because common stereotypes hold that eating large quantities of food is "unfeminine," women eat less in the presence of attractive men (Mori, Chaiken, & Pliner, 1987). Similarly, because stereotypes portray modesty to be a feminine virtue, women tend to offer lower estimates of their ability in public compared with private settings (Berg, Stephan, & Dodson, 1981; Gould & Slone, 1982). And because aggressiveness is considered "unfeminine," women become less aggressive when they are observed and personally identified. However, men show no such change (Lightdale & Prentice, 1994).

Men as well as women conform to gender stereotypes, particularly when they are being watched. Men are more helpful during emergencies, for example, particularly when they are being observed and when the person who needs help is a woman (Eagly & Crowley, 1986). This suggests that men enact the gender-stereotypic role of "masculine valor," particularly when they are being observed. Similarly, in conformity experiments, men stick up for their beliefs and resist group pressures more in public than in private settings (Eagly, Wood, & Fishbaugh, 1981). Apparently, men feel especially motivated to show that they "can't be pushed around" when others are watching them. The general principle seems to be that both women and men are more likely to live up to gender stereotypes when they are being observed by others and when they interact with attractive members of the opposite sex.

There are additional settings that serve to make gender stereotypes salient. One is when a person is the "token"—the sole male or female—in a group. Imagine, for example, that you are the only woman seated on a jury, or sitting on a corporate board, or elected to a state supreme court. Token status tends to emphasize one's role as male or female, and it encourages the "token" to think about how she comes across "as a woman," or how he comes across "as a man." Similarly, when people take on roles that violate traditional gender stereotypes (a woman in an engineering faculty, a male kindergarten teacher), they may be forced to think more about their own gender than their coworkers do. People in such situations may have to choose between enacting gender stereotypes ("Look, I'm feminine, even though I'm an engineering professor!") or rejecting them and facing the disapproval that results.

It's important to emphasize that we don't need to think *consciously* about gender stereotypes for them to influence our thoughts and actions. Much recent research shows that well-learned stereotypes—and gender stereotypes are probably the most overlearned and entrenched stereotypes we possess—can be "primed" (i.e., triggered) by transient cues we are not even aware of (Fiske, 1998). All the factors just described—public observation, the presence of attractive members of the opposite sex, token status, gender-role violations—may serve as unconscious primes to gender stereotypes. When gender stereotypes come to mind, our internal "gender gyroscope" often directs us to behave as they dictate. Other common primes to gender stereotypes include sexist jokes, sexist language (e.g., referring to people in general as "he" rather than "she"), and gender stereotypic content in the mass media—including gender-stereotypic sexual images. The general principle is, When men and women are in settings that trigger gender stereotype, they are more likely to act in accordance with those stereotypes (Deaux & Major, 1987).

Self-Fulfilling Prophecies and Behavioral Confirmation

Not only do people act consistently with their gender stereotypes, but they also influence others to do the same. Much social psychological research has shown that people can induce others to act consistently with their beliefs (Olson, Roese, & Zanna, 1996). This process is sometimes referred to as a *self-fulfilling prophecy* (Jussim, 1986; Merton, 1948) or as *behavioral confirmation* (Snyder, 1981). Consider the following example: Based on gender stereotypes, you decide that that your student Mary is not good at math. Through your words and demeanor you convey your doubts to Mary. Mary begins to doubt her own ability and in fact does not perform well on her math tests. Your initial assessment of Mary's math ability is confirmed. What you fail to realize, however, is that your actions contributed to Mary's poor performance.

Gender stereotypes can often become self-fulfilling prophecies. Chapter 3 described an experiment in which pairs of college men and women—sitting in separate rooms and communicating by lights—negotiated how to divide masculine and feminine tasks between them. Women "chose" fewer feminine tasks when their partners falsely believed they were males, and they "chose" more feminine tasks when their partners (correctly) thought they were women (Skrypnek & Snyder, 1982). Translate this experiment to a real-life domain: Do married women "choose" to launder clothes and vacuum carpets because they love to do these tasks or because they are induced to do so by their husbands' (and society's) expectations? Of course, women as well as men may internalize gender stereotypes. One study found that both women and men were more likely to assign "feminine" tasks to women and "masculine" tasks to men (Lewis, 1985). The division of labor fostered by gender stereotypes may become an "unconscious ideology" accepted by both women and men, even when it is patently unfair (Bem & Bem, 1971).

Men may more readily influence women to behave in gender stereotypic ways than vice versa. Why? Because men tend to hold more sexist beliefs than women do, men may be particularly likely to induce women to behave in gender-stereotypic ways. Conversely, because women have greater sensitivity to nonverbal cues then men do, women may be better than men at reading their partner's expectations (Christensen & Rosenthal, 1982). And as we shall see later, because women tend to have lower-status positions than men have, women may need to accommodate male higher-ups' stereotypes more than the other way around.

Although subtle nonverbal cues (frowns and smiles, cold and warm tones of voice) are undoubtedly important in conveying information about how we expect others to behave, there are more direct means of influencing women and men to behave consistently with gender stereotypes. Studies of group problem solving and leadership show that group members often praise men's suggestions and solutions more than women's (Altemeyer & Jones, 1974; Butler & Geis, 1990; Ridgeway, 1982). Conversely, people interrupt and ignore women more than men (Bunker & Seashore, 1975). You may recall that men tend to show more instrumental behaviors and women more expressive behaviors in group settings (see Chapter 1). One likely reason for this is that people discourage assertiveness in women but encourage it in men. To influence others, women often must adopt a warm, friendly, smiling (i.e., expressive) demeanor (Carli & Bukatko, 2000). Otherwise, their influence attempts are viewed as illegitimate and "unfeminine."

People use "sticks" as well as "carrots" to keep others in line as men and women. For example, they deal harshly with women who break the rules of "feminine" behavior. "Feminists" are judged to be unlikable and unattractive (Haddock & Zanna, 1994). Brashness and self-promotion are disliked in women but not in men (Rudman, 1998). Women who show a "masculine," directive style of leadership are judged to be less likable than men who show the same style of leadership (Eagly, Makhijani, & Klonsky, 1992). Thus one reason women may choose not to behave in assertive, "masculine" ways is that they know from experience that such behavior will backfire on them. When deciding how to behave in work settings, women often face a "damned if you do, damned if you don't" dilemma (Geis, 1993). Success in the competitive world of business, government, and academia requires women to be forceful, assertive, and "aggressive"; however, these traits are often deemed "unfeminine," and women who show such traits are often disliked (Carli, 1990; Crawford, 1988).

Men who violate gender stereotypes may also receive harsh treatment. For example, men who opt to stay home as "house husbands" may be viewed as weak, henpecked, and ineffectual. Men who work in professions that violate gender stereotypes (e.g., as nurses, elementary school teachers, interior decorators) may have their masculinity questioned, often because of fears about homosexuality. In many different ways, people convey the message that feminine behavior is unacceptable in men and masculine behavior is unacceptable in women. Is it any surprise then that most men come to act in masculine ways and that most women come to act in feminine ways?

Stereotype Threat: When Negative Stereotypes Undermine Performance

There is a third way in which gender stereotypes may influence women and men. When stereotypes question the abilities of one sex ("women aren't good at math," "men are inept with infants"), they may undermine the performance of individual women and men. This phenomenon has been labeled *stereotype threat* (Steele, 1997).

Imagine you are a college woman taking the math Graduate Record Exam (GRE) in a room full of men. Your "token" status primes the stereotype that "women aren't good at math," and this triggers anxiety and worry about how you'll perform on the test. Furthermore, you may worry about how your friends will react if you receive a disappointing score. If you do badly, you reason, you'll have proven the detested stereotype true. Your anxiety and distracting thoughts may be particularly likely if you identify with the task (you are a math major) and if good performance is important to you (you're hoping to get into a good graduate school). Your anxiety ends up interfering with your test performance.

Two experiments by Steven Spencer, Claude Steele, and Diane Quinn (1999) confirmed the sequence just described. University of Michigan women and men were asked to work on a test that contained difficult GRE math questions. Some participants were told that the test showed gender differences, and others were told that the test showed no gender differences. Presumably, women who thought the test showed gender differences would be worried about the stereotype that "women are not good at math." The results supported the stereotype threat hypothesis. When negative stereotypes about women's math ability were made salient, women performed worse than did men on the challenging math test. However, when women were "relaxed" about gender stereotypes, they performed as well as men did. Other experiments show that when token status in work groups and even the mere presence of men in work groups can trigger negative gender stereotypes that undermine women's math performance (Inzlicht & Ben-Zeev, 2000).

Decades before these experiments took place, British novelist Virginia Woolf (1929/1957) intuitively understood the phenomenon of stereotype threat:

> There was an enormous body of masculine opinion to the effect that nothing could be expected of women intellectually. Even if her father did not read out loud these opinions, any girl could read them for herself; and the reading, even in the nineteenth century, must have lowered her vitality, and told profoundly upon work. There would always have been that assertion—you cannot do this, you are incapable of doing that—to protest against, to overcome.

BROADER SOCIAL FACTORS: SOCIAL ROLES AND STATUS DIFFERENCES

No discussion of the "nurture" of gender would be complete without mention of broader social forces that mold the lives of women and men.

We consider two factors here: the powerful social roles that channel women's and men's behaviors, and pervasive status differences that exist between women and men.

According to Alice Eagly's social role theory (Eagly, 1987; Eagly, Wood, & Diekman, 2000), when we observe differences in men's and women's behavior, these differences result from the social roles that men and women occupy, not from innate differences between the sexes. Social role theory describes three central components to contemporary gender roles: (a) women are more often homemakers and men breadwinners, (b) women tend to work in different occupations than men do; and (c) women often have lower status than men do. Social role theory proposes that each of these aspects of gender roles contributes to gender stereotypes and to sex differences in the behavior.

For example, the role of homemaker cultivates expressive traits (being warm, sensitive, and nurturant), whereas the role of breadwinner and worker cultivates instrumental traits (being independent, competitive, and assertive). In one study, college students were asked to judge the personality traits of men and women who stayed at home as parents, and of men and women who worked full time. They judged homemakers—whether male or female—to be gentler and kinder, and they judged full-time workers—whether female or male—to be more assertive and competitive (Eagly & Steffen, 1984). This study suggests that judgments of women's and men's traits are more a function of their roles as homemaker and worker than of gender per se.

The second component of gender roles prescribes different kinds of work for men and women. Men are more likely than women to work in some occupations (e.g., military officer, politician, business executive), and women in others (e.g., nurse, librarian, elementary school teacher). These occupational roles lead to gender stereotypes (e.g., "men are aggressive," "women are helpful and nurturant"). Common sense may tell us that men and women *choose* different kinds of work because of their differing traits, but social role theory warns us that we may have the causal sequence backward. Powerful social roles have forced men and women into different occupations. Working men and women then behave differently *because* of their imposed occupational roles, and as a result, people form gender stereotypes based on these observed differences.

The mistake people make, according to social role theory, is in attributing men's and women's behavior (men's aggressiveness, women's helpfulness) to gender and not to social roles. One recent study showed that male-dominated occupations are judged to require stereotypic masculine traits (such as assertiveness and physical strength) and female-dominated occupations are judged to require stereotypically feminine traits (such as sensitivity and physical attractiveness)

(Cejka & Eagly, 1999). But is this really so? When male workers went off to combat during World War II, "Rosie the Riveter" and her sisters did just fine at "male jobs." Today, as more and more women gain admission to the formerly male bastions of corporate management, law, medicine, and academia, we realize that women have what it takes to do these jobs. According to social role theory, past social roles channeled women into selected kinds of work, and people inferred "women's traits" from this fact. The mistake lay in not realizing that it was the invisible hand of social roles that led to women's "choices," not their innate traits or preferences.

The different occupational roles of men and women have often been confounded with status differences—the third main component of gender roles. The job of secretary (traditionally female) carries much less power than the job of executive (traditionally male), and the job of nurse (traditionally female) carries less authority than the job of doctor (traditionally male). Domestic roles—both at home ("housewife") and in the work world ("maid," "janitor")—typically carry low status, and such roles have traditionally been assigned more to women than to men. Although many in our society give lip service to the importance of child care, most men remain unwilling to trade in their careers to work as full-time fathers, perhaps because they regard child care as a low-status undertaking. And although the wage gap between women and men has decreased in our society, women still receive less pay than men do for equivalent work, and in a capitalistic society like ours, status is gauged in part by salary. The reasons for the status differences between women and men are complex and in part reflect sexist ideologies and institutions. The point to emphasize here is that existing status differences contribute to gender stereotypes and to behavioral differences between women and men.

In one experiment, Alice Eagly and Valerie Steffen (1984) found that people in high-status roles are judged to be more assertive, independent, and dominant (i.e., to have more stereotypically masculine traits) than people in low-status roles. Not surprisingly, people in high-status roles (manager, executive) are also judged to be more influential, whereas people in low-status roles (secretary, clerk) are judged to be more easily influenced by others (Eagly & Wood, 1982). Of course, these are exactly the kinds of stereotypes that people hold about men and women. The implication is that common gender stereotypes are really stereotypes about high-status versus low-status people.

The different-status explanation for gender differences has been studied intensively in relation to nonverbal behavior. When interacting with others, women smile more and show more eye contact than men do. Women are more accurate in judging facial emotions than men are. In contrast, men maintain more personal space in social interaction than women do (see Chapter 1). One explanation for these differences is that women show nonverbal behaviors characteristic of low-status people, whereas men show nonverbal behaviors characteristic of high-status, powerful people (Henley, 1977; LaFrance & Henley, 1997).

A relatively subtle nonverbal difference between men and women is that men tend to engage in more eye contact while talking, whereas women tend to engage in more eye contact while listening. The first style of eye contact is more characteristic of high-status, powerful people (e.g., bosses), whereas the second style is more characteristic of low-status people (e. g., subordinates). A number of experiments suggest that when women are assigned to powerful roles (e.g., as supervisors) they show powerful styles of eye contact. However, in equal-status interactions, men show the "powerful" style of eye contact more often than women do (Dovidio, Ellyson, Keating, Heltman, & Brown, 1988). Such findings indicate that unless the social setting assigns women power, gender serves as a kind of "diffuse status cue," with women seen to be less powerful than men (Ridgeway & Diekema, 1992; Wagner & Berger, 1997).

To compensate for their lower status, women may engage in warmer styles of influence and persuasion (e.g., they smile more, maintain more eye contact) and are less forceful and "abrasive"). Otherwise, they risk not succeeding in influencing others (Ridgeway, 1982; Ridgeway & Diekema, 1992; Shackelford, Wood, & Worchel, 1996). Recall that one difference between women's and men's behaviors in groups is that women engage in more expressive, socio-emotional behaviors, whereas men engage in more instrumental, task-oriented behaviors (see chapter 1). One explanation for these differences is the unequal status women and men possess. Again, the mistake people make is in attributing behavior to women's and men's traits ("women are expressive," "men are assertive") rather than to power differences between women and men (Carli, 1991).

CODA

Gender affects virtually every aspect of our lives: the clothes we wear, the decoration of our rooms, our hobbies and interests, our favorite school subjects, our work and careers, our ways of interacting with others, and our roles in family life. Why is gender so overwhelmingly important? It is tempting to answer that it is because women and men are born with different natures.

According to evidence presented in this chapter, however, the reason gender is so important is because it is ceaselessly drilled into us from birth on—by our parents, teachers, and peers; by the mass media; by a host of social institutions. We amplify the impact of social learning

when we label ourselves as males and females, develop gender stereotypes, and internalize self-concepts as males and females. Aiding and
abetting the process is a society that enforces gender roles and status
differences between the sexes. The environmental gender juggernaut is
so pervasive, so ubiquitous, that it becomes invisible to many of us. We
are like the proverbial fish in water—we cannot see our environment
for what it is. Our surroundings are so saturated with gender lessons
that gender becomes second nature to us, which we readily confuse
with "nature" itself.

And so we suffer from an illusion—that gender is innate rather than
a product of relentless, ongoing, and ever-present environmental
forces. Scientific research can help us to see past the illusion. It can
help us to realize that, like the veil to Madame Bovary's hat, our behavior as men and women is constrained by many cords; it quivers before
countless past and present gusts.

SUMMARY

Social learning theories propose that children learn to behave as boys
and girls as a result of rewards, punishments, and imitation. Sex-typed
play is one of the earliest differences to emerge in girls' and boys' behaviors. Research shows that parents encourage sex-typed play in children, that fathers encourage sex-typed play more strongly than mothers, and that parents encourage sex-typed play more in boys than in
girls. In addition, parents may restrict girls more than boys, encourage
more independence in boys than in girls, encourage different emotions
in boys and girls, and assign different tasks to boys and girls. All these
factors lead boys and girls to behave differently.

Teacher, peer, and media influences are important in molding
gender-related behaviors. Teachers sometimes treat boys and girls differently, although the reasons for this are not always clear. Peer influences may be especially important in molding children's sex-typed behaviors. In early and middle childhood, boys and girls interact mostly
with members of their own sex, and this sex segregation intensifies differences between boys and girls. Boys in particular seem to police one
another, encouraging masculine behaviors and ridiculing feminine behaviors. The mass media are saturated with gender stereotypic images,
and children learn common gender stereotypes and sex-typed behaviors by watching television.

Children progress through definite stages of gender understanding.
By age 2½, most children accurately label themselves as boys or girls,
and by age 3½, most children understand that gender is stable over
time. Between ages 3 and 4, children internalize standards of sex-typed

conduct and acquire an inner "gender gyroscope" that guides their behavior as boys and girls. By age 6 or 7, most children achieve gender constancy—a mature understanding that gender is stable and not influenced by superficial changes in body appearance or dress. Gender knowledge has social origins and social consequences. Accurate gender labeling increases children's attention to same-sex models, helps gender stereotypes to develop, and permits children to learn about gender from their social environments. As children move into middle childhood, their gender stereotypes become more accurate and extensive, but also more flexible. Social factors such as parents' gender beliefs, peer influences, sibling influences, and media influences affect gender knowledge and stereotypes.

Once in place, gender stereotypes influence people's behavior in many ways. People try to act consistently with gender stereotypes, particularly in settings that make gender salient. People often influence others—both in subtle and not-so-subtle ways—to act consistently with gender stereotypes. Finally, negative stereotypes about the abilities of men and women may undermine individuals' performance in affected domains.

Broad social factors lead women and men to behave differently. Social role theory proposes that the behaviors of women and men are more a function of gender roles than of innate traits. Traditional gender roles prescribe three commonly observed patterns of behavior: (a) women are more often homemakers and men more often workers; (b) women and men tend to have different occupations; and (c) women tend to have lower-status positions than men have. As a result, traditional roles foster different behaviors in women and men (e.g., more expressive behaviors in women and more instrumental behaviors in men), and these behaviors lead us to form gender stereotypes and to mistakenly attribute gender differences to innate traits rather than to the invisible hand of social roles.

Status differences between women and men also produce different behaviors in women and men (e.g., different nonverbal behaviors, different behaviors in groups). However, these different behaviors are a function of status, not of innate differences between the sexes.

Taken together, the research summarized here shows that social and environmental factors have a powerful influence on many of the phenomena described by the term *gender*.

6

Cross-Examinations

I dogmatise and am contradicted, and in this conflict of opinions and sentiments I find delight.

—Samuel Johnson

NATURE and NURTURE came together one day to have tea in an outdoor café. As they sat and observed the people about them, their conversation turned to the nature of women and men. The following is a transcript of their impromptu discussion.

Nature: I'm glad we finally have a chance to sit down for a civilized cup of tea. I don't have to tell you that it gets a little wild where I'm from.

Nurture: I can see by the stains on your clothes. I don't wish to criticize, but you really shouldn't stick your fingers out when you lift your cup.

Nature: Well, I haven't had the benefit of your upbringing.

Nurture: Anybody can learn, with the proper environment.

Nature: It takes some native ability, too.

Nurture: Let's not start that again!

Nature: You remember the last big fight we had?

Nurture: What were we discussing that time?

Nature: Intelligence!

Nurture: Well, for heaven's sake, let's stay away from that topic today. Let's chat about something that's not controversial, like all the rest of these people. Let's have a normal conversation for once. Did you overhear those women over there, discussing fashions and recipes? Those are safe topics. I have a great new recipe for a vegetarian casserole I can share it with you, if you're interested. And listen to that group of men over there, arguing about football and cars. What do you think? How will the 49ers do this year?

Nature: It just goes to prove what I've said all along. Men and women have different natures.

Nurture: Oh no, not again! Well you have to admit that I tried to steer us into a safer topic! But now that you've said what you've said, I must respond to your gratuitous comment. I'm sure it comes as no surprise to you to learn that I disagree with you. For an elemental force, I find you to be really behind the times. This is the 21st century! We've moved past the sort of essentialist nonsense you just spouted about the nature of gender!

Nature: I don't think it's nonsense to say that men and women have different natures. I just read a book, *Gender, Nature, and Nurture,* by a fellow from California. . . .

Nurture: Yes, I believe I read the very same book. Quite interesting. Made a number of good points about the importance of nurture. But some of the arguments on the other side seemed a bit strained to me.

Nature: Really! My take on the book was just the opposite. There were a number of excellent points about biological influences on men and women's behavior. But, much of the stuff about nurture seemed rather far-fetched to me. Wordy, too. That fellow needed a good editor.

Nurture: You're right there. The chapter on biology could have been pruned down considerably. It was quite repetitious. And many of its arguments were specious to boot. All that stuff on animal research—about hormones affecting the nervous system, sexual behaviors, and so forth. Let's be realistic—we know that human beings are much more complex than lower animals. We have higher thought processes and culture. We are conscious, thinking beings.

Nature: I didn't know *you* were human.

Nurture: Don't be ridiculous. I am what makes humans human. Without the benefit of nurture, humans would be no better than animals. Let me use sex as an illustration.

Nature: By all means! I like to talk about sex!

Nurture: That doesn't surprise me. But to return to what I was saying, as we all know, the mating of animals is largely reflexive. But human sexuality is largely learned. When people make love, they have feelings, fantasies, and romance. Human sexuality is molded by cultural influences; it is *socially constructed*. That California fellow really needs to read some Foucault.

Nature: But you are ignoring a fundamental fact: People *are* animals. We eat and drink, we breathe and bleed. We have all the basic bodily functions. We are DNA-based organisms, and we have evolved, just like amoebas, lizards, and rats.

Nurture: I didn't know *you* were human.

Nature: I am *everything*. I embrace the whole spectrum of living things. That's my point exactly. People are a part of *nature*. There's no escaping it.

Nurture: But you overstep yourself. You are *not* everything. That's your problem. You think everything can be reduced to DNA—to genes, hormones, and nerve impulses. To you, everything is a Darwinian struggle, "red in tooth and claw." But let me tell you, there's more to human beings than their biological parts. And there's more to men and women than their genes and genitals. There are emergent properties you don't acknowledge—things like consciousness, beliefs, language, and culture. These things are learned, and they cannot be readily explained by biology.

Nature: I'll concede this much—that consciousness, language, and culture complicate things. But biology *can* have a direct influence on human behavior, despite the factors you cite. Cultures across the world vary in their cuisine; however, people all over the world like sweet and fatty foods. Cultures provide variations on a theme, but the basic themes are biologically set.

Nurture: I thought we were talking about gender.

Nature: Okay, let's talk about gender. Let's return to one of my favorite topics—sex. You read that fellow's book. The evidence is quite clear: Across the world, despite cultural variations, men are more interested in casual sex than women

"... but I'm high in the dominance hierarchy ..."

A Darwinian pick-up line.
Has evolution led men and women to prefer different traits in a mate?

are, and they prefer youth and beauty in a mate more than women do. In contrast, women are more interested in a mate's wealth, status, and dominance than men are. These differences must be due to biological factors.

Nurture: But you're ignoring the fact that men have more power and status the world over.

Nature: Well, *why* do men have more power and status?

Nurture: I repeat, men have more power and status the world over. And people who have power and status can pick young, attractive things for dates and mates. On the other hand, if you are economically dependent—as women traditionally have been—then it's important for you to mate with someone who has power, money, and status. In the past, when women married, they acquired a standard of living as well a mate. But things have changed, now that women are less oppressed and more economically independent ..."

Nature: Women *still* prefer good earnings and status in a mate more than men do, according to recent research.

Nurture: Well that will change, as the two sexes come closer to achieving equality.

Nature: You seem to have forgotten David Buss's (1989) study of 37 cultures across the world. The sex differences he found in mating preferences were quite consistent across cultures, and this implies that there are biological factors at work. I know you don't want to hear these words, but I'm going to say them anyhow: There *are* biologically determined sex differences in human sexual behaviors and mate preferences.

Nurture: I'm glad you brought up Buss's research, because there was a very interesting article in the June 1999 issue of the *American Psychologist* by Alice Eagly and Wendy Wood. It challenged Buss's evolutionary position, using Buss's own data. . . .

Nature: You read a lot for an elemental force.

Nurture: Don't be silly! I am synonymous with cultural learning. Of course I keep up with current knowledge!

Nature: You needn't be so touchy!

Nurture: As I was saying before you so rudely interrupted, Alice Eagly and Wendy Wood analyzed David Buss's own data from more than 30 different cultures, and they showed that the size of sex differences in mate preferences depends on women's status in those cultures. Sex differences in preferences for a mate's earning potential, for example, were particularly large in societies in which women had low status and education. However, sex differences were smaller in societies in which women had higher status and more education. Clearly, what you claim is a biologically determined sex difference varies a lot, depending on cultural and economic factors. Eagly and Wood showed that gender differences in mate preferences are really a matter of sex differences in status and education, and not a matter of biology!

Nature: But was there any culture in which men valued the earning prospects of a mate *more* than women did?

Nurture: Well, no. . . .

Nature: There you go! Of course there are cultural variations in mate preferences. No one denies that. But there are still consistent sex differences, despite all the cultural variations. And the only plausible explanation for these consistencies is biology. They are *caused by nature*, in short.

Nurture: You just don't understand what I'm saying!

Nature: I understand you all right; however, I'm looking at the data in a different light. You want to emphasize cultural variations in sex differences and argue from them that culture creates sex differences. However, I want to emphasize *cross-cultural consistencies* in sex differences and argue that only biology can explain these consistencies.

Nurture: I must remind you that cross-cultural consistencies in sex differences can result from sexist institutions and social roles that are common across cultures.

Nature: Okay then, let's look at another example—sexual orientation. You must agree there's a huge sex difference there. Most men are sexually attracted to women and most women are sexually attracted to men. Surely you admit this is primarily caused by biological factors.

Nurture: Not necessarily. As I was telling you before, human sexuality is socially constructed. In most cultures, people are taught heterosexuality from birth on. Clearly, there have been some cultures that practiced homosexuality and bisexuality more than we do—in ancient Greece, for example.

Nature: But you are familiar with the evidence. Variations in prenatal androgen exposure affect masculine and feminine sexual behaviors in rodents and monkeys. Studies of humans exposed to unusual levels of sex hormones also show a link between prenatal hormones and adult sexual orientation. Recent research on physical traits such as otoacoustic emissions, finger-length ratios, and hip-to-waist ratios again suggest that biological factors are linked to adult sexual orientation. Furthermore, family linkage and behavior genetic studies show that sexual orientation runs in families and is influenced by genetics. And finally, Simon LeVay (1991) demonstrated that there may even be brain differences between gay men and straight men, and I am excited to report that there is a new study that shows the same thing (Byne et al., in press). The evidence is really overwhelming—don't you think?—that biology plays an important role in sexual orientation.

Nurture: Not necessarily. You talk about human "sexual orientation" is if it were some immutable, fixed thing. You are clearly unable to escape your essentialist moorings. Let me quote from Anne Fausto-Sterling's (1992) excellent book, *Myths of Gender*, which argues against LeVay and others of his ilk who wish to make sexual orientation a simple, gender-linked trait:

> Human behavior . . . is much more complex than [LeVay] admits. How can he explain the football hero—masculine

to the core—who is nevertheless gay? And what about the highly feminine lesbian, the straight man who fantasizes about having sex with a man while making love to his wife or who experiences sexual arousal from anal penetration, the lesbian who fantasizes about penile penetration while making love to her lady friend, or the well-known phenomenon of situational homosexuality that occurs in institutions such as prison? These examples reiterate that human sexuality is not an either/or proposition. Nor do sex roles necessarily mirror sexual orientation (p. 249).

Nature: Whew, that's a real mouthful! Did you memorize all that?

Nurture: Yes. I'm a quick learner.

Nature: You must be. But to return to Fausto-Sterling, I think she is mixing apples, oranges, and rutabagas in that passage. Let me try to untangle some of it. First of all, I must say that it seems quite strange for a social constructionist like Fausto-Sterling to describe *any* man as "masculine to the core." However, for once I find myself in agreement with her, for I do believe that some men are "masculine to the core" and that some women are "feminine to the core." Why? Because it is in their biological natures!

In response to the "straight man" who fantasizes about having sex with a man while making love to his wife, my answer is simple. Chances are, he's not really a "straight man"! Similarly, the "lesbian" who fantasizes about penile penetration while making love to her "lady friend" is not truly a "lesbian"—she's either a heterosexual woman experimenting with lesbianism or she's bisexual. And the man who gets turned on by anal penetration when making love with his wife? It's very simple—if he's sexually attracted to men and if he's fantasizing about anal penetration, he's probably gay. If he's turned on by women and simply likes that kind of stimulation, in addition to others, he's probably straight. And situational homosexuality, as occurs in prisons, is no big deal. The question is, what do these men prefer once they are out of prison? If they resume sexual relations with women, chances are they are straight. If they continue having relations with men, chances are they are gay.

Fausto-Sterling creates unnecessary conceptual confusion when she fails to distinguish between *sexual behaviors*, which of course are molded by social forces and environmental opportunities, and *sexual de*sires. When I speak of human sexual orientation, I am speaking, most fundamentally, of one's sexual desire for men or for women. This is the aspect of sexual orientation that I believe is most influenced by biology.

Nurture: Now I am going to trap you with your own words!

Nature: Uh oh!

Nurture: You just defined "sexual orientation" in a totally different way from most of the animal studies you admire so much. In these studies, "sexual orientation" is defined in terms of mounting behaviors and sexual presenting. Do these behaviors assess "desire for males" or "desire for females"? I think not.

Nature: You may be right. However, you must admit it's hard to assess a rat's desires.

Nurture: Then admit that you are measuring quite different things in animal and human studies. And if you admit this, then you must admit also that studies on the effects of sex hormones on animals' "masculine" and "feminine" sexual behaviors don't tell us very much about human sexual orientation.

Nature: Are you through?

Nurture: For now.

Nature: Then I want to make one final comment about Fausto-Sterling. I believe she is simply wrong when she claims there is no relation between sexual orientation and other aspects of gender. There may indeed be some gay football heroes who are "masculine to the core." But I suspect they are rare. Recent research shows there are strong links between sexual orientation and various measures of masculinity and femininity. Furthermore, children who are gender nonconformists—feminine boys and masculine girls—are much more likely than gender-conforming children to grow up to be homosexual adults. All this evidence points to the strong likelihood that there are biological factors that influence both sex-typed behaviors and sexual orientation.

Nurture: Not so fast! You forget that there are gay and lesbian subcultures that influence the adoption of supposedly "masculine" and "feminine" behaviors, just as mainstream society socializes the masculine and feminine behaviors of the majority. However, it is my observation that gender role-playing has decreased in the gay and lesbian communities.

Nature: I just don't understand your resistance on this topic. It seems so obvious to me that biology influences sexuality. If biological evolution molded any aspect of gender, wouldn't it be sexual behavior and, in particular, sexual orientation? *If sex is about anything, it's about sex.* That is to say, if "male" and "female" have any biological purpose whatsoever, it is reproduction and genetic recombination. Darwinian evolution is all about reproduction. I think you are being simply wrongheaded when you refuse to acknowledge that biological evolution molded sexual orientation and other aspects of human sexuality.

Nurture: Okay, I'm wrongheaded. But I repeat, there's much more to human sexuality than is dreamt of in your philosophy!

Nature: Okay, I don't want to beat a dead horse. Let's move on.

Nurture: That sounds like a good metaphor for your theorizing, although it seems you're beating dead rats more than horses. But neither provides a particularly good model for *human* sexuality.

Nature: Okay, let's move on. I would like to ask you a more general question about gender. And be honest now. Are you really claiming that there are no biological differences between men and women?

Nurture: No, obviously not. After all, men have penises and women have vaginas.

Nature: *And that's it?* Sometimes you make me want to scream!

Nurture: Well, why don't you go howl with some hyenas. It seems to me that you have more in common with them than with human beings.

Nature: I warn you, I *am* going to scream!

Nurture: Please don't! There aren't any hyenas here. Only people. It's not like we're out in the jungle somewhere. Look, I'll concede a point, just to calm you down. I do believe there are some biological differences between women and men, beyond the fact that men have penises and women have vaginas.

Nature: Finally, I am hearing some sense from you! I'm telling you, my blood pressure was going through the ceiling just a second ago!

Nurture: You really need to control yourself better!

Nature: I'm going to take 10 deep breaths now. Here goes . . . 1, 2, 3 . . . Okay, that's better. Whew! Now that I've calmed down a bit, tell me, what are the other sex differences you think are due to biology?

Nurture: First of all, men are bigger than women and have greater upper-body strength. Second, women carry babies, and they lactate and nurse.

Nature: *And that's it?*

Nurture: Don't be silly. That's enough. Do you realize how important these differences have been over the history of the human race? In prehistoric times, men were more responsible for hunting and warfare because of their greater size and strength and because they were not tied down by pregnancy and lactation. On the other hand, women were more responsible for child care and close-to-home foraging because they were tied down by pregnancy and nursing.

Nature: Ah, I think I'm going to hoist *you* by your petard.

Nurture: You read Shakespeare? You didn't seem the type to me.

Nature: I am not going to deign to respond to that. Look, you said that men are bigger than women and that men have greater upper-body strength than women. But why is this so? Evolutionary theory is the only reasonable explanation for these differences. The reason men are bigger and stronger is because of sexual selection. Ancestral men must have competed with one another for status and mates. I can give you some papers to read. . . .

Nurture: Don't bother. I read more than you think. So what if men are bigger than women? Look, I'm not a member of the Flat World Society. I believe in biological evolution. I do *not* believe, however, that evolution directly explains sex differences in human behavior. You promulgate an altogether too deterministic and reductionistic form of evolutionary theory for my taste. I repeat, the only evolved sex differences that I'm willing to concede to you is that men evolved to be larger and to have greater upper-body strength and that women evolved to give birth and lactate. All the rest is learned and cultural. I don't have to restate it. Reread that book we were discussing earlier, particularly the chapter entitled, "The Case for Nurture."

Nature: You are so infuriating!

Nurture: Go howl with your hyenas!

Nature: No, I refuse to be goaded. And I'm not going to let go of what I just said. The best explanation for why men are larger than women is sexual selection. And if human males

did indeed evolve to be physically larger than women because of sexual selection, then they most likely also
evolved to possess a cluster of related behavioral traits,
such as male-on-male aggression, dominance, and status
seeking. These are the traits that helped ancestral males
get mates in the past.

Nurture: Oh, all this ranting and raving about "ancestral males"! It
gets so tiresome. Were you there during this mythical "ancestral past"? No, of course not. You and your evolutionary
friends incessantly make up these "just-so stories," which
explain everything under the sun, *after the fact*. But you fail
to see the obvious environmental explanations right under
your noses.

Nature: You folks do pretty well with just-so stories yourself. For
years you preach that gender differences and gender variations are a matter of parental treatment. Then psychologists look carefully into this claim, and low and behold,
they find that parents treat boys and girls more alike than
different. Furthermore, they conclude that when parents *do*
treat boys and girls differently, it may be *in response to the
children's behavior* rather than because of any desire to enforce gender stereotypes.

Then you and your friends come up with a new
dogma—that sex differences are caused by the mass media. But influences like parental rearing and the mass media should make same-sex siblings more similar to one another in their masculinity and femininity. However,
behavior genetic studies show that same-sex siblings in a
given family are no more similar than strangers are, once
you account for genetic influences. You people make up
just-so stories too, when they suit your purposes. It's just
that your just-so stories are always environmental ones.

Nurture: Look, you clearly didn't read that book very carefully. No
one denies that gender socialization is a very complex
process. It depends on parents, teachers, and the mass media. Children's peers are also very important. And to make
matters even more complex—and this supports what I said
earlier—people are conscious, thinking beings. People
have self-concepts. They learn gender stereotypes. And
then there's also the whole matter of sexist institutions.
Let's face up to the complexity. We don't need to accept
your simplistic alternative—that all observed sex differences are due to biology.

Nature: You simply didn't understand the compelling evidence for biology presented in that fellow's book.

Nurture: I understood it! I also understood all the flaws in that evidence. First of all, there's the problem of overgeneralizing from animals to human beings. And then there are all those claims about testosterone levels being linked to people's aggressiveness, criminality, personality, and visual-spatial abilities. Well, any introductory psychology student could criticize those findings. They're all correlational! We don't know what causes what. You would like to conclude that testosterone *causes* aggression and dominance and so on. But correlational studies don't allow such cause-effect inferences. Aggressiveness may elevate testosterone levels, rather than high testosterone levels causing aggressiveness.

Nature: But there's a lot of convergent evidence by now, from an awful lot of studies on testosterone. . . .

Nurture: I am not finished! And then, all that research about people with atypical hormones and genes is hopelessly flawed, too. You folks claim that CAH girls are masculinized because of high prenatal androgen levels. But these girls often *appear* different at birth. Their genitals are often masculinized and then surgically "corrected." The parents of CAH girls know about their daughters' condition. Sometimes these girls are even mistaken for boys at birth. It's clear to me that there are lots of ways in which parents may treat CAH girls differently from non-CAH girls.

Nature: But some studies have taken genital masculinization into account, and this doesn't seem to affect their findings. And research on girls exposed to DES does not suffer from the confounding problem of genital masculinization.

Nurture: The results of that research are much weaker.

Nature: But . . .

Nurture: Don't interrupt me! I'm not finished! Then you and your friends go on and on about people with androgen insensitivity. When testosterone doesn't organize the nervous system, you claim, people develop as females. But you ignore the obvious fact that androgen-insensitive individuals *look like females,* and therefore they are reared and treated as females. So it's obvious to me, the reason androgen-insensitive people are feminine is because of socialization.

Nature: What about reductase-deficient boys who grow penises at puberty?

Nurture: Some of them look genitally ambiguous, and they may be reared differently from normal girls.

Nature: What about Reiner's (2000) work on pelvic defect boys?

Nurture: Too preliminary. Hasn't even been published in a reputable journal yet. Let's wait and see if it's for real.

Nature: What about the "John/Joan" case? For years you and your friends have claimed that this case proved that gender identity is learned and a product of socialization. You argued that a genetic boy could become a girl, if he were reared as a girl from an early enough age. Now it turns out that "Joan" was never really comfortable as a female and has reverted back to being a male. Biology won out! Admit it!

Nurture: It's only a single case study and therefore not definitive. Furthermore, "John" was castrated at a relatively late age, and his parents were probably conflicted over the whole matter. It doesn't necessarily prove anything.

Nature: But there are other similar cases reported in the literature.

Nurture: And I remind you that in at least one of these cases, an XY individual was castrated and reared as a girl, and she *accepted* a female gender identity (Bradley, Oliver, Chernick, & Zucker, 1998).

Nature: But I remind you that even with her female gender identity, this individual was sexually attracted to women and worked in a masculine job—as a mechanic, or something like that.

Nurture: Notice how you focus only on the facts that support your case.

Nature: You should talk! You pick and choose only studies that are consistent with your point of view!

Nurture: You should talk! You ignore half a century's worth of research on gender socialization from psychology, sociology, and anthropology.

Nature: That's not true! I simply see flaws in that research.

Nurture: Like what?

Nature: We both read the same book, so we can agree on some things. Remember those studies on similarities between parents and children? Working mothers produce children who are less sex-typed. Siblings influence their brothers' and sisters' sex-typed behaviors. I don't have to repeat all those findings. I'm sure you're familiar with them.

Nurture: Yes, it's clear that parents and siblings have a big effect on children's masculinity and femininity.

Nature: But what's the nature of the effect? None of these studies ever mentions the possibility that parents and children are similar because of *shared genes*. We cannot understand the impact of parental rearing without acknowledging the possibility of genetic influences. There is a fundamental flaw in most existing research on gender socialization, and that flaw is that the research never even considers the possibility that parents and their children *share genes*. This fundamental flaw renders much socialization research uninterpretable. Admit it!

Nurture: I will not.

Nature: Furthermore, behavior genetic research shows that common family influences on sex-typed behaviors are very weak. Gender socialization—which you seem to think is so overwhelmingly important—just doesn't have the powerful effects it should have on all the boys and on all the girls in a family. The evidence is clear that boys and girls bring strong predispositions—*genetic* predispositions—to gender socialization. One might even say that they bring different *natures* to gender socialization.

Nurture: You really need to read that book again and review the evidence about how parents encourage different kinds of play in boys and girls. . . .

Nature: I'm glad you brought up the topic of play. First of all, I insist that you acknowledge that parents may be *responding* to girls' and boys' different toy preferences rather than creating them. The evidence *is* clear. As early as researchers can observe children, boys and girls show different toy preferences and play styles. There must be something innate going on here. Did you know that even monkeys show sex differences in their "toy" preferences and play styles? Male monkeys engage in more aggressive, rough-and-tumble play; females play more with doll-like toys (Meaney, Stewart, & Beatty, 1985).

Nurture: Look, I'm not willing to concede anything to you about sex-typed toy play *in human beings*. Forget about monkeys. Human gender socialization starts at birth. Even if there are sex differences in children's toy preferences by the second year of life, these children have already had more than a year to *learn* those differences, a year of parents' handing them different toys and encouraging different play activities.

Nature: That's an implausible explanation for such an early, pervasive, and cross-species sex difference.

Nurture: Is it more plausible that there are "doll centers" in girls' brains and "truck centers" in boys' brains?

Nature: That's putting it in a derisive way. But yes, there are innate predispositions—which ultimately must have some physiological basis—leading boys and girls to prefer certain kinds of activities to others. More subtly, perhaps there are innate predispositions that make certain kinds of learning easier or more likely in males or in females. This conceptualization should satisfy you, I would think, for it acknowledges that the environment plays a role, too. Certain kinds of learning may be more biologically prepared in boys, and other kinds more in girls. The notion that certain kinds of learning may be "biologically prepared" is a respectable notion in psychology.

Nurture: Yes, but psychologists talk about biologically prepared kinds of learning in relation to species, not in relation to the two sexes. I think your use of this concept just boils down to biological determinism in another guise—you are saying in effect that boys are biologically "primed" to learn truck play and girls to learn doll play.

Nature: What about sex differences in occupational preferences? I refer you to Chapters 1 and 2 of the book we both read. Men prefer "realistic" occupations; they like being mechanics, farmers, and plumbers. Women prefer social and artistic occupations; they like being social workers, teachers, nurses, and editors.

Nurture: But a lot of men prefer those occupations too!

Nature: But on average, men more strongly prefer thing-oriented occupations, and women more strongly prefer people-oriented occupations. This difference is quite large. And I'm sure you recall that recent behavior genetic research indicates that over 50 percent of individual differences on the people-things dimension are due to genetic influences. Surely, you can't believe that the huge observed difference between men and women on the people-things dimension is due entirely to environmental factors?

Nurture: I do indeed. The fact that individual differences are highly heritable *within each sex* does not necessarily tell us anything about the causes of gender *differences*. I believe that gender socialization is the reason why women and men prefer different kinds of occupations.

Let me remind *you* of Jacquelynne Eccles's research (Eccles et al., 1993) that found that parents have different expectations for their daughters' and sons' math performance and furthermore that these expectations influence girls' and boys' estimates of their own abilities. Eccles's research helps explain why men are more likely than women to choose "thing-oriented" fields like engineering and natural sciences.

In addition, there are also other powerful situational pressures, as you very well know. For example, it is obvious that university science and engineering departments create notoriously hostile environments for women to work in and to learn in. It is no wonder that women avoid these settings and their related occupations. And I remind you that powerful social roles have continually channeled women into low-status occupations throughout history. Until gender stereotypes are abandoned and gender roles dismantled, we cannot say with any certainly what the true occupational preferences of women and men are.

Nature: I'm glad you brought up Jacquelynne Eccles's research, for you must be aware that a number of recent studies have used Eccles's data to investigate the power of self-fulfilling prophecies (Madon et al., 1998; Jussim & Eccles, 1995; Jussim, Eccles, & Madon, 1996). In general, these studies have shown that teachers have pretty realistic assessments of their students' abilities, and that self-fulfilling prophecy effects are pretty weak. I think you overestimate the power of gender stereotypes to guide people's occupational choices, and you underestimate people's innate preferences.

Nurture: Preferences need not be "innate." The studies on self-fulfilling prophecies that you mention in no way invalidate Eccles's findings that parents have different expectations for sons and daughters and that these expectations affect sons' and daughters' beliefs about their own competencies.

Nature: But consider this: Women's occupational pursuits *have* changed enormously over the past several decades, at least in industrialized countries. The women's movement has had a major impact. Women have gained more and more access to higher education. As a matter of fact, a *majority* of all college students in the United States are now women. Women have entered high-status occupations in ever increasing numbers. Nonetheless, there remain large sex differences on the people-things dimension. Most women just don't seem drawn to fields like engineering and physics.

Nurture: You're wrong. It varies from country to country. In Hungary, half the university physics teachers are women (Dresselhaus, Franz, & Clark, 1994). And I remind you, gender differences in occupational choices are still confounded with status differences between the sexes.

Nature: But women are drawn to *some* high-status occupations, like medicine, law, and the social and biological sciences. I believe this is because these fields are more on the "people" side of the people-things dimension. Don't you think that *some* of the sex differences on the people-things dimension may be due to biological factors?

Nurture: I do not.

Nature: How about all the research on sex differences in visual-spatial ability? These differences are consistently found and they are quite large, at least for certain kinds of spatial ability. Men score a lot better on mental rotation tests than woman, for example.

Nurture: But women do better on spatial location tests than men.

Nature: That's true.

Nurture: I still don't believe any of these differences are due to biology. Girls and boys have very different learning experiences throughout childhood. They play with different kinds of toys. They participate in different kinds of sports. They take different math and science classes.

Nature: Could some of these childhood difference *result* from differences in visual-spatial abilities rather than causing them? Recall that sex differences in visual-spatial ability are quite consistent across cultures. Recent work suggests that these differences are present in young children, and there is intriguing recent evidence that nonhuman primates also show sex differences in spatial abilities (Kimura, 1999). Surely biology must play a role in all this.

Nurture: I don't think so.

Nature: Well, just as a thought experiment, I'd like you to suspend your disbelief for just a second. Imagine that there were a biologically based sex difference in certain kinds of visual-spatial abilities. Do you think that this could lead men and women—*on average*—to prefer different kinds of occupations?

Nurture: I reject the premise of your question.

Nature: But it's just a thought experiment.

Nurture: You know, for years people have claimed that "men's work" and "women's work" were dictated by native abilities and innate preferences. And usually, women were portrayed as having some kind of "deficit" in comparison with men. But this is just hogwash. Jobs do not have genitals!

        I refer you to a compelling article by Janet Shibley Hyde (1990) that offers some calculations to refute just the kind of argument you are making. She assumed—for the sake of discussion—that to be an engineer, a person requires spatial abilities in the top 5 percent of the population. Assuming a d value of 0.40 for sex differences in overall spatial ability, then 7.35% of men and 3.22% of women would have the requisite level of spatial ability to be an engineer. This suggests the ratio of male to female engineers should be around 2:1. But in fact, the ratio is more like 20:1. This means that there must be other factors—*social factors*—that lead to such huge differences in the number of men and women who pursue careers in engineering.

Nature: But those "other factors" could very well be other innate abilities and traits. Hyde's assumptions are mere conjecture, as I'm sure you'll agree. But let me play her game just the same. First, I'd like to point out that some sex differences in spatial ability are larger than her assumed d value of 0.40. More importantly, there are sex differences in other abilities that are also very important for success in engineering, such as math ability and mechanical aptitude. Furthermore, men on average are more *thing-oriented* than women are, and this difference is large. If we combine the effects of all these sex differences—in visual-spatial ability, math ability, mechanical aptitude, and people versus thing orientation—it becomes more understandable why the male-to-female ratio in engineering is 20:1.

Nurture: You are adjusting your assumptions to fit your conclusion.

Nature: Just as Hyde was. However, at least Hyde acknowledged that professions like engineering do in fact require exceptional skills and abilities in certain domains. To be an outstanding engineer or physicist, for example, it is not sufficient simply to be above average in math ability. You must be *outstanding* in math.

I'm sure you are familiar with Camilla Benbow and Julian Stanley's (1983) well-known research on gifted boys and girls. They found that the higher children's math abilities are, the more lopsided the sex ratios are. For example, in a study of the SAT math scores of gifted 13-year-olds, Benbow and Stanley found the following sex ratios: Twice as many boys as girls scored above 500; 4 times as many boys as girls scored above 600; and 13 times as many boys as girls scored above 700.

And this illustrates a more general point—that modest *mean* sex differences on a trait can result in very large sex differences at extreme values of the trait. To use another example, although there may be only a modest *mean* sex difference in aggressiveness, there may simultaneously be very large sex differences in extreme forms of aggression, such as homicide.

Nurture: I completely reject Benbow and Stanley's conclusions. Furthermore, I think their conclusions were harmful to girls' self-esteem and math performance. As I'm sure you know, in their original 1980 *Science* article, Benbow and Stanley argued that boys may be better than girls at math because of biological factors. They made this outrageous claim without having directly assessed any biological factors in their study. Their claim was immediately taken up by the mass media. Jacquelynne Eccles and Janis Jacobs (Eccles & Jacobs, 1986) found that mothers who had been exposed to the media misinformation lowered their estimates of their daughters' math abilities. Scientists need to be careful when they make damaging claims.

Nature: I believe that Benbow and Stanley did present their conclusions cautiously. However, not only must scientists be careful when presenting and interpreting their data; they also need to consider *all* reasonable theories. Theories must be judged on the basis of scientific validity, not political correctness. Many gender scholars summarily reject all biological explanations. That's not science—that's ideology!

Nurture: If you were one of the girls listening to the media blitz on "innate male mathematical superiority," you'd change your tune about the need for caution in making unfounded claims about biological gender differences.

Nature: You know, I think you're setting yourself up for a big fall.

Nurture: What are you talking about now?

Nature: You're always criticizing biological theories, and you're always stating that the biological research is primitive and flawed. . . .

Nurture: I'm glad *you* used those words. You are so right! The brain sciences are still in their infancy. Our understanding of the biology of human behavior *is* quite primitive. There is much we do not understand, including the neural bases of memory, learning, thought, emotion, and sexuality. Even if there were some *bona fide* gender differences in brain structure—and the current evidence on this topic is highly debatable, in my opinion—who knows what these differences mean?

Berkeley neuroscientist Marc Breedlove (1994) has put it very well. All psychological phenomena—including learning, memory, and motor skills—must be a function of the brain. However, to say that behavior is a function of the brain is not to say that behavior is "innate." The human brain is extraordinarily plastic. It is influenced by experience. To observe that a brain structure or a brain process is *correlated* with gender does not necessarily imply that brain differences *cause* gender differences. Gender differences in brain structure may *result from* gender differences in learning, experience, and socialization.

Nature: But more and more research is honing in on gender-linked biological processes, particularly prenatal androgen levels. And the evidence is growing stronger and stronger that these processes influence later behaviors. I don't need to repeat it all for you. There is Udry's (2000) research on links between prenatal androgen exposure and sex-typed behaviors in adult women, research on people with abnormal exposure to sex hormones, and research on castrated boys reared as girls. Then too, there's the recent flurry of research on finger-length ratios, otoacoustic emissions, and hip-to-waist ratios, which are thought to be biological markers of prenatal androgen levels. You must admit that these biological markers are unlikely to be influenced by socialization, and yet they correlate with gender-related traits and behaviors in adults.

Nurture: The kinds of research you cite are very preliminary. The findings haven't settled down yet, and I'm not ready to accept that these studies have convincingly demonstrated biological causes of gender-related behaviors.

Nature: Well, this brings me back to my earlier comment that you're setting yourself up for a fall.

Nurture: You never explained what you meant by that.

Nature: It's clear to me that biological knowledge is increasing at an exponential rate. The Human Genome Project will soon generate huge advances in knowledge about the biological causes of human behavior. I foresee major discoveries about the genetics and biology of gender in the near future. People with their heads in the sand—like yourself, I'm afraid—are going to be surprised by many of these soon-to-come findings. By summarily rejecting all biological influences on gender, you are setting yourself up to be refuted.

Nurture: Look, the biological determinists have been declaring victory for more than a century now, but their evidence remains muddy and unconvincing. I suspect it will remain so for a very long time to come. And you ignore the fact that psychologists, sociologists, and anthropologists also continue to study gender. Undoubtedly, there will be major advances in their research as well.

Nature: I'll make this prediction to you. Social science in the 21st century will need to be biologically informed, or it will be doomed to failure. Now note, I'm not saying that biology will supplant the social sciences, but I am saying that social sciences need to form a strong partnership with biology. I recommend Edward O. Wilson's (1998) fascinating book, *Consilience*, in which he argues for the unity of all sciences.

Nurture: Isn't that the same Edward O. Wilson who is the father of modern sociobiology? I'm not likely to accept *his* philosophy of science. He's always been guilty of overgeneralizing from animals to human beings, and he's always making grandiose claims about the power of evolutionary theory to explain human social behavior. I think Wilson should stick to his original love—studying ants—and leave the study of people to others!

Nature: As I said before, you may choose to stick you head in the sand.

Nurture: But perhaps *you* are the ostrich here! I haven't heard you discuss any social psychological research on gender. Anyone who's serious about the topic of gender knows that social forces create, enforce, and sustain the behavior of women and men. Read that *Gender, Nature, and Nurture* book again. People act in ways that are consistent with gender stereotypes.

Nature: But a lot of recent research shows that gender stereotypes are often quite accurate (Eagly & Diekman, 1997). People are not *making up* what they believe about men and women. Social reality creates gender stereotypes more than gender stereotypes create social reality.

Nurture: Alice Eagly's social role theory acknowledges that *apparent* social reality creates gender stereotypes. But let's extend your analysis a step further. Gender stereotypes sometimes reflect social reality, but social reality is often created by the powerful and invisible hand of *social roles*. Change gender roles and you will change women's and men's behavior. And ultimately, you will change the gender stereotypes that result.

Nature: You go on and on about self-fulfilling prophecies and behavioral confirmation. But all the social psychology experiments you cite are really only plausibility demonstrations. All they show is that, under very controlled and ideal experimental circumstances, social psychologists can demonstrate statistically significant behavioral confirmation effects. But these are not necessarily *large* effects. I told you before that recent research shows that self-fulfilling prophecy effects are often quite weak in real-life settings.

The same criticism applies to "stereotype threat" experiments on women's math performance, which are often conducted on high-ability women from elite universities. However, we don't know how much these effects occur in real-life settings. Furthermore, if you look closely at stereotype threat experiments—and I'm sure you have—you'll notice that they often don't study subjects' *raw test scores*. Rather, they statistically "correct" test scores based on subjects' previous SAT performance. In addition, some of these experiments compute test scores in strange ways—for example, as the *proportion* of questions a person gets right out of those questions attempted. This is not how *real*

SAT or GRE tests are scored. If you want to claim that stereotype threat effects are large and significant in the real world, you'd better conduct studies that use real-life tests and testing procedures on representative populations of women and men. Deep down, I think the stereotype-threat effect has been oversold. We'll see if it stands up to replication in real-life settings.

Nurture: You make me so mad! You want to dismiss every careful piece of research that demonstrates the social origins of gender differences.

Nature: No, I simply want you to be as critical of social psychological research as you are of biologically oriented research. Furthermore, even assuming that there are stereotype-threat effects, what do you suggest as a remedy? Should women have extra points added to their SAT math scores? That hardly seems fair. Not to mention it would bolster negative attributions about women's math abilities. Should universities stop requiring SAT math scores, even though these scores are quite useful for selecting engineering and natural science students? That's really throwing the baby out with the bath water! Do you want women to take tests only in all-women groups? What attributions will women make about their abilities if they require special test-taking settings, and furthermore, what happens later when women must solve math problems in real-life mixed-sex settings?

Nurture: You're really getting way offtrack here! The central point I was trying to make is that gender stereotypes have the power to undermine women's performance in some settings. The key point is that we don't need to propose innate sex differences to explain sex differences in test performance.

Nature: You know, I don't know if you're doing women a favor by portraying their performance as being so sensitive to environmental pushes and pulls. It seems as though you are portraying—inadvertently, I'm sure—women as the "weaker sex."

Nurture: You are really making my blood boil now! Let me be clear with you, stereotype threat can affect men as well women. One recent study showed that *white men* performed worse on a math test when they were induced to compare their performance with Asian men (Aronson, Lustina, Good, Keough, Steele, & Brown, 1999). This happened because common stereotypes portray Asian students to be better at math than White students. I guess men can be the "weaker sex" too, when the stereotypes are stacked against them.

Nature: You know, this discussion triggers a much broader complaint I have about psychological approaches to gender. According to many psychologists, everything's a matter of thought processes. Psychologists make it seem as if people *think* their way into gender.

Nurture: But they do, in an important sense. I keep telling you, thought processes are important in human beings. Gender *is* a matter of beliefs, stereotypes, and expectations.

Nature: But you are ignoring an important finding in the developmental literature. Children display sex-typed behaviors *before* they achieve the ability to label their own or others' genders correctly.

Nurture: But no one ever argued that gender labeling is the *only* route to sex-typed behavior. Conditioning, reinforcement, and modeling are important too, particularly when children are very young. And I must remind you that when children are able to label gender accurately, their behaviors *are* affected. For example, gender labeling can affect sex segregation and aggression in girls.

Nature: Sometimes. But again, sex-typed toy preferences and play *precede* gender labeling.

Nurture: I like the metaphor used by that California fellow. Gender labeling provides a "second-stage rocket booster" to children's gender development, and the internalization of gender standards provides a "third-stage rocket booster." Look, it's clear that thought processes are important in the development of gender. You can't tell me that boys are born feeling that doll play is repellent, embarrassing, and disgusting. Even if boys are born with a preference for certain kinds of play—which I don't believe—this cannot explain why boys derogate girls' toys and play.

Nature: Well, there certainly are some interesting psychological processes going on there, which could be related to the development of in-group and out-group feelings.

Nurture: And these are *cognitive* processes, which social psychologists have studied intensively.

Nature: I still think you and your psychologist friends have grossly overestimated the impact of cognition on gender-related behaviors. In my view, gender cognitions are often epiphenomena—they float above gender-related behaviors. They come after the fact. I remind you once again that sex-typed behaviors *precede* accurate gender labeling in children, and the relation between children's gender *beliefs* and sex-typed *behaviors* is often quite weak.

Nurture: But I remind you that experiments on adults show a clear link between gender stereotypes and behavior. Consider all the studies on self-fulfilling prophecies, behavioral confirmation, and stereotype threat.

Nature: But as I told you before, these experiments are plausibility demonstrations rather than demonstrations of real-life effects. Let's use the "Baby X" studies (Stern & Karraker, 1989) as an example. For the purpose of experimental control, researchers briefly present the same baby—sometimes labeled as a male and sometimes as a female—to adults who are asked to judge or interact with the baby. In other words, the researchers present the adults with standard "stimulus materials," so that any differences in their reaction to the baby "boy" or "girl" can be attributed to gender labeling and gender stereotypes. But in real life, you are not faced with standardized *hes* and *shes*. Rather you are faced with actual boys and girls, who do in fact behave in different ways, have different preferences, and respond to your actions in different ways.

Consider also studies on the effects of gender stereotypes on judgments of adult men and women. Experimenters present us with impoverished stimulus materials—a photograph of a person or a person described by a few trait words or by a transcript—and then ask us to judge this "person," who has been labeled as either as "John" or "Joan." But in real life, we do not judge such phantom people. Rather, we judge people who behave, talk, and interact with us, who provide us with a huge amount of rich, individuating information. Research shows that when we judge people based on lots of information, the information wins out and stereotypes have only weak effects (Kunda & Thagard, 1996).

Nurture: Even if the effects of stereotypes on people's judgments are weak—which, by the way, I don't buy—stereotypes exert their effects over and over again, and these cumulative effects may be much stronger than any single effect. If teachers hold even weak beliefs that boys are more able than girls in math, then imagine the cumulative effect of these beliefs, when teachers interact hour after hour, day after day, and year after year with girls and boys. It's not as easy to assess the "real-life" effects of stereotypes as you suggest. For every argument you present that the real-life effects of stereotypes are weak, I will counter with an argument demonstrating that these effects are strong.

Nature: I don't think we're going to make any headway here.

Nurture: Not if you remain as pigheaded as you've been.

Nature: Okay, let's turn to another topic, then. The *Gender, Nature, and Nurture* book argued that the strongest evidence for biological contributions to sex differences existed for sexuality, visual-spatial ability, and aggression. We've already discussed the first two. But what about the last one? Surely you must believe that biology contributes to sex differences in physical aggressiveness?

Nurture: Not necessarily.

Nature: But the evidence is so consistent and varied. Sex differences in aggression occur at an early age, and if anything, they are stronger in children than in adults. Our closest primate relatives show sex differences in aggression. Testosterone levels are related to aggression in both animals and humans. Cross-culturally, men are more aggressive than women are, and these differences are particularly large when you focus on extreme forms of aggression such as homicide, violent assault, and warfare.

Nurture: Much of this can be explained by greater male size and upper-body strength. It can also be explained by sexist institutions, patriarchy, social roles, and gender socialization—particularly, the socialization of masculinity. We don't need to postulate that men have a higher innate level of aggressiveness than women do.

Nature: But body size cannot explain greater male aggressiveness in young children.

Nurture: Learning and socialization can explain sex differences in young children's aggression. Furthermore, I think you overemphasize the cross-cultural consistencies. There are some cultures—think of the Amish, for example—in which *both* sexes show very low levels of aggression.

Nature: I don't doubt that both men and women in some cultures display low levels of aggression—often in response to very strong social pressures and ideologies. Absolute levels of aggression undoubtedly vary a lot across cultures, but this doesn't negate the fact that sex differences are also very consistent across cultures. I wish someone would do a careful study of aggression in Amish communities. I'm willing to bet that the rates are higher in men than women, even among the Amish.

Nurture: I'll take you up on that. Let's place a bet on it!

Nature: I accept! If you win, I'll treat the next 10 times we meet for tea.

Nurture: Okay. However, I don't think I can endure 10 more meetings with you.

Nature: But we must keep meeting until this is resolved!

Nurture: I doubt if this will ever be resolved. To return to what we were discussing, for example, I still don't accept that males are *innately* more aggressive than females. The socialization of boys to be tough and aggressive is so pervasive that it's premature to accept any biological explanations.

Nature: I'm afraid that there's no empirical evidence that will serve to convince you that *any* human sex difference is influenced by biological factors.

Nurture: And deep down, I'm afraid there's no evidence that will convince you that human gender differences are the result of learning, socialization, and environmental forces.

Nature: What do you make of the fact that some sex differences— and again, aggression is a good example—are so strong and pervasive?

Nurture: Notice how much you always focus on *differences*. You never acknowledge that there is enormous variation within each sex. All the behaviors you focus on—aggression, visual-spatial performance, occupational choices, sexual orientation—show enormous variability within each sex. Your constant harping on *differences* obscures this fundamental fact!

Nature: This is not my intent at all! Remember, the *Gender, Nature, and Nurture* book said that there were two sides to gender: differences between the sexes and individual differences in masculinity and femininity. Masculinity and femininity are all about within-sex variations. And I remind you that behavior genetic research suggests that much of this variation results from genetic factors.

You may wish to take refuge in the fact that there is a lot of variability among men and among women. But I think this is a false refuge, because these variations—which you take as evidence of the nonreality of gender—are sometimes themselves due to gender-related traits!

Nurture: I view within-sex variability as evidence against simplistic, bipolar, either-or, dichotomous constructions of gender. Society wants to divide humanity into two essential categories: male and female. But reality is not nearly so simple. I refer you to Anne Fausto-Sterling's recent book, *Sexing the Body* (2000). Did you know that even in genetic and anatomical terms, a significant number of people are intersex—neither purely male nor purely female. Such individuals include CAH females, androgen-insensitive males, Turner's syndrome females, reductase-deficient males, true hermaphrodites (people with both male and female reproductive organs or genitals), and other kinds of people as well.

Nature: Well surely, such individuals must be a small minority.

Nurture: Fausto-Sterling estimates that 1.7% of the population is intersex. This is not a trivial number. In the United States alone, this represents millions of people.

Nature: But you are getting offtrack. Let's return to the topic of variations among men and variations among women.

Nurture: Intersex people represent one kind of gender variation. I can see why you're uncomfortable. My discussion of intersex individuals questions the very categories of "male" and "female," which are so important to you.

Nature: You are wrong. I am not uncomfortable. Nonetheless, I do think that the biological categories of "male" and "female" make sense. They are not merely social constructions. The fact that there are genetic, physical, and developmental anomalies that affect a small percentage of people does not alter the validity of this fundamental biological classification. But again, I would like to return to the topic of variations within each sex.

Nurture: By all means.

Nature: You would like to argue that variations within each sex somehow negate the essential categories of "male" and "female." But I think that this argument is false. Even if there are variations in sexual orientation within each sex, for example, this should not blind us to the fact that there are still huge differences *between the sexes.* The same is true of physical aggressiveness, visual-spatial ability, and people versus thing orientation.

On one level you are right. The more within-sex variation there is on any given trait, the smaller the sex differences (i.e., d statistics) will be for that trait. However, the more important point is this: Within-sex variations are sometimes themselves *gender related.* That is, within-sex variations are sometimes themselves related to maleness and femaleness, and at a deeper level, they are probably related to the same biological processes that are linked to sex itself—prenatal hormone levels, sex-linked brain structures, and so on.

In a strange way, variations within each sex offer us a backdoor way of examining the nature and nurture of gender. The very fact that some men are gay, for example, or interested in interior design, or terrible at doing mental rotations shows that monolithic gender socialization—which you claim to be so overwhelmingly powerful—does not "take" in some people. I suspect that genetic and biological factors provide the explanation for why the behavior of significant numbers of men and women "goes against the tide" of gender socialization.

Nurture: You are sounding like James Dabbs (2000) now: "If [boys] are not masculine, it is more likely because of physiology than parenting." Give me a break!

Nature: But it's true. And there's yet another way that within-sex variations offer us a backdoor entry into probing the nature and nurture of gender. As I've noted before, the socialization factors most emphasized by psychologists and sociologists—parental treatment, social models, and mass media effects—should show themselves as *common environmental effects* in behavior genetic studies of masculinity and femininity. That is, these "nurture" factors should equally affect all the boys and all the girls in a given family. They should therefore make all the boys in a given family more similar to one another in masculinity and all the girls more similar to one another in femininity. *But behavior genetic studies show that this is not true!*

Something is fundamentally wrong with the classic socialization accounts of gender. Gender socialization does not inevitability and inexorably lead to sex differences and within-sex homogeneity. Rather, it interacts with the biology and temperament of individual boys and girls. And therefore, behavior genetic studies—which are often portrayed to be about genetics—actually tell us something very important about the *socialization* of gender.

Nurture: I think you place altogether too much faith in behavior genetic studies. Their analyses are based on debatable statistical assumptions about how genes and environments work. Personally, I believe in much more interactive and epigenetic models of development.

Nature: What do you mean by that?

Nurture: At all levels of human development—the genetic, the cytoplasmic, the hormonal, the embryological, the individual, the family, the social and cultural—there are complex feedback loops whereby events at one level influence events at other levels. In such complex systems, it's not possible to distinguish between "nature" and "nurture." There are no simple, linear, cause-effect sequences. Genes direct the production of proteins and hormones, but environmental events—for example, being stressed—in return influence hormones, which then serve to "turn on" some genes and "turn off" others. The causal arrows go in all directions, across all levels. Environmental factors—nutrition, infectious diseases, maternal stress levels—influence embryological development, and embryological development in turn influences environmental factors—the maternal immune system, for example. Individuals seek out certain environments, which can then influence the action of genes and hormones. No level and no factor is walled off from another, and no factor is causally preeminent.

Nature: Well, at least biological factors have a place in your epigenetic system.

Nurture: Of course they do! I never have denied that we are embodied creatures. What I deny is the primary and preeminent role you assign to biological factors. In your system of thought, biology is always the "cause," and behavior is the "consequence." I'm afraid the truth is not nearly as simple as that.

Nature: I've heard a number of writers offer the following analogy— that asking whether behavior is more influenced by nature or nurture is like asking whether the area of a rectangle is more influenced by its width or height.

Nurture: The point is that they're both important, right?

Nature: Right. However, this analogy goes only so far, I think.

Nurture: Damn! I thought that we would finally be able to end our conversation on a note of agreement.

Nature: End our conversation? But there's still a potful of tea left! Don't you want to hear the limits of the rectangle analogy?

Nurture: I doubt if I have a choice.

Nature: I find it scientifically unsatisfying to say, "Both things count," and to leave it at that. If the science of gender is to advance, we must understand *how* nature and nurture have their effects, and more subtly, under what conditions nature has more of an effect and under what conditions nurture has more of an effect.

Nurture: Well, I hate to sound churlish, but I have always felt that you've been exceedingly vague in specifying the precise mechanisms by which biology has its "effects" on gender. I hear all this talk about hormones, but no one has spelled out—to my satisfaction, at least—exactly how hormones "affect" aggression, spatial ability, or whatever. You folks talk about sex differences in the hypothalamus, in the corpus callosum, and so on, but no one has come even close to proposing the neural circuitry of sexuality, or of cognitive abilities, or of anything, for that matter.

Nature: Sadly, I must agree with you here. Biological theories have been weak in specifying the mechanisms by which genes, hormones, and brain structures affect gender-related behaviors. I'd like to believe that this deficiency results from the relative immaturity of biological psychology. I expect much progress will soon be made.

Nurture: We'll see.

Nature: But I'd still like to return to my dissatisfaction with the rectangle analogy. Let me use some examples to illustrate my point. No one doubts that having five fingers on each hand requires both nature (human genes) and nurture (decent nutrition, shelter, oxygen to breathe). But in most normal environments, children will end up with five fingers on each hand, and thus it is a legitimate shorthand to say that the number of fingers on the human hand is an evolved trait and that, at the individual level, this trait is genetically determined. Similarly, no one doubts that learning a human language requires both nature (a functioning human brain) and nurture (a functioning social environment). But most children who grow up in a reasonably normal social environment will learn a native language, and thus it is a legitimate shorthand to say that the *particular language* a child learns to speak is socially determined.

The same point can be made about individual differences. It takes both nature (human genes) and nurture (good nutrition and shelter) to achieve adult height. But still, behavior genetic research informs us that, for people reared in reasonably normal environments, most of the variation in people's height is genetically determined. Conversely, although most people who grow up in the United States learn to speak fluent English, it's fair to assume that most of the variations in their accents are socially and environmentally determined.

So yes, it is true that both nature and nurture play essential roles in all human behavior, including gender-related behavior. But it is still legitimate to probe into the relative contributions of nature and nurture to specific kinds of traits and behaviors, among people who inhabit reasonably normal social and physical environments.

Nurture: But I must constantly remind you that current "normal" social environments are sexist environments. We may not be able to learn some key facts about the nature and nurture of gender until women achieve full equality in our society— that is, until currently "normal" environments become abnormal!

Nature: At last we have found a point on which we can agree! A fascinating social experiment is now in progress. Economic transformations and the modern women's movement have triggered what appear to be irreversible changes in women's and men's roles. Although this social experiment will take years to play out, when it is done, it will offer new—perhaps even *definitive*—evidence about the relative roles of nature and nurture in producing the phenomenon we call "gender."

Nurture: Amen! But I would like to amend one thing you just said.

Nature: What's that?

Nurture: When talking about gender research, never use the word *definitive!*

Nature: Finally, something we can agree on whole-heartedly!

SUMMARY

Cross-examination reveals weaknesses on both sides of the nature-nurture debate. Both sides are at times guilty of selectively reviewing evidence, and both sides are tempted to make causal conclusions based on correlational data.

Partisans on the nature side sometimes overgeneralize animal results to human beings and underemphasize plausible environmental explanations for research findings. Furthermore, they often fail to specify the precise mechanisms by which biological factors influence gender-related behaviors.

Partisans on the nurture side of the debate fail to acknowledge that correlations between parents' and children's gender-related behaviors may be due to genetic as well as environmental factors. They also fail to acknowledge that not only do environments influence gender-related behaviors, but genetic predispositions likely influence the environments people choose to be in. Recent behavior genetic findings that common environmental effects on gender-related behaviors are weak throw doubt on classic socialization accounts of gender.

Although social psychological processes such as self-fulfilling prophecies and behavioral confirmation are offered by nurture theorists as explanations for sex differences, recent research suggests that these processes may be weak in real-life settings. Furthermore, experiments on self-fulfilling prophecies, behavioral confirmation, and stereotype threat are often conducted on limited populations in controlled, artificial settings. Thus, they are best viewed as "plausibility demonstrations" rather than as conclusive demonstrations of real-life processes.

Nature theorists may at times be guilty of overly simplistic and reductionistic explanations of gender, whereas nurture theorists may embrace explanations that are so complex, relativistic, and hermeneutic that they are scientifically unsatisfying.

Continued changes in the roles of men and women will provide new data about the effects of nature and nurture on gender, and ongoing research will bring a clearer resolution to the nature-nurture debate.

7

Gender, Nature, and Nurture: Looking to the Future

Successful investigations of the process of gender embodiment must use three basic principles. First, nature/nurture is indivisible. Second, organisms—human and otherwise—are active processes, moving targets, from fertilization until death. Third, no single academic or clinical discipline provides us with the true or best way.

—*Sexing the Body*
Anne Fausto-Sterling

Gender is complex; it changes over time. Figure 7.1 fleshes out this assertion by tracing several tracks of gender development, which proceed in tandem over an individual's life. These tracks include cascades of biological influences, family influences, peer influences, cultural and social influences, and influences originating from the individual's own ongoing thoughts, feelings, and behaviors.

Among the biological and genetic factors listed in Figure 7.1 are genes, prenatal sex hormones and brain organization, ongoing genetic and hormonal effects across the life span, hormonal and physical changes of puberty, and the biological processes of childbirth and parenthood. Family influences include parental socialization, sibling influences, and gender roles and stereotypes transmitted by families. Peer influences include the effects of classmates, friends, and coworkers. Broader social and cultural factors include teacher attitudes and influences, mass media effects, the structure of educational and work settings, and the influences of government, political, and social organizations. All these myriad influences come together to mold the behavior

FIG. 7.1 Parallel Tracks of Gender Development and their Complex Interactions

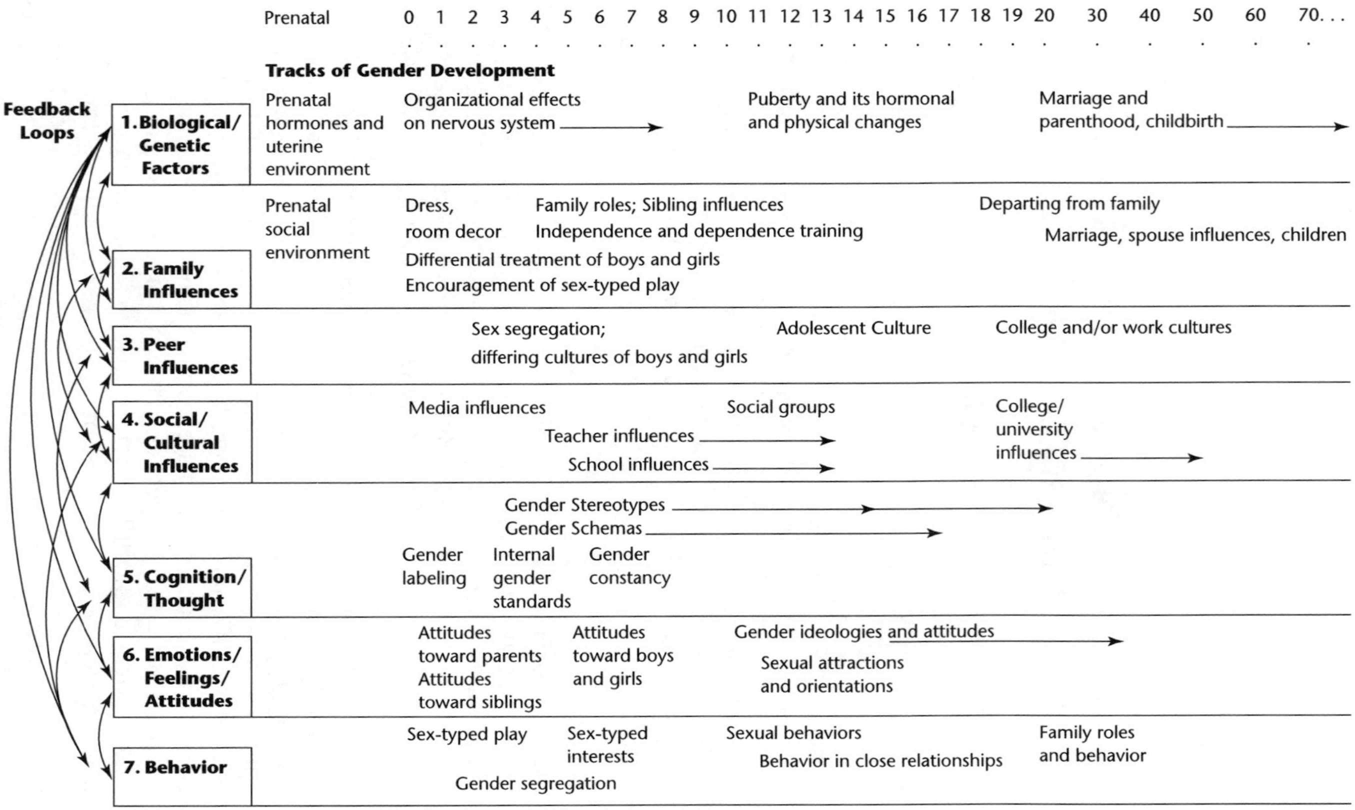

Tracks of Gender Development

Timeline (years): 0 1 2 3 4 5 6 7 8 9 10 11 12 13 14 15 16 17 18 19 20 30 40 50 60 70...

Prenatal — Puberty and its hormonal and physical changes — Marriage and parenthood, childbirth

1. Biological/Genetic Factors
- Prenatal hormones and uterine environment
- Organizational effects on nervous system →

2. Family Influences
- Prenatal social environment
- Dress, room decor
- Differential treatment of boys and girls
- Encouragement of sex-typed play
- Family roles; Sibling influences
- Independence and dependence training
- Departing from family
- Marriage, spouse influences, children

3. Peer Influences
- Sex segregation; differing cultures of boys and girls
- Adolescent Culture
- College and/or work cultures

4. Social/Cultural Influences
- Media influences
- Teacher influences →
- School influences →
- Social groups
- College/university influences →

5. Cognition/Thought
- Gender labeling
- Internal gender standards
- Gender constancy
- Gender Stereotypes
- Gender Schemas →

6. Emotions/Feelings/Attitudes
- Attitudes toward parents
- Attitudes toward siblings
- Attitudes toward boys and girls
- Gender ideologies and attitudes →
- Sexual attractions and orientations →

7. Behavior
- Sex-typed play
- Gender segregation
- Sex-typed interests
- Sexual behaviors
- Behavior in close relationships
- Family roles and behavior

Feedback Loops

of individual males and females, to produce the phenomenon we term *gender.*

The complexity of gender has implications both for theories of gender and for public policies that relate to gender. This final chapter will explore the future of gender research, and it will examine how the nature-nurture debate relates to real-life public policy questions.

CAUSAL CASCADES AND CAUSAL THICKETS

The developmental tracks portrayed in Fig. 7.1 constantly interact with one another, often in complex ways. They form causal "thickets"—hard-to-analyze tangles of influences that interact via many interlocking feedback loops. Consider the following examples: Genes held in common by parents and children influence how parents treat their children and also how children respond to parents (Tracks 1 and 2 interact). Biological predispositions in girls and boys foster sex segregation, and conversely, sex segregation amplifies biological predispositions in girls and boys (Tracks 1 and 3 interact). Parental socialization molds the ways children interact with their peers (Tracks 2 and 3 interact). Peer influences determine which TV shows children watch and the resulting gender messages children take from TV (Tracks 3 and 4 interact). Parent and teacher stereotypes influence the educational choices of boys and girls, which then influence their subsequent occupational choices (Tracks 2 and 4 interact). Work and educational settings influence individuals' gender stereotypes, stress levels, and even hormone levels (Tracks 1, 4, and 5 interact). The list of possible interactions goes on without end, with feedback loops swirling in all direction, all inextricably intertwined.

Gender as a Complex Causal Cascade

The interweaving developmental processes—the causal thickets—portrayed in Fig. 7.1 suggest three major conclusions:

1. It is often hard to partition the overall causes of gender into two clear categories labeled "nature" and "nurture."

2. On a practical level, changing any single causal factor in gender development may produce at best modest effects, if all the other factors that create and sustain gender remain in place. And predicting the effect of a change in any single factor is often difficult, for its effects can ripple through the total system in unexpected ways.

3. On a more theoretical level, the whole of gender development is often greater than the sum of its parts.

Stanford University psychologist Eleanor Maccoby (1998) offers a concrete example of the emergent complexity of gender development when she discusses the relationship between family gender socialization and childhood sex segregation:

> [W]hatever effect parents have on their children's playstyles is magnified by the formation of same-sex groupings; there is a feedback loop. Here is a plausible scenario: Individual boys, each prenatally sensitized (or primed by parents) to respond positively to overtures for rough, arousing play, will choose each other as playmates, and when they engage in play, will build up a dyadic or group process that is more distinct from female-type play than their individual tendencies would dictate. And girls, individually sensitized by their parents to others' feelings, or in a state of greater readiness to receive socialization inputs of this kind from their parents, will use these developed attributes to build a new and distinctively female type of interaction with their playmates.
>
> I am arguing that the whole is greater than the sum of its parts—that the merging of individual children, with their individual socialization histories, into a group, will produce a new form of interaction that is different from what they have experienced with their parents. Once the male group process is set in motion, its very existence increases the likelihood that boys will preferentially choose (or be chosen) to participate in it, and that girls will avoid it. In a similar way, girls who originally select other girls on the basis of individual playstyle compatibility or because they share a gender category, will construct forms of reciprocal interaction that can only occur in female dyads or groups once these are formed. Participating in these forms of interaction will make girls more likely to seek out other girls with whom they have experienced satisfying forms of female-typical interaction. And by virtue of the same-sex group interaction that occurs, a group identity, a group esprit, is built up, distinctive to all-girl or all-boy groups. (pp. 296–297)

Maccoby proposes that early parental socialization—fathers' high levels of rough-and-tumble play with their sons and parents' high levels of verbal discussion with daughters—may have more powerful consequences as children increasingly interact with peers. Although Maccoby acknowledges that biological factors can influence boys' and girls' styles of play, innate readiness and sensitization are seen as always requiring environmental "stimulation" to show themselves. Nature needs nurture, and nurture needs nature, according to this point of view.

Maccoby's proposed causal cascade can be summarized as follows: Parental socialization of boys and girls, in interaction with biological predispostions, leads boys and girls to interact in distinctive ways with their peers, and this in turn fosters sex segregation and the development of distinctively different "boy cultures" and "girl cultures."

Here are some additional causal cascades that may contribute to the development of gender:

- Cascade 1: Both biological predispositions and early social learning lead to sex-typed toy preferences in children, which in turn lead to sex differences in child-parent and child-peer interactions and to the development of different motor skills and cognitive abilities in boys and girls. Ultimately, this cascade affects the classes children take in school and the occupations they choose as adults.

- Cascade 2: Genetic predispositions influence boys' and girls' playstyles, which influence children's preference for male or female playmates. Most boys prefer to play with other boys, but some prefer instead to play with girls. Similarly, most girls prefer to play with other girls, but some prefer instead to play with boys. Playing in largely same-sex versus opposite-sex groups influences individuals' attributions of arousal, their developing erotic reactions to peers, and ultimately, their adult sexual orientation (see Bem, 1996, 2000, for a more complete description of this "exotic become erotic" theory of sexual orientation).

- Cascade 3: Adults' beliefs about boys' and girls' math abilities affect children's self-concepts and feelings of self-competence regarding math, which then influence the classes boys and girls take, which ultimately influence later choices of college majors and adult careers.

- Cascade 4: Biological predispositions, doll play, and mass media influences lead girls to be more interested in babies than boys are. As a result, girls learn more about babies, spend more time with them, and develop the skills needed to care for babies and young children. Parents and neighbors foster this early bias by often assigning girls the task of babysitter and surrogate parent. After marriage and childbirth, both men and women agree that that women are "naturally" more suited to caring for babies than men are, and in family life, women—even full-time working women—assume much more responsibility for child care than men do.

- Cascade 5: Parental treatment, sex-typed grooming, physical cues such as body shape and voice pitch, and constant social classification by gender lead toddlers to quickly learn the categories of "male" and "female." Children readily apply these labels to themselves and their peers, and they use these labels to organize gender-related behaviors they observe in themselves and others. After achieving accurate gender labeling, children exaggerate the sex differences they perceive in others, and they develop in-group feelings toward their own sex and out-group feelings toward the other sex. With the internalization of gender standards that occurs between ages 3 and 4, perceived differences between the sexes are transformed into moral imperatives. Then, children believe not only that boys and girls *are* different but also that they *should* be different.

Causal Cascades and the Nature-Nurture Debate

When applied to the nature-nurture debate, the notion of a causal cascade raises a central question: In a complex, interacting, dynamic, causal system—like that portrayed in Fig. 7.1—is it ever possible to partition the causes of any particular gender-related behavior exclusively into one of two simple and mutually exclusive categories: nature or nurture? The answer suggested by Fig. 7.1 is, probably not.

Why not? One reason is that causes are rarely "pure" in the sense that they have just biological or just environmental antecedents. For example, gene expression (a seemingly biological "cause") is influenced by both DNA codes and environmental factors (e.g., cellular environments, uterine environment, external stressors). Social "causes," such as parental treatment and peer influences, are influenced by both biological factors (e.g., parents' genes and peers' X and Y chromosomes) and social factors (e.g., gender roles and cultural traditions). An individual's choice of settings (e.g., a child's choice of male or female playmates) is genetically as well as socially influenced. Individuals' levels of sex hormones can be influenced by environments (e.g., by stress, by success, by the presence or absence of members of the opposite sex) as well as by sex chromosomes.

Assigning causes to "nature" or to "nurture" depends, in part, on how far back you want to look in the causal chain. It depends on the particular developmental instant at which you take your causal snapshot. To illustrate, the relative influence of nature and nurture on physical aggression probably differs, both quantitatively and qualitatively, for 3-year-olds and for adults.

In developmental terms, there is one way in which nature seems to have a head start on nurture: an individual's prenatal development, which is largely biologically driven, precedes his or her exposure to social environments. However, even in the case of prenatal development, environments (e.g., the uterine environment, the mother's social setting) can have significant impacts on the developing fetus. Still, these environmental inputs are likely to have their immediate effects on the fetus through biological mediators such as hormone levels, immunological factors, blood chemistry, physical traumas, or infectious agents.

Recent behavior genetic research suggests that the heritability of adult intelligence (estimated to be about 50% to 80%) is higher than the heritability of childhood intelligence (about 40% to 50%) (Jensen, 1998; McClearn, et al., 1997; McGue, Bouchard, Iacono, & Lykken, 1993). The greater genetic contribution to variations in adult intelligence may result from the fact that adults have greater freedom to *choose* their intellectual (or nonintellectual) environments than children do. After all, children *must* go to school, and some children are exposed, against their wills, to "enrichment" programs prescribed by their parents. But after leaving home, people are freer to "do their own thing." Intelligent people tend to place themselves in settings that continue to develop their intellect; nonintelligent people do not.

The heritability of masculinity and femininity may similarly vary with age. A somewhat feminine boy may be pressured by peers and parents to behave in an acceptably "masculine" manner as a child, but when he leaves home, he may be freer to express his "true self." The broader point is this: There may be no *overall* answer to behavior genetic questions such as, "What is the heritability of masculinity-femininity?" Instead, there may by multiple answers that depend on age and other factors. Similarly, there may be no global answers to the following nature-nurture questions: How much are sex differences in aggression due to socialization? To what degree are sex differences in visual-spatial ability influenced by hormonal variations? To what degree are individual differences in sexual orientation due to variations in social environments? The answer to each question may vary, depending on other factors such as age, education level, social milieu, and cultural background. This does not mean that nature-nurture questions are meaningless. Rather it means that we should expect a range of answers to such questions.

In discussing possible factors that influence the relative impact of nature and nurture, we should not ignore the obvious—that one such factor may be gender itself. The causal cascades sketched out in Figure 7.1 may sometimes differ for males and females. The following findings are consistent with this hypothesis: Parents police gender more strongly in sons than in daughters (see Chapter 5). The process of childhood sex segregation is more extreme and intense in boys than it is in girls, and boys seem to police other boys' gender-related behavior more strongly than girls police girls (see Chapters 1 and 5). Boys' sex-typed behaviors appear to be more impervious to adult influences than girls' sex-typed behaviors are (see Chapter 5). After achieving gender labeling, young girls show behavioral effects (e.g., reduced levels of aggression) that boys do not (see Chapter 5).

Sociologist Richard Udry (2000) has recently proposed that girls, because of their lower testosterone levels, may be more responsive to gender socialization—whatever direction it takes—whereas boys may be more rigidly channeled by innate factors. In a similar vein, psychologist Roy Baumeister (2000) has proposed that women's sexual behavior may be more variable, flexible, and responsive to social factors, whereas men's sexuality may be more fixed, rigid, and driven by innate factors. Recent emotion research suggests that women's subjective emotions are more responsive to social feedback, whereas men's emotions are more "read out" from their current physiological states (Roberts & Pennebaker, 1995). Men and women appear to respond to stress differently. Women show more of a "tend and befriend" response, which leads to social interaction and comparison, whereas men show more of a "fight or flight" response, which leads more often to social isolation (Taylor et al., 2000). Taken together, these varied findings suggest that in a host of ways, women's gender-related behaviors may be more responsive to "nurture" (social environments, social comparisons, social pressures), and that men's may be guided more by "nature" (genes, hormones, inner physiology).

Perhaps it's no accident, then, that female gender theorists have tended to emphasize the "nurture" of gender (the influence of socialization, gender-schemas, and social roles; see Bem, 1981b; Deaux & Major, 1987; Eagly, 1987; Maccoby, 1998), whereas male gender theorists have tended to emphasize the "nature" of gender (evolutionary pressures, genes, hormones, and brain structures; see Buss, 1999; Geary, 1998; Kenrick, 1987). Like the rest of us, gender scientists form their intuitions, based in part on their own life experiences, and the life experiences of female and male scientists differ, on average, just as do the experiences of women and men more generally.

Will future researchers succeed in developing a "unified field theory" of gender that accounts for the development of gender in all people at all times? Or will they need instead to develop subtheories of gender: theories for males and females; theories for toddlers, teenagers, and adults; theories for disadvantaged and middle-class people; theories for people from individualist and collectivist cultures? To date, most gender theorists have striven to create "all purpose" theories (e.g., social learning theories, gender schema theories, social role theories) that attempt to explain the development of gender in *all people*, using universal theoretical principles. However, the truth may turn out to be more complex than this. Rather than developing a universal theory of gender and honing in on a single answer to the nature-nurture question, researchers may instead need to be satisfied with multiple theories and multiple answers. They may come to learn that different causal cascades lead to gender in different ways, in different groups, at different stages of life.

Cascades, Fulcrums, and Social Interventions

The notion of a causal cascade raises an important practical question: If our goal is to effect real-life change in gender-related behaviors (e.g., to encourage girls to study math and natural sciences or to dissuade boys and men from aggressive behaviors), where should we intervene to produce the largest effects? Do the causal thickets portrayed in Fig. 7.1 give us guidance? Are there especially sensitive points in the causal web—what I'll call *fulcrums*—where modest interventions can lead to large outcomes? Or, on the other hand, is the thicket of factors leading to gender so over-determined—with so many interlinked "causes" pushing in the same direction—that the system as a whole possesses an inertia that resists quick and easy "fixes"? Is childhood sex segregation the "key" to sex typing? Which is more important, parental rearing or peer pressures? Can parents change children's gender-related behaviors if teachers do not cooperate? What role does each "thread" play in the overall "web" of gender?

The term *cascade* implies a sequence of interlocking causal events, where small initial effects may combine, over time, to produce large ultimate effects. Psychologists Richard Martell, David Lane, and Cynthia Emrich (1996) demonstrated such a process in a study that investigated gender-related hiring bias. These researchers conducted a computer simulation that postulated a business hierarchy—like those found in many corporations—with eight job levels and with fewer employees in top-level jobs than in lower-level jobs. They further assumed that both men and women varied randomly in their qualifications (e.g., in their test scores, their job experience) but that the two sexes were, on average, equally qualified. Company officials who decided on promotions were slightly biased ($d = 0.2$) in favor of men. In operational terms, this meant that the simulation boosted each male worker's job qualification score by a few points.

The organization started with equal numbers of men and women at each job level. New employees always started at the bottom, and higher-level employees were selected from the most qualified people at the next lower level. Twenty employment cycles were simulated, and 15% of the employees were lost to attrition at the start of each cycle. Although the simulation started with equal numbers of men and women at all job levels, by the 20th cycle, 53% of the lowest-level workers but only 35% of the highest-level workers were women. Assuming a somewhat higher level of gender bias ($d = 0.45$), the simulation generated an even more extreme result. After 20 promotion cycles, 58% of the lowest-level workers but only 29% of highest-level workers were women.

This principle—that repeated small effects can produce large cumulative effects—has been discussed earlier. For example, Chapter 1 described a meta-analysis showing that men, on average, end up with slightly better outcomes than women after face-to-face negotiations (Stuhlmacher & Walters, 1999). Although this difference is small ($d = 0.09$ to 0.25, depending on the kind of negotiation), it could lead to more sizable differences over the course of repeated negotiations—for example, repeated salary negotiations over the course of an entire career. Like compound interest, small advantages build over time.

Or consider a second example. If a child has a slight preference to play with same-sex peers during early childhood, then as the "choice tournament" for playmates repeats, day after day, this slight bias accumulates; more and more of the child's friends are same-sex friends. Later, when children form into groups, these groups become increasingly sex segregated, based in part on small biases in individual boy's and girl's preferences. The increasing sex segregation of boys' and girls' groups serves to amplify differences in boys' and girls' styles of play and thereby further strengthens preferences for same-sex playmates.

Or consider a third example. After marriage, a husband and wife both pursue their respective careers. When the possibility for promotion and increased work responsibilities arise, a bias exists in favor of pursuing the husband's promotion over the wife's, particularly if the promotion involves moving to a new city or working some distance from home. Over time and with repeated promotions, husband-wife differences in career success compound.

Although the examples just discussed tend to emphasize small environmental causes that snowball over time, the same can be true of biological causes. Indeed, because genes and hormones may produce fairly constant "biases" toward certain kinds of behavior (toward rough play, toward aggressiveness, toward verbal communication of feelings, toward playing with mechanical toys and objects), their effects—even if small—may steadily accumulate over the course of a lifetime. It may be hard to counter such biological biases with environmental interventions—such as brief classroom programs or "gender-neutral" parenting—because the cascading biological tendencies operate 24 hours a day, inside and outside school, inside and outside the home. Although social pressures may come and go, genes and hormones—in an important sense—are forever.

Although theorists often tend to portray nature and nurture as standing in opposition to one another, in fact nature and nurture often reinforce one another. For example, biological factors (e.g., toward rough play in boys) may foster childhood sex segregation, and simultaneously, social and cultural factors also may foster sex segregation. Male biological predispositions toward physical aggressiveness are often amplified by cultural learning. Sex differences in visual spatial abilities may be exaggerated by the play and school activities that boys and girls are channeled into. Clearly, biological and social factors that work in concert will be more potent than biological and social factors that oppose one another, and the mutually reinforcing effects of nature and nurture will accumulate more rapidly than will effects that do not superimpose.

It's important to note that a cascade is not simply a process in which repeated small causes yield large cumulative effects. It is also a process in which causal factors at one level trigger *increasingly complex* chains of causal events at subsequent levels. These multiplying consequences then become causes themselves, feeding back to influence and alter their original causes (see Fig. 7.1). Such proliferating feedback loops of cause and effect are ubiquitous at the cellular level. For example, DNA is "read" by chemicals in the cell, which then construct new proteins based on DNA "instructions." The synthesized proteins then feed back to influence ongoing chemical reactions in the cell and to turn on and turn off segments of DNA. Rather than viewing DNA as the chemical "mastermind" that directs all other processes in a cell, we might more accurately envision that everything causes everything else, in an unimaginably complex, self-regulating, Rube Goldberg machine.

To complicate matters even further, the causal factors that feed back to influence DNA expression do not exist just at the cellular level. Feedback loops also cut across causal levels (like those portrayed in Fig. 7.1). For example, events in the adrenal glands can affect DNA expression in brain cells. Mothers' stress levels and immune reactions can feed back to influence the action of DNA in fetal cells. Even external and social environments—stress, nutrition, and the presence of a sexual partner—can influence DNA expression in one's cells (see Gottlieb, Wahlsten, & Lickliter, 1998).

Lest the notion of intertwined causal cascades seem hopelessly complex—to the point of suggesting impenetrable causal thickets that are inaccessible to analysis—we should note, optimistically, that science has often made great progress by imposing artificial simplicity on very complex causal systems (e.g., atomic nuclei, living cells, marine ecologies, planetary climates, and spiral galaxies). Scientists enforce simplicity on complexity, in part, by developing theories that everyone knows to be oversimplifications. Such theories can nonetheless provide useful approximations to reality.

Although specific theories of gender often strive for simplicity, gender theories as a whole may sometimes seem to be a study in confusion and contradiction. It is certainly true that current theories embrace a broad diversity of viewpoints (see Chapter 3). However, there is strength in diversity. Contemporary nurture theories have moved beyond simple socialization accounts of gender to propose models that include the influence of social roles, sex segregation and peer influences, gender schemas and stereotypes, and current social settings. And nature theories have moved beyond the simplistic notions that "anatomy is destiny" or "heredity is destiny." They now probe gender in increasingly subtle ways, from the vantage points of evolutionary psychology, behavior genetics, molecular biology, and neuroendocrinology. Most contemporary biological theorists acknowledge that environments interact with biological factors at all levels of analysis.

Both nature and nurture now have seats at the theoretical table, and so the really hard work now begins—to specify, in nitty-gritty detail, exactly how the many biological and social-environmental factors identified by recent theories weave together to create the complex tapestry known as gender.

Causal Cascades and the Two Faces of Gender

The term *gender* serves as a kind of shorthand for two different phenomena: (a) sex differences in behavior and (b) individual differences in masculinity and femininity (see Chapters 1 and 2). This raises an obvious question: Are the causal cascades sketched out in Fig. 7.1 the same for these two sides of gender? More specifically, are the causal factors that generate sex differences in behavior the same as those that generate individual differences in masculinity and femininity?

Let's consider these questions in relation to a specific finding—that masculine people are more likely to die at any given age than feminine people (Lippa, Martin, & Friedman, 2000). Is this finding relevant to the topic of *sex differences*? The answer is almost certainly yes. Epidemiological studies consistently show that men die at a younger age than women do. In the United States, for example, the mean difference in life expectancy for men and women is 6 or 7 years. Thus the finding that masculinity is linked to mortality is matched by the parallel finding that men, on average, die sooner than women do.

But are the causal factors that lead to sex differences in mortality the same as the causal factors that lead masculinity to be linked to mortality within each sex? We don't yet know the answer to this question. However, I believe that the answer is likely to be yes. Some of the common causal factors may be biological (e.g., men have higher testosterone levels than women do, and similarly, masculine individuals have higher testosterone levels than feminine individuals). Other common factors may be behavioral (e.g., men smoke more than women do, and similarly, masculine individuals smoke more than feminine individuals). And still other common factors may be environmental (e.g., on average, men work and play in more dangerous settings than women do, and similarly, masculine individuals work and play in more dangerous settings than feminine individuals do). If the factors that lead masculinity to be linked to mortality strongly overlap with the factors that lead to sex differences in mortality, then masculinity and maleness (and similarly, femininity and femaleness) will prove to have deep as well as surface similarities.

Comparing causal factors responsible for sex differences with those responsible for within-sex variations may be worthwhile when studying other sorts of behaviors as well. For example, are the causal factors that lead men and women to have different sexual orientations the same as the factors that lead to individual differences in sexual orientation within each sex? Are the causal factors that lead men, on average, to be more physically aggressive than women the same as factors that lead to individual differences in aggression within each sex? Are the causal factors that lead men and women, on average, to choose different kinds of occupations the same as factors that lead to individual differences in occupational choices within each sex? The answer to each of these questions is not clear, but the very act of posing such questions encourages researchers to study and compare the causal cascades that contribute to the two sides of gender.

Some sex differences may actually *result* from differences between subgroups of men and women that are defined in terms of their masculinity and femininity levels. Once again, the masculinity and mortality study provides a concrete example. Lippa, Martin, and Friedman (2000) found that men in their study were more likely to die than women at any given age. Further analyses showed, however, that sex differences in mortality were strongest for masculine men and feminine women, but they were much smaller for feminine men and masculine women. Thus, what appeared to be a "sex difference" may have in fact been largely a difference between just some men (those high in masculinity) and some women (those high in femininity).

Consider another example. Sex differences in homicide rates may be due primarily to differences between some men (hypermasculine men) and women, but not between most men and women. Thus what appears to be a "sex difference" from one perspective may appear, from another perspective, to be largely a difference between subgroups of men and women. Or consider another example: Sex differences in sexual orientation (an individual's degree of sexual attraction to men or to women) may be stronger for some groups of men and women (masculine men vs. feminine women), and weaker for others (feminine men vs. masculine women). These examples suggest that research on sex differences should move beyond the simple question, "Do men differ from women?" to consider the more subtle question, "Which men differ most strongly from which women?"

There is a final way in which the study of sex differences is linked to the study of masculinity and femininity: The very size of sex differences may depend, in part, on individual differences in masculinity and femininity. Recall that the most common measure of sex differences, the d statistic, depends both on mean differences between the sexes and on the amount of variation observed within each sex (see Chapter 1). The more variation there is within each sex—variation that is due in part to individual differences in masculinity and femininity—the smaller the d statistic.

This statistical point brings us back to the nature-nurture debate, for the relative magnitude of sex differences and within-sex individual differences may provide another way to probe the relative impact of nature and nurture. The following thought experiment will make this clearer. Imagine a society in which all boys are sent at an early age to military camps where they are trained to be stoic, competitive, and aggressive. In contrast, all girls remain at home, where they are sequestered, shrouded in confining robes, kept illiterate, and educated only to raise children and carry out domestic tasks. Such a gender-polarized society would likely produce very large differences between the two sexes and strong homogeneity within each sex.

In contrast, imagine a society in which boys and girls are treated exactly alike from birth on. Boys and girls attend the same schools, study the same curricula, and play the same sports. Both boys and girls wear the same unisex clothes and all read the same nonsexist children's books. Parents give boys and girls the same toys to play with, and teachers treat boys and girls alike. Such a society would probably produce much smaller differences between the two sexes, but it would permit much more variability within each sex.

Thus, to the extent a culture's gender socialization practices influence both sex differences in behavior and individual differences in masculinity and femininity, we should expect a negative relationship, across cultures, between the magnitude of sex differences and the magnitude of within-sex variations in gender-related behaviors. However, to the extent that biological factors are responsible for both sex differences and individual differences in masculinity and femininity, then the magnitude of sex differences may often be unrelated, across cultures, to within-sex variations (think of sex differences and within-sex variations in height as an example).

In short, the relation between sex differences and variations in masculinity and femininity, across cultures, gives researchers another tool for studying the contributions of nature and nurture to gender. Once again we see that although sex differences and variations in masculinity and femininity are conceptually distinct, they are intimately intertwined, like so many other aspects of gender.

GENDER, NATURE, AND NURTURE: SOME REAL-LIFE CONCERNS

We acknowledge a biological difference between men and women, but in and of itself this difference does not imply an oppressive relation between the sexes. The battle of the sexes is not biological. (Editorial Collective, 1977)

But then again, maybe the "battle of the sexes" is biological, at least in part. For example, if evolution has molded women to seek devoted, faithful mates but simultaneously has molded men to enjoy "sowing their wild oats," then men and women may bring an evolved conflict to their sexual relationships. And if men tend to be bigger and stronger than women, then biology may contribute, indirectly at least, to male violence against women. The "battle of the sexes" is certainly social as well as biological, fought over a host of issues such as equal pay for equal work, corporate "glass ceilings," educational opportunities, programs to stop sexual harassment and violence, the availability of parental leave and day care, and child custody.

The remainder of this chapter briefly examines the nature-nurture debate in relation to a number of current real-life controversies that swirl around the topic of gender. Should working mothers receive more parental leave and more flexible work hours than should working fathers? Should boys and girls receive identical treatment in school? Should boys and girls participate in the same sports? Should women serve as combat soldiers? Does gender equity require gender equality? Should we aspire to equality of *outcomes* for the two sexes or equality of *opportunities*? Should standards—for college admissions, for political office, for job promotions, for enrollment in the military—be the same for men and women?

Our goal is not to resolve these difficult questions but rather to consider how different assumptions about nature and nurture may suggest different answers to these perennial public policy questions.

Rearing Girls and Boys

When psychologist Sandra Bem gave birth to her daughter and son in the 1970s, she knew at once that she was determined to rear them in a completely nonsexist manner (see Bem, 1998, for a personal account). With her husband, Daryl, she instituted a carefully thought-through program to counter traditional gender socialization:

[We] did everything we could for as long as we could to eliminate any and all correlations between a person's sex and other aspects of life. For example, we took turns cooking the meals, driving the car, bathing the baby, and so on, so that our own parental example would not teach a correlation between sex and behavior. This was easy for us because we already had such well-developed habits of egalitarian turn-taking. In addition, we tried to arrange for both our children to have traditionally male and female experiences—including, for example playing with both dolls and trucks, wearing both pink and blue clothing, and having both male and female playmates. This turned out to be easy, too, perhaps because of our kids' temperaments. Insofar as possible, we also arranged for them to see nontraditional gender models outside the home. (p. 104)

Bem tells how, when her daughter Emily was very young, she would repeatedly drive past a local construction site where a woman worked as part of the crew, because she wanted Emily to see nontraditional role models and to learn that women and men could do in any kind of work. Bem limited her children's TV viewing to three hours a week to reduce their exposure to limiting gender stereotypes, and she gave her children nonsexist children's books to read, even to the point of "doctoring" books with magic markers and whiteout to change the mostly male characters into female ones.

In raising Emily, Bem tried to counter common cultural attitudes about women's physical appearance and female beauty:

I felt that a girl in our society would especially need to be inoculated against the ubiquitous message that there is something fundamentally wrong with the female body in its natural form. Why else, after all, would we women have to watch our weight so meticulously, shave our legs and underarms, douse ourselves in perfume, cover ourselves with makeup, augment or diminish our breasts, curl or straighten our hair, and so on ad nauseum? So when Emily asked for the first time, at about age three, why some very made-up woman in a restaurant had "all that stuff" on her face, all I could say, and I think I said it with a perfectly straight face, was that the woman wanted to look like a clown. As outrageous as this now sounds to me, the reason I said it was that I didn't want Emily, at such a tender age, to have to conceptualize the wearing of all that makeup as a necessary part of being a grown-up woman. (p. 127)

When Emily was young, her nonsexist upbringing did in fact seem to influence her behavior. For example, Emily did not show the same degree of sex segregation that other children in her kindergarten class did:

When Emily was five years old, her kindergarten teacher told us that she functioned as a kind of bridge between the girls in the class and the boys, who would otherwise not have been playing with one another so productively. I doubt that Emily was still playing the same role in high school, but she did still have at least as many male friends as female friends, just as she had in kindergarten and nursery school. I don't know whether her ability to get on so well with boys had anything to do with her experience in rough-and-tumble physicality, because the boys she was friendly with were rarely the roughest. But whatever the reason, I was glad that, at every age, she constructed both a self and a social world big enough to incorporate both sexes. (p. 129)

Of course, Bem was not a typical mother. She was a prominent gender theorist and a passionate feminist. Furthermore, she and her husband were academics who lived in liberal university towns that provided supportive milieus for her feminist goals. Most parents do not have Bem's determination to constantly combat gender stereotypes and to rear their children in nonsexist ways. Indeed, many conservative parents would probably look aghast at Bem's child-rearing practices, and they would strive instead to rear their children in more traditional ways.

Although Emily and Jeremy Bem grew up to hold nonsexist attitudes and to be "gender benders" who violated traditional gender norms as young adults, both children nonetheless showed many sex-typed interests. Emily's passions were creative writing, drama, and the arts, whereas Jeremy's forte was theoretical mathematics, computer science, and physics. Of course, a sample of one boy and one girl reared in a non-gender-stereotypic home does not a scientific study make. Still, it appears that even though Emily and Jeremy were strongly influenced by their nonsexist upbringing, each brought unique (biological?) predispositions that interacted with their unorthodox upbringing.

The nontraditional rearing of Emily and Jeremy raises a host of broader theoretical and practical questions. Among these are: How much do nature and nurture influence children's gender development, and is it possible to easily change the course of gender development by changing rearing practices?

Childhood Gender Segregation: Can It Be Reduced?

In describing the consequences of her unorthodox child-rearing practices, Sandra Bem (1998) noted that Emily preferred male playmates as much as female ones as a young girl and that Jeremy actually preferred the company of girls. Did Emily and Jeremy's unusual upbringing lead them to seek out opposite-sex peers, and did their atypical playmate preferences influence their later gender development? We can never know the answers to these specific questions.

However, we do know that many studies indicate that childhood sex segregation is an important factor—a fulcrum—that contributes to early sex differences (see Chapter 5). Is it possible to reduce, or even eliminate, children's tendency to segregate by sex? If it were possible, would it be desirable to do so? As described in Chapter 5, attempts to reduce sex segregation in classroom settings have not proven to be very successful. It may be possible for teachers, with unlimited resources and constant surveillance, to bring boys and girls together. For example, teachers could assign students to alternate by sex in classroom seating, and they could always assign children to mixed-sex groups. On the playground, adult monitors could assign both girls and boys to participate in all activities—hopscotch and baseball, jump rope and football. Gender integration would be constantly encouraged, and even enforced.

Of course, children don't spend all their time at school. Would boys and girls be allowed to choose their own friends? If so, then sex segregation would probably emerge despite teachers' best efforts. Would sex-segregation be permitted outside school—in Boy Scout and Girl Scout groups, in Little League teams and ballet troupes? If so, then again, sex segregation would probably result. Would children be allowed to choose their own hobbies and activities—to collect Barbie dolls or baseball cards, to take dance lessons or karate lessons, to bake cakes or assemble model airplanes? If so, then children would probably choose their friends partly based on shared interests, and again sex segregation would likely result. Would children be allowed to pursue their individual preferences for rough-and-tumble versus more sedate styles of play? If so, then once again, sex segregation would likely result.

To prevent sex segregation would require strict regulation of children's lives, to the point of forcing many boys and girls to participate in activities they disliked. Although parents and teachers sometimes force children to do things they would rather not do, the rigid control of children's friendships and activities necessary to eliminate sex segregation would probably strike most American parents as excessive. Furthermore, even if parents and teachers wished to eliminate sex segregation—which many do not—they could not possibly monitor children 24 hours a day. It seems likely that reasonable efforts to eliminate childhood sex segregation would be doomed to failure.

In most real-life settings, childhood segregation by sex will remain a powerful reality—a reality that is probably fostered, at least in part, by biological factors. The real decision facing adults who supervise children is not whether to eliminate sex segregation, but rather, whether to reduce it in some situations, some of the time. Despite its resistance to change, childhood sex segregation may very well constitute a fulcrum in early gender development. Change it and you would likely alter the course of many of the other causal cascades that follow.

Historically, the one institution in the United States (excluding the family) that has most successfully brought boys and girls together in relatively equal-status settings is the public school system (see Tyack & Hansot, 1990). At school, boys and girls learn the same subject matter, and they have, more or less, the same responsibilities and assignments. Girls and boys intermingle in classrooms and during extracurricular activities. Indirectly, public education for large numbers of girls has undoubtedly contributed to the huge advances in women's rights that have occurred over the past century. Given the role of public education in integrating the two sexes and fostering gender equity, it is therefore ironic that same-sex education has increasingly been proposed as a remedy for problems facing America's educational systems.

Gender in the Classroom

A number of studies have indicated that girls receive less attention and encouragement than boys do in classroom settings (Sadker & Sadker, 1995). Teachers sometimes show gender bias when they call on boys more than girls, ask boys more complex questions, and listen longer to boys' responses. Compounding the problem, teachers and counselors have often channeled girls into lower-status educational tracks, majors, and careers (see American Association of University Women Educational Foundation, 1992). Boys may contribute to gender inequities in the classroom. Due to their greater assertiveness, they may sometimes end up "hogging" instructional resources—lab equipment, computers, audio-visual aids. And because boys are, on average, more disruptive than girls are in classroom settings, their very presence may detract from learning.

In all fairness, it is important to note that boys as well as girls face serious problems in school. Indeed, some contemporary observers argue that boys may be more educationally "at risk" than girls are (Sommers, 2000). For example, boys experience more reading problems than girls do, they are more likely to drop out of school, and on average, they receive poorer grades than girls do. Perhaps because of these problems, young men now constitute a minority of enrolled college students in the United States. Young men of all ages suffer disproportionately from an array of problems—attention deficit disorder and hyperactivity, drug and alcohol abuse, violent assault and homicide.

Solutions for the Problems Faced by Girls and Boys in the Classroom.   Are there solutions to the different (and shared) problems faced by girls and boys in school? If girls are in fact shortchanged in many coed classrooms, then all-female education might constitute one solution. In same-sex schools, girls would not have to compete with boys for classroom resources, teachers' attention, or leadership positions. Furthermore, girls might experience a more comfortable, collaborative, and cooperative learning environment, and they would not have to "play up" to male egos or seek the attention of male peers. Finally, girls would not have to choose between academic achievement on the one hand and societal notions of "femininity" on the other.

Of course, there are other ways to create educational equity for girls. One is to educate teachers and administrators about the problem of gender bias in educational settings and to develop institutional guidelines on how to treat the two sexes equally in mixed-sex classrooms. Other approaches include instituting special programs for girls, such as workshops that encourage girls to study science and math, classes and field trips that expose girls to successful female role models, and classes in women's studies.

Programs to address the problems facing boys in school include additional special education teachers and classes, special assistance for boys who are poor readers, after-school tutoring programs, workshops to teach boys social skills and ways to deescalate violent confrontations, and after-school activities (such as sports leagues) to help vent and channel male energy, competitiveness, and aggression.

The nature-nurture question is clearly relevant to discussions of how to best educate boys and girls. If environmental factors completely account for differences in boys' and girls' educational choices and outcomes, then environmental changes can reduce and even eliminate gender inequities and sex differences in the classroom. On the other hand, if genetic and biological factors contribute to some sex differences in academic behavior and outcomes, then perhaps special programs must be tailored to each sex.

Many education researchers view the study of math and science as especially critical for later academic and job success, particularly in today's high-tech, information-based economy. How then should educators encourage girls, who seem less interested than boys in mathematics and the natural sciences, to take more classes in these subjects? A gender-neutral solution might be to require more math and science classes of *all* students, and to counsel all students about the importance of math and science classes for future job success. A more gender-differentiated solution would be to develop special programs for girls that encourage them to take math and science classes and to develop instructional methods that are particularly suited to teaching girls—methods that make use of cooperative, group learning and of mathematics word problems that appeal to girls' interests.

If research suggests that some kinds of instructional techniques (e.g., group-based, cooperative instruction) are more effective for girls, whereas other kinds of instruction (competitive, individual-oriented instruction) are more effective for boys, then which kind should be implemented in a mixed-sex classroom? Should educators employ a Goldilocks "just right" strategy that uses mixed techniques? Or should they educate girls separately from boys and tailor instructional strategies to each sex's on-average learning styles? This brings us back to the topic of same-sex schooling.

The Value of Same-Sex Schooling. Many feminists view all-male schools, such as elite military academies, as bastions of male privilege. If all-male schools are objectionable, can all-female schools then be ideologically acceptable? One possible response is that all-female schools compensate for past inequities whereas all-male schools serve to preserve them. While there may be some truth in this argument, valuing all-female schools while devaluing all-male schools violates the principle of equal treatment for girls and boys. It also is logically inconsistent.

Does all-female education actually benefit girls? A number of studies suggest that women's colleges foster academic and career successes in their graduates and that all-girl junior and senior schools encourage girls to develop more positive attitudes toward "masculine" subjects such as science and math (for a review, see American Association of University Women Educational Foundation, 1998). Girls attending same-sex schools also report that they experience more social support and that their classes have better order and discipline.

However, some of the positive effects of all-female education may be due to self-selection. The girls and women who attend such schools—which are sometimes also religious schools—probably differ in many ways from girls and women who attend coeducational schools. They may be more serious, more academically oriented, more religious, and more conservative. Same-sex education removes girls from the influences of a heterosexual adolescent peer culture, which often emphasizes appearances, sex appeal, dating, and nonacademic social and extracurricular activities (Riordan, 1990). As a result, the self-esteem of girls in all-female schools may be based more on their academic achievement and less on their physical attractiveness and "sex appeal." Same-sex education may also help reduce the problem of teen pregnancy.

On the other hand, the evidence is quite weak that girls in same-sex schools actually learn more than girls in coed schools do. Existing research suggests that attending same-sex schools has little effect on girls' gender stereotypes. There has been little research on the effects of same-sex schooling on girls' later relationships with men. However, it seems obvious that same-sex schooling reduces girls' opportunities to interact with male peers. As a result, it may encourage female-typical styles of communication and interaction, and it may serve to extend the "female culture" of childhood into adolescence and beyond. Is this good or bad? On the positive side, same-sex schools provide girls with a nurturing and supportive environment. More negatively, they may not prepare girls for the more rough-and-tumble mixed-sex academic and corporate worlds they are likely to encounter later in life.

Some educators have recommended that schools experiment with a small number of all-girl classes, particularly in science or math. Such experiments can have paradoxical and unintended side effects, however. If participation is elective, then the existence of one or two all-female classes guarantees that girls not enrolled in these classes will attend math and science classes with higher-than-usual numbers of males. The possible advantage of same-sex classes for some girls, then, might create disadvantages for other girls who find themselves in mostly male classrooms. (Recall research on stereotype threat, described in Chapter 5, which shows that "token" female status in a group can trigger negative gender stereotypes and thereby undermine women's math performance.) Boys would also find themselves in increasingly male-dominated science and math classes. This could have the effect of fostering their negative stereotypes about women, particularly if they come to view girls as requiring "special" math and science classes. Mostly male classes might also amplify the "male culture" of early childhood and adolescence and increase male behavior problems.

Same-sex education has been proposed for boys as well as for girls. Research suggests that same-sex schools may provide boys with higher levels of structure and discipline than coed schools, and they may also reduce adolescent boys' tendency to "grandstand" for girls' attention. At the same time, all-male settings may help continue the "male culture" of childhood, which emphasizes toughness, dominance hierarchies, and loyalty to tribal peer groups. Furthermore, when boys are separated from girls, it may become easier for them to regard girls as sex objects, and more difficult for them to view girls as intellectual peers and future work colleagues.

Thus there is a paradox: Whatever benefits same-sex education may bring, it also extends childhood sex segregation to later stages of life and thereby perpetuates the male and female cultures of childhood. Probably the best recommendation, given today's state of uncertainty about the advantages and disadvantages of same-sex education, is to experiment cautiously with same-sex schooling in selected populations of boys and girls.

A final cautionary note: Even if research shows that same-sex education provides some benefits, these benefits may turn out not to result from same-sex education per se but rather from correlated factors. Same-sex schooling may be effective because it provides students with individualized attention in small schools and classes. In addition, it may encourage classroom order and discipline, emphasize academics over extracurricular activities, and "break up" some of the more negative aspects of peer culture. But with sufficient will and resources, these same results could be achieved in coed schools.

Sexual Harassment and Assault: Are They Male Problems?

A recent (and controversial) book argued that male tendencies to sexual violence, coercion, and rape have an evolutionary basis (Thornhill & Palmer, 2000). Although the reasons why men engage in sexual violence are open to debate, the empirical data are not: Men engage in sexual violence at much higher rates than women do, and women are much more frequently the victims of sexual violence than men are.

The nature-nurture debate is relevant to this real-life problem in the following sense: If biological predispositions—for example toward greater male sexual urgency, dominance, and aggressiveness—contribute to the problem of male sexual violence and coercion, then special educational and legal programs that particularly target young men may be required. And if girls and women are more often the victims of sexual violence, then special education programs—in self-defense, risk prevention, and assertiveness—that particularly target girls and women may be required.

A gender-neutral strategy would be to socialize and educate boys and girls alike, to inform them of the ethics and legal consequences of abusive sexuality, and to teach them ways to protect themselves against sexual harassment and assault. More sex-differentiated strategies might be to monitor and restrict girls more than boys, to segregate the sexes (e.g., at summer camps, in dormitories, and at school), and to provide boys with special educational programs (e.g., about the consequences of sexual assault to victims and the legal consequences for perpetrators) and special extracurricular activities (e.g., sports, youth groups) that channel male energies and that monitor adolescent males after school. Those who believe that biological factors contribute to male sexual violence would probably opt more for the gender-differentiating strategies just listed, whereas nurture theorists would likely opt more for gender-neutral strategies.

Chapter 5 described how girls tend to be sheltered and protected more than boys and how this constitutes a kind of dependence training for girls. Because of fears about their sexual assault and abuse, many parents are unlikely to grant as much independence to their daughters as to their sons. Girls could be taught self-defense strategies and self-assertion. In a sense, this would constitute a socialization program designed to "masculinize" girls in certain ways. And boys could be taught to be less impulsive and more sensitive and compassionate—in a sense, to be more "feminine." Men's sexual callousness may sometimes be aggravated by their participation in all-male groups (gangs, fraternities, all-male sports teams, military groups), and so the problem of sexual violence intersects, in some ways, with the phenomenon of sex segregation.

Husbands and Wives: The Nature and Nurture of Close Relationships

Most people, regardless of their gender, find their greatest fulfillment in close and intimate personal relationships. However, men and women may, on average, behave differently in close relationships. How much is this difference due to nature, and how much is it due to nurture, and does the answer to this question affect the potential happiness that men and women can find in close personal relationships with one another?

As described in Chapter 1, men and women look for somewhat different qualities in a mate. Men emphasize youth and beauty more than women do, and women seek out status and good earning potential in a mate more than men do. At the same time, men and women seek many of the same traits in a mate—kindness, fidelity, intelligence, honesty, and a sense of humor. Research suggests, consistent with social stereotypes, that men are more interested than women in sex for sex's sake, whereas women are more interested in committed, intimate, emotional relationships, which include sex as one part of a larger intimacy (Roscoe, Diana, & Brooks, 1987). Sex differences in sexual styles and desires are likely influenced, at least in part, by biological factors (see Chapter 4).

Traditionally, women have served as "gatekeepers" to sexual intimacy in heterosexual relationships, and this role certainly has strong cultural as well as possible biological causes. Women are still subject to sexual double standards that stigmatize them for engaging in sexual behavior that is accepted and even admired in men. And of course, women get pregnant and men do not. For whatever reason, women take a more cautious approach to sexuality, on average, than men do.

If sexuality is socially constructed and the routes to intimacy are learned, then men and women may find increasingly common ground in their close relationships. On the other hand, if there are real and sometimes strong sex differences in aspects of sexuality, then many men and women may need to negotiate their sexual relations, and they may often experience some degree of conflict.

Rearing Children.   Men and women don't seem to differ in their desire for children. However, men and women do differ, on average, in how they interact with their children. Although male participation in child care has increased in recent years—at least in industrialized countries like the United States—women still bear the brunt of child care (Bronstein & Cowan, 1988).

The biological realities of pregnancy and breast-feeding ensure that most mothers invest more time and energy in their babies than fathers do. These biological facts of life may also cause women to experience stronger bonding with their babies than men do. This is not to say that fathers don't love their children. But the nature of the mother-child bond may differ, on average, from the nature of the father-child bond. During early and middle childhood, fathers often play the role of occasional playmate and giver of discipline to their children, whereas mothers more often play the role of nurturer, mediator, caregiver, and "executive" who manages the child's life (Bronstein, 1988; Lamb, Pleck, Charnov, & Levine, 1987; Youniss & Smollar, 1985). Mothers seem to be more intimately connected with their children's lives, and they monitor the comings and goings of their children more closely than fathers do (Maccoby & Mnookin, 1992).

Except in unusual cases, mothers and fathers are equally capable of taking care of young children. However, men and women may bring somewhat different skills and dispositions to the task. Whether as a result of nature or nurture, women are on average more socially perceptive than men are, and mothers are more nonverbally "in tune" with their babies and young children than fathers are (Huang, 1986; Lamb, Frodi, Frodi, & Huang, 1982). On personality tests, women report that they are more tender-minded and agreeable than men, whereas men report that they are more assertive and aggressive than women (see chapter 1). Consistent with these self-reports, fathers are more likely than mothers to roughhouse with children, to command respect and obedience from children, and to deliver imperative commands to their children (Bronstein, 1988). As described in Chapter 5, fathers are more likely to treat sons and daughters differently than mothers are, and fathers are more disturbed by feminine behavior in their sons than mothers are. On average, fathers police gender in their children more strongly than mothers do.

Divisions of Labor. Husbands and wives must divide duties and chores between themselves. In some families, tasks are equally shared. In others, the division of labor is gender based and gender stereotypical. For example, husbands may be more responsible for outside work and wives for inside work. On an interpersonal level, husbands may be more responsible for disciplining children and keeping family members—particularly boys—"in line," whereas wives may be more responsible for mediating disputes, maintaining warm family relationships, and boosting and maintaining family members' moods.

Some gender-based divisions of labor in families are likely related to other kinds of sex differences—for example, sex differences in nurturance, aggressiveness, assertiveness, interpersonal sensitivity, and people versus thing orientation (see Chapter 1). To the extent that these differences have biological bases, it is likely that husbands and wives will continue to show somewhat different behaviors and roles in family life. On the other hand, to the extent that the behaviors of husbands and wives are determined by gender socialization and gender roles, then the possibility exists for a future in which husbands and wives divide tasks according to their individual abilities and preferences, not according to gender.

Harmony, Disharmony, and Divorce.   In the United States, almost 50% of all new marriages end in divorce. Do the two sexes bring different interpersonal styles to marital harmony and disharmony, and if so, are these differences due to nature or to nurture? Although social stereotypes portray women to be the more "romantic" sex, a number of studies suggest that men are more quick to "fall in love" and they take longer to "fall out of love" (Choo, Levine, & Hatfield, 1997; Peplau & Gordon, 1985). Of course, *love* may mean somewhat different things to the two sexes. For men, erotic attraction may be a relatively more important component of love, whereas for women, intimacy and friendship may be relatively more important components (Hendrick & Hendrick, 1986). These differences are linked to sex differences in sexuality and interaction styles described earlier in Chapter 1.

Some studies suggest that women are better than men at "taking the pulse" of relationships—monitoring their relationship's strengths and weaknesses and foreseeing problems and even breakups (Rubin, Peplau, & Hill, 1981). Such findings are consistent with the notion that women are, on average, more interpersonally sensitive than men are, and that women are more people-oriented—that is, they reflect on, ruminate about, and analyze human feelings and relationships more than men do. If such differences are learned, then men and women may, in the future, aspire to relationships in which each is equally tuned in to the ebb and flow of interaction. On the other hand, if such differences have biological bases, then men and women may be destined to remain, on average, on somewhat different wavelengths in close relationships.

Some of the interaction patterns that men and women bring to close relationships may reflect patterns developed in same-sex childhood groups. For example, men may worry more than women about dominance, independence, and saving face in relationships, whereas women may focus more on verbal negotiation, sharing intimate information, developing reciprocal roles, and cooperation. Perhaps men's and women's different experiences in sex-segregated childhood groups contribute to a common pattern observed in troubled marriages—the intrusive, verbally "pestering" wife versus the avoidant, distant, "stonewalling" husband (Gottman, 1994).

This pattern may relate to another finding: When stressed, women display more of a "tend and befriend" response, whereas men show more of a "fight or flight" response (Taylor et al., 2000). Women often want to "talk things out," negotiate, and verbally resolve conflicts. In contrast, men often want instead to "flee" a conflict situation, particularly if fighting is not perceived to be an option. Research suggests that men show more physiological arousal than women do during marital conflicts, though on the surface they may appear inexpressive (Gottman & Levenson, 1988). This finding is consistent with research (see Chapter 1) that men are more often "internalizers" who maintain facial calm while churning inside, whereas women are more often "externalizers" who show their feelings facially but don't churn so much internally.

The differing interaction styles of men and women and the different strategies men and women use to resolve conflicts may result from both nature and nurture. Whatever their causes, the differing communication styles of men and women require continual accommodation on both sides (see Tannen, 1990)

Child Custody. Although both men and women are capable of caring for young children, the legal system in the United States favors mothers over fathers in child custody cases. This was not always true. Until the late 19th century, American society adopted British legal precedents, which held that a man's wife and children were, in essence, his property. As a result, when a marriage dissolved, custody of the children was usually awarded to the father. This made a kind of sense in agrarian societies, in which fathers worked at home and children served as laborers. With the advent of the industrial revolution, however, men left the home to work in factories and mills, and women assumed responsibility for child care. By 1916, social attitudes had changed to the point that the Washington State Supreme Court could write the following opinion in a child custody case:

> Mother love is a dominant trait in even the weakest of women, and as a general thing surpasses the paternal affection for the common offspring, and moreover, a child needs a mother's care even more than a father's. For these reasons courts are loathe to deprive a mother of the custody of her children, and will not do so unless it be shown clearly that she is so far an unfit and improper person to be intrusted with such custody as to endanger the welfare of the children (*Freeland v. Freeland*, 1919; cited in McNeely, 1998).

Although modern courts and lay people would probably not state the matter quite so extremely, many probably agree, in essence, with the doctrines set forth by the Washington Supreme Court—that mothers are more essential to young children's well-being than fathers are and that a mother's love is more responsive to a young child's needs than a father's love is.

Over the course of the 20th century, and particularly since World War II, women have increasingly entered the workforce. At the same time, women have remained the primary caretakers of young children. Many feminist organizations decry the gender inequities of parenting, and they strongly advocate more male participation in child care. At the same time, wives often oppose husbands who seek primary (or even joint) custody of children during divorce proceedings. Feminist groups are ambivalent about child custody rights for fathers, perhaps because child custody is one of the few areas in which women possess power compared with men. Whatever the ideological rationale, women end up with primary custody of children after divorce more than 90% of the time (for reviews, see Maccoby & Mnookin, 1992; McNeely, 1998).

Although many people still believe that, all things being equal, young children are better served by living with their mothers, the exclusion of fathers has had negative consequences for children. Fathers may distance themselves from children with whom they have no close emotional ties, and if fathers feel that their role is simply one of "writing checks," they may be tempted to withdraw child support and eventually to abandon their children. Unfortunately, child custody cases too often serve as means for embittered spouses to get back at one another for real and imagined past injuries rather than as means to serve the needs of children. Given the legal system's tendency to favor mothers in child custody cases, fathers often end up feeling victimized by the process.

If there are biological factors that predispose mothers to be more responsive caretakers of young children, then perhaps the legal system is right to award custody more frequently to mothers than to fathers. At the same time, the child custody system must strive to ensure that fathers remain involved in their children's lives. Fathers may play a more critical parenting role during some stages of children's lives (e.g., during a boy's middle childhood and adolescence) than others. Further research and legal reforms are necessary if conflicts between mothers' and fathers' desires for child custody are to be resolved wisely (Maccoby & Mnookin, 1992).

If a person's skill as a parent is strongly influenced by socialization, then one recommendation should be uncontroversial: We need to train both sexes—through family role models, media role models, and formal instruction—how to be better parents.

Gender in the Workplace: Parental Leave, Day Care, and "Mommy Tracks"

The increasing participation of women in the workforce has created a number of public policy dilemmas. Should men and women be expected to act the same in the workplace? Do women and men bring distinctive styles to work settings, and are these differences desirable? Should employers treat working mothers differently from working fathers? How should companies and employees deal with sexuality in the workplace?

The demands of parenthood clearly are biologically different for women and men. Pregnancy and childbirth affect mothers more than fathers. Working mothers must often deal simultaneously with the physiological demands of pregnancy and the physical and psychological demands of work. Women must decide how much maternity leave to take, and then they must worry whether their absence will affect their careers. If mothers choose to breast-feed their babies, they are faced with additional decisions: how soon to return to work and whether it is possible to breast-feed and work at the same time. After recovering from the physical stress of childbirth, women are usually more responsible for child care than their husbands. (And it's important to remember that many new mothers do not have husbands with whom to share child care responsibilities.)

The biological facts of pregnancy, childbirth, and breast-feeding may require public and corporate policies that treat women differently from men, at least in certain regards. Maternal leave must be sufficient for women to give birth, recover, and bond with their infants without worrying about the security of their jobs or paychecks. Of course, some would argue that what's really required is adequate *parental leave*, and that both husbands and wives (and unmarried parents as well) should be free to care for newborn children. The availability of affordable quality day care would provide important help to many working women.

One controversial suggestion for dealing with the conflict that management women experience between the demands of motherhood and the demands of work is for companies to create two career paths for women: a "mommy track" for women who want to tone down their career goals a bit while they're rearing young children, and a "non-mommy track" for women who want to pursue their careers full tilt without any concessions to motherhood (Schwartz, 1989). The mommy track would entail greater time flexibility, more time off, and certain job features (e.g., little travel) that would make rearing children easier, whereas the non-mommy track would be the "no holds barred" default career path that men typically pursue. Pursuing the non-mommy track would seem to require mothers to be superwomen who heroically juggle

"Have you and Tim picked out a name for the career obstacle yet?"

*"Mommy tracks" and other matters: Should companies treat working
mothers differently from other employees?*

all their responsibilities at once. Pursuing the non-mommy track would
probably encourage some women to remain childless—at least, during
critical periods of their career development.

The proposal of a corporate mommy track generated strong protests
from some women, who argued that child care should not be a predominantly female responsibility and that parent tracks should apply to
men as well as to women. The nature-nurture question lurking behind
the mommy track controversy is this: Do biological factors lead women

to be more physically and psychologically invested in child care, or is parenting purely a function of socialization? Can we envision a future society in which men and women equally participate in child care and childrearing? If not, should society create options, like the mommy track, that accommodate women's unique role as mothers?

As with other aspects of gender, the policy debates over women's work roles interact with other public policy questions. For example, if the legal system continues to favor women in child custody decisions, then divorced women who work will face different pressures, on average, than divorced men who work. And if women continue to hold lower-paying and lower-status jobs compared with men, then many married couples will be tempted to sacrifice women's careers more than men's careers to accommodate the demands of rearing children.

In the past *women's work* has been defined, at least in part, in terms of occupations (e.g., teaching, nursing, and secretarial work) that are "portable," in case the family must move, and with flexible hours that can be matched to children's schedules. As is true for other causal cascades in the gender system, there are interlocking feedback loops here that sustain the status quo on various levels. Greater commitments to child care lead some women to pursue low-status jobs, and they lead others to pursue high-status jobs, but with reduced energy or commitment. Women's low-status jobs perpetuate gender stereotypes and serve to lock women more firmly in their roles as providers of child care and homemakers. Whatever its merits, one virtue of the mommy track is that it aids women who wish to have children *and* enter into high management positions; thus it may help to reduce gender segregation in elite corporate occupations.

Political Animals: Men and Women Who Govern

In the millennial year 2000, 13% of the members of the United States House of Representatives and 9% of the members of the United States Senate were women. These statistics were comparable to those from other industrialized countries. The percentage of women legislators was highest in countries with the most liberal attitudes toward gender, such as Denmark (37%), Finland (37%), the Netherlands (33%), Norway (36%), and Sweden (42%) (United Nations Development Programme, 2000). Political parties in Sweden have gone so far as to declare an informal 40/60 rule, which holds that in nominating candidates for legislative seats, neither sex should receive less than 40% or more than 60% of the nominations. However, even in Sweden, women do not comprise 50% of the legislature.

Why are women less likely than men to occupy elected and appointed government positions? There are many environmental explanations. Throughout much of the 20th century, women simply did not receive the education or work experience that would prepare them for positions of power. Powerful social pressures shunted women into limited roles. "Old boy networks " and outright prejudice excluded women from the corridors of power. Katherine Graham (1997), former owner of the *Washington Post*, tells in her autobiography how, after dinner parties for the political elite of Washington during the 1960s, she was expected to leave the room and "go off with the women" when the men began to talk politics.

There may also be biological predispositions that feed into the gender gap in politics. Males may be biologically primed to form dominance hierarchies, to compete for status, and to jockey for power. Evolutionary theories propose that sexual selection has led to male status-seeking and power-seeking. Former United States Secretary of State, Henry Kissinger put in bluntly when he stated, "Power is the ultimate aphrodisiac."

The biological facts of pregnancy and breast-feeding have caused women, traditionally, to be tied down by child care for extended periods of their lives. Rising to power often entails long periods of time working one's way up in political and government hierarchies, and women have faced, on average, more interruptions in this process. Throughout most of history, women have also had to contend with doubtful electorates who viewed being male as an essential prerequisite for high elective office. It is important to recall that women's right to vote is a recent historical achievement.

Women who manage to work their way up in political and government organizations may bring a somewhat different style to leadership than men do. Chapter 1 summarized research suggesting that women show more social-emotional and democratic styles of leadership, whereas men show more task-oriented and autocratic styles of leadership. Given that political success requires the ability to negotiate and compromise, the skill to forge consensus among allies and adversaries, and interpersonal perceptiveness, it would seem that in many ways, women are ideally suited to politics.

Old stereotypes have portrayed women as reluctant to exercise power in a tough-minded fashion and as overly subject to hormonal vicissitudes. However, female leaders and such as Golda Meir, Indira Gandhi, Margaret Thatcher, and Madeleine Albright belie such stereotypes. These examples of tough women leaders raise an interesting question in the nature-nurture debate: Is leadership style a function of biological sex, or is it rather a function of power and status? As more women occupy high government positions, will they behave as men traditionally have, or will they develop new, distinctively female styles of leadership?

Recent political polls and election results have shown evidence for a "gender gap" in the electorate's political attitudes and voting habits

(Norrander, 1999; Studlar, McAllister, & Hayes, 1998; Trevor, 1999). On average, women are more focused on social issues such as child care, education, and healthcare, whereas men are more focused on "power" issues such as military preparedness and law and order. Men tend to be more conservative, and women more liberal. Part of the "gender gap" in politics seems to flow from the different experiences of women and men in daily life. Women are more responsible than men are for child care. They monitor children's day-to-day activities, including educational activities, more often than men do. Women are responsible for their families' medical needs, and when family members—including parents—require care, women are more likely than men to provide it. Working women are more responsible than men are for difficult decisions about child care, and women must face the real-life consequences of unwanted pregnancies much more directly than men do.

All of these examples suggest that although biology may not influence politics in a direct sense, the biological realities of being male or female may have indirect consequences on the political concerns of men and women. The cascades of consequences that follow from childhood sex segregation, and the differing childhood cultures of boys and girls probably affect adult politics as well. For example, boys' competitive, risk-taking participation in hierarchical groups undoubtedly has parallels in the approaches that men take towards politics. It is probably no accident that men frequently use sports and military metaphors (to be a "good team player," to "hit a home run," to "do an end run," to "take no hostages") when describing political events.

In contrast, women's earlier experiences in cooperative, verbal-negotiating groups may influence their approaches to politics and lead women to display a more democratic, consensus-based style of leadership than men do. Our discussion of men and women in politics shows once again that the various strands of gender are interwoven in complex ways.

Women and Men in the Military: The Battles of the Sexes

BERLIN—Germany welcomed the first women into its military combat forces Tuesday, ending a long tradition of an all-male army, and top officers said the move would have a positive effect on morale.

"Male soldiers will make much more of an effort than they have in the past," said Harald Kujat, the general inspector to the army.

The first induction of 244 female volunteers began with most entering the army, some the air force and a handful the navy.

Germany had long opposed allowing women into its front-line combat forces. The government changed its policy after one woman sued and won a European Court of Justice decision last January for the right to serve in combat forces. Previously, women were allowed to serve only in musical and medical formations.

The European Court of Justice in Luxembourg said the ban on women bearing arms in the German army went against the European Union's principle of sexual equality.

The ruling, however, said exceptions were possible "where sex constitutes a determining factor to access to certain special combat units."

Many of the female inductees said they looked forward to the new era, but they were also apprehensive.

"I am very nervous and don't know what to expect," said Sylvia Siebenhauer, a new recruit. "Both men and women are going to have to change their attitudes. I don't think it will be easy. But I am going to do the best I can." (Women Enter German Combat Forces. *Los Angeles Times,* Jan. 3, 2001, from Reuters)

As of the late 1990s, women made up about 15% of the active military forces of the United States. Thus women constituted a relatively small minority of military personnel, even though almost 90% of the U. S. military's more than 1 million jobs were officially open to women. Statistics for other industrialized countries were comparable. Women made up 10% of Canada's armed forces, 6% of France's armed forces, 7% of Great Britain's armed forces, and 8% of the Netherlands' armed forces (International Institute for Strategic Studies, 2000). Germany permitted women to participate only in musical and medical units—that is, until 2001.

When the women's movement blossomed in the late 1960s and early 1970s, the right to participate in military combat was probably not uppermost in feminists' minds. However, equality is equality, and the issue of women in the military raises fundamental questions about women's rights, the ability of the two sexes to do the same work and to work together, and the nature and nurture of gender. Do biological factors exist that disqualify women from serving in combat roles? Testifying before the Senate Armed Services Committee on the role of women in the military, former Marine Corps commandant General Robert H. Barrow delivered an impassioned affirmative answer to this question:

Exposure to danger is not combat. Being shot at, even being killed, is not combat. Combat is finding . . . closing with . . . and killing or capturing the enemy. It's *killing.* And it's done in an environment that is often as difficult as you can possibly imagine. Extremes of climate. Brutality. Death. Dying. It's . . . uncivilized! And women *can't do it!* Nor should they even be thought of as doing it. The requirements for strength and endurance render them *unable* to do it. And I may be old-fashioned, but I think the very nature of women disqualifies them from doing it. Women give life. Sustain life. Nurture life. They don't *take* it. (Should Women be Sent into Combat? *New York Times,* July 21, 1991)

Many people agree with Barrow. Polls show that although a majority of Americans think many military jobs should be open to women—including jobs that expose women to danger, such as working on warships and in combat aircraft—at the same time, most Americans do not think that women should participate in hand-to-hand combat. Why not? Although many Americans might not state it as bluntly as General Barrow did, they probably entertain many of his doubts and reservations.

Do women "have what it takes" when it comes to hand-to-hand combat? Maybe this is the wrong question. Many men don't "have what it takes" either. The real question is, "Do *some women* have what it takes?" Currently, the U.S. military tests physical fitness by using separate norms developed for each sex. Thus women don't have to achieve the same number of sit-ups, pushups, or running speeds as men do in order to be declared "fit." Is this unfair? Not necessarily. For military men, fitness is graded by age. Forty-year-old men do not have to do as many sit-ups or push-ups or run as fast as a 20-year-old man to be declared "fit." Fitness is relative, and it seems reasonable to calibrate physical fitness by sex and age.

But are most women "fit" to endure the rigors of frontline combat? This is a trickier question to answer. In terms of physical strength, most women do not match most men. Of course, modern warfare, like many other aspects of modern life, depends less on brute physical strength and more on technological prowess. Women may be as capable as men to pilot fighter jets and to launch cruise missiles. However, do as many women as men *desire* to be fighter pilots? It is here that the nature and nurture of gender may come critically into play, by molding dispositions like aggressiveness, competitiveness, risk taking, and thrill seeking—dispositions that may contribute to a person's desire to be a fighter pilot or combat soldier in the first place.

Most people who advocate "equal rights" for women in the military are not advocating "equal outcomes" for the two sexes. It is not necessary that half of all combat forces be composed of men and half of women. Rather, women should have the same opportunities as men, and women who qualify should be able to serve in military jobs. To many people, the very essence of women's roles seems at odds with military culture. While it may be possible to envision a "kinder and gentler" government or corporation, a "kinder and gentler" combat force seems a contradiction in terms.

But then again, maybe the contradiction is more apparent than real. Combat is only one aspect of military service. Most military personnel, during most of their military careers, do not engage in military combat. Military service also involves management, procurement, record keeping, conflict management, education, and learning complex technological systems. No one would argue that such activities are the exclusive province of either men or women, and indeed, it seems likely that women may have the edge over men in some of these domains. Clearly, the trend in recent years has been for women and men to achieve greater equality in the military. Future military actions will put new gender policies to the ultimate test.

CODA

The nature-nurture debate is relevant to a number of public policy questions: Should schools treat boys and girls alike? What are the advantages and disadvantages of same-sex education? Do biological factors contribute to male sexual violence? Are mothers better caretakers of young children than fathers? Should mothers be favored over fathers in child custody cases? Are men and women on different "wavelengths" in close relationships? Should working women be treated differently from working men? Do men and women bring different skills and traits to politics? Should men and women serve equal roles in the military? Answers to these questions will be guided both by scientific research and by public opinion about the nature and nurture of gender.

SUMMARY

Gender results from a complex cascade of biological and social-environmental factors. Biological factors include genes, hormones, and neurophysiology. Social-environmental factors include the influences of family, peers, teachers, and media, and the effects of social roles and institutions. Because various causal factors constantly interact with one another, it is often difficult to partition the causes of gender precisely into two categories labeled "nature" and "nurture."

Still, nature-nurture questions are worth posing, if we are willing to accept a range of answers. The relative impact of nature and nurture may vary depending on factors such as age, social class, cultural milieu, and gender itself. The future task of gender researchers is to specify exactly how a host of biological and social-environmental factors weave together to create the complex tapestry known as gender.

The causal cascades that influence sex differences in behavior and individual differences in masculinity and femininity may differ. Analyzing the relationship between sex differences and within-sex variations in gender-related behavior, across cultures, may provide new information about the influence of nature and nurture on gender.

The nature-nurture debate is relevant to many public policy issues: gender equity in schools, the advantages and disadvantages of same-sex schooling, sexual coercion and violence, the success and failure of close relationships, parenting styles and child custody, and gender equity in the workplace, in politics, and in the military. Both scientific research and public opinion about the nature and nurture of gender will influence future public policy decisions concerning these issues.

References

Abramovitch, R., Corter, C., & Lando, B. (1979). Sibling interaction in the home. *Child Development, 4*, 997–1003.

Abramovitch, R., Corter, C., & Pepler, D. J. (1980). Observations of mixed six sibling dyads. *Child Development, 51*, 1268–1271.

Ackerman, P. (1997). Intelligence, personality, and interests: Evidence for overlapping traits. *Psychological Bulletin, 121*, 219–245.

Adorno, T. W., Frenkel-Brunswik, E., Levinson, D. J., & Sanford, R. N. (1950). *The authoritarian personality.* New York: Harper & Row.

Allen, L. S., & Gorski, R. A. (1992). Sexual orientation and the size of the anterior commissure in the human brain. *Proceedings of the National Academy of Sciences USA, 89*, 7199–7202.

Allessandri, S. M., & Lewis, M. (1993). Parental evaluation and its relation to shame and pride in young children. *Sex Roles, 29*, 335–343.

Altemeyer, B. (1981). *Right-wing authoritarianism.* Winnipeg, Ontario: University of Manitoba Press.

Altemeyer, B. (1988). *Enemies of freedom: Understanding right-wing authoritarianism.* San Francisco: Jossey-Bass.

Altemeyer, B. (1998). The other "authoritarian personality." In M. P. Zanna (Ed.), *Advances in experimental social psychology* (Vol. 30, pp. 47–92). San Diego, CA: Academic Press.

Altemeyer, R. A., & Jones, K. (1974). Sexual identity, physical attractiveness and seating position as determinants of influence in discussion groups. *Canadian Journal of Behavior Science, 6*, 357–375.

American Association of University Women Educational Foundation. (1992). *The AAUW Report: How schools shortchange girls.* Washington, DC: American Association of University Women.

American Association of University Women Educational Foundation. (1998). *Separated by sex: A critical look at single-sex education for girls.* Washington, DC: American Association of University Women.

American Psychiatric Association (1994). Diagnostic and statistical manual of mental disorders. (4th ed.). Washington, DC: Author.

Anderson, L. R., & Blanchard, P. N. (1982). Sex differences in task and social-emotional behavior. *Basic and Applied Social Psychology, 3,* 109–139.

Annett, M. (1985). *Left, right, hand and brain: The right shift theory.* Hillsdale, NJ: Erlbaum.

Antill, J. T. (1983). Sex role complementarity versus similarity in married couples. *Journal of Personality and Social Psychology, 45,* 145–155.

Arad, S. (1998). *The Big Five, gender-related traits, and health risk factors.* Unpublished master's thesis, California State University, Fullerton.

Archer, D., & McDaniel, P. (1995). Violence and gender: Differences and similarities across cultures. In R. B. Rubak & N. A. Weiner (Eds.), *Interpersonal violent behaviors: Social and cultural aspects* (pp. 63–87). New York: Springer.

Archer, J. (1991). The influence of testosterone on human aggression. *British Journal of Psychiatry, 82,* 1–28.

Aronson, J., Lustina, M. J., Good, C., Keough, K., Steele, C. M., & Brown, J. (1999). When men can't do math; Necessary and sufficient conditions in stereotype threat. *Journal of Experimental Social Psychology, 35,* 29–46.

Asch, S. E. (1956). Studies in independence and conformity: 1. A minority of one against a unanimous majority. *Psychological Monographs, 70,* (Whole No. 416).

Ashmore, R. D. (1990). Sex, gender, and the individual. In L. A. Pervin (Ed.), *Handbook of personality: Theory and research* (pp. 486–426). New York: Guilford.

Ashmore, R. D., Del Boca, F. K., & Wohlers, A. J. (1986). Gender stereotypes. In R. D. Ashmore & F. K. Del Boca (Eds.), *The social psychology of male-female relations* (pp. 69–119). Orlando, FL: Academic Press.

Bagemihl, B. (1999). *Biological exuberance: Animal homosexuality and natural diversity.* New York: St. Martin's Press.

Bailey, J. M., & Bell, A. P. (1993). Familiality of female and male homosexuality. *Behavior Genetics, 23,* 313–322.

Bailey, J. M., & Benishay, D. (1993). Familial aggregation of female sexual orientation. *American Journal of Psychiatry, 150,* 272–277.

Bailey, J. M., Dunne, M. P., & Martin, N. G. (2000). Genetic and environmental influences on sexual orientation and its correlates in an Australian twin sample. *Journal of Personality and Social Psychology, 78,* 524–536.

Bailey, J. M., & Pillard, R. C. (1991). A genetic study of male sexual orientation. *Archives of General Psychiatry, 48,* 1089–1096.

Bailey, J. M., Pillard, R. C., Dawood, K., Miller, M. B., Farrer, L. A., Trivedi, S., & Murphy, R. L. (1999). A family history study of male sexual orientation using three independent samples. *Behavior Genetics, 29,* 79–86.

Bailey, J. M., Pillard, R. C., Neale, M. C., & Agyei, Y. (1993). Heritable factors influence sexual orientation in women. *Archives of General Psychiatry, 50,* 217–223.

Bailey, J. M., & Zucker, K. J. (1995). Childhood sex-typed behavior and sexual orientation: A conceptual analysis and quantitative review. *Developmental Psychology, 31,* 43–55.

Bakan, D. (1966). *The duality of human existence.* Chicago: Rand McNally.

Bandura, A. (1977). *Social learning theory.* Englewood Cliffs, NJ: Prentice-Hall.

Bandura, A., & Huston, A. C. (1961). Identification as a process of incidental learning. *Journal of Abnormal and Social Psychology, 63,* 311–318.

Bandura, A., Ross, D., & Ross, S. A. (1963). A comparative test of the status envy, social power and secondary reinforcement theories of identificatory learning. *Journal of Abnormal and Social Psychology, 67,* 601–607.

Barber, N. (1995). The evolutionary psychology of physical attractiveness, sexual selection, and human morphology. *Ethology and Sociobiology, 16,* 395–424.

Barry, H., Bacon, M. K., & Child, I. L. (1957). A cross-cultural survey of same sex differences in socialization. *Journal of Abnormal and Social Psychology, 55,* 327–332.

Barry, R. J. (1980). Stereotyping of sex roles in preschoolers in relation to age, family structure, and parental sexism. *Sex Roles, 6,* 795–806.

Baruch, G. K., & Barnett, R. C. (1981). Fathers' participation in the care of their preschool children. *Sex Roles, 7,* 1043–1055.

Bassoff, E. S., & Glass, G. V. (1982). The relationship between sex roles and mental health: A meta-analysis of twenty-six studies. *Counseling Psychologist, 10,* 105–112.

Baucom, D. H., Besch, P. K., & Callahan, S. (1985). Relation between testosterone concentration, sex role identity, and personality among females. *Journal of Personality and Social Psychology, 48,* 1218–1226.

Baumeister, R. F. (2000). Gender differences in erotic plasticity: The female sex drive as socially flexible and responsive. *Psychological Bulletin, 126,* 347–374.

Baumeister, R. F., & Sommer, K. L. (1997). What do men want? Gender differences and the two spheres of belongingness: Comment on Cross and Madson (1997). *Psychological Bulletin, 122,* 38–44.

Beal, C. R. (1994). *Boys and girls: The development of gender roles.* New York, NY: McGraw-Hill.

Becker, B. J. (1986). Influence again: Another look at studies of gender differences in social influence. In J. S. Hyde & M. C. Linn (Eds.), *The psychology of gender: Advances through meta-analysis* (pp. 178–209). Baltimore: Johns Hopkins University Press.

Becker, B. J., & Hedges, L. V. (1984). Meta-analysis of cognitive gender differences: A comment on an analysis by Rosenthal and Rubin. *Journal of Education Psychology, 76,* 583–587.

Bellinger, D., & Berko-Gleason, J. (1982). Sex differences in directives to young children. *Sex Roles, 8,* 1123–1139.

Bem, D. J. (1996). Exotic becomes erotic: A developmental theory of sexual orientation. *Psychological Review, 103,* 320–335.

Bem, D. J. (2000). Exotic becomes erotic: Interpreting the biological correlates of sexual orientation. *Archives of Sexual Behavior, 29,* 531–548.

Bem, S. L. (1974). The measurement of psychological androgyny. *Journal of Consulting and Clinical Psychology, 42,* 165–172.

Bem, S. L. (1975). Sex role adaptability: One consequence of psychological androgyny. *Journal of Consulting and Clinical Psychology, 42,* 155–162.

Bem, S. L. (1981a). *Bem Sex-Role Inventory professional manual.* Palo Alto, CA: Consulting Psychologists Press.

Bem, S. L. (1981b). Gender schema theory: A cognitive account of sex typing. *Psychological Review, 88,* 354–364.

Bem, S. L. (1985). Androgyny and gender schema theory: A conceptual and empirical integration. In T. B. Sonderegger (Ed.), *Psychology and gender: Nebraska Symposium on Motivation, 1984* (pp. 179–226). Lincoln, NE: University of Nebraska Press.

Bem, S. L. (1987). Masculinity and femininity exist only in the mind of the perceiver. In J. M. Reinisch, L. A. Rosenblum, & S. A. Sanders (Eds.), *Masculinity/femininity: Basic perspectives* (pp. 304–311). New York: Oxford University Press.

Bem, S. L. (1993). *The lenses of gender: Transforming the debate on sexual inequality.* New Haven, CT: Yale University Press.

Bem., S. L. (1998). *An unconventional family.* New Haven, CT: Yale University Press.

Bem, S. L., & Bem, D. J. (1971). Training the woman to know her place: The power of a nonconscious ideology. In M. H. Garskof (Ed.), *Roles women play: Readings toward women's liberation* (pp. 84–96). Belmont, CA: Brooks-Cole.

Bem, S. L. & Lenney, E. (1976). Sex typing and the avoidance of cross-sex behavior. *Journal of Personality and Social Psychology, 33,* 48–54.

Bem, S. L., Martyna, W., & Watson, C. (1976). Sex typing and androgyny: Further explorations of the expressive domain. *Journal of Personality and Social Psychology, 34,* 1016–1023.

Benbow, C. P., & Stanley, J. C. (1980). Sex differences in mathematical ability: Fact or artifact? *Science, 210,* 1262–1264.

Benbow, C. P., & Stanley, J. C. (1983). Sex differences in mathematical reasoning abilities: More facts. *Science, 222,* 1029–1031.

Bender, B. G., Linden, M. G., & Robinson, A. (1994). Neurocognitive and psychosocial phenotypes associated with Turner syndrome. In S. H. Broman & J. Grafman (Eds.), *Atypical cognitive deficits in developmental disorders: Implications for brain function* (pp. 197–216). Hillsdale, NJ: Erlbaum.

Benton, D. (1992). Hormones and human aggression. In K. Bjoerkqvist & P. Niemelae (Eds.), *Of mice and women: Aspects of female aggressiveness* (pp. 37–48). San Diego, CA: Academic Press.

Berenbaum, S. A., & Hines, M. (1992). Early androgens are related to childhood sex-typed toy preferences. *Psychological Science, 3,* 203–206.

Berg, J. H., Stephan, W. G., & Dodson, M. (1981). Attributional modesty in women. *Psychology of Women Quarterly, 5,* 711–727.

Berry, J. W. (1966). Temme and Eskimo perceptual skills. *International Journal of Psychology, 1,* 207–229.

Bettencourt, B. A., & Miller, N. (1996). Gender differences in aggression as a function of provocation: A meta-analysis. *Psychological Bulletin: 119,* 422–447.

Bigler, R. S. (1999). Psychological interventions designed to counter sexism in children: Empirical limitations and theoretical foundations. In W. B. Swann, J. H. Langlois, & L. A. Gilbert (Eds.), *Sexism and stereotypes in modern society: The gender science of Janet Taylor Spence* (pp. 129–151). Washington, DC: American Psychological Association.

Birnbaum, D. W., & Croll, W. L. (1984). The etiology of children's stereotypes about sex differences in emotionality. *Sex Roles, 10,* 677–691.

Bishop, K. M., & Wahlsten, D. (1997). Sex differences in the human corpus collosum: Myth or reality? *Neuroscience and Biobehavioral Reviews, 21,* 581–601.

Blanchard, R. (1997). Birth order and sibling sex ratio in homosexual versus heterosexual males and females. *Annual Review of Sex Research, 8,* 27–67.

Blanchard, R., Zucker, K. J., Siegelman, M., Dickey, R., & Klassen, P. The relation of birth order to sexual orientation in men and women. *Journal of Biosocial Science, 30,* 511–519.

Block, J. H. (1978). Another look at sex differentiation in the socialization behaviors of mothers and fathers. In J. Sherman & F. L. Denmark (Eds.), *The psychology of women: Future directions of research* (pp. 29–87). New York: Psychological Dimensions.

Bolton, R. (1994). Sex, science, and social responsibility: Cross-cultural research on same-sex eroticism and social intolerance. *Cross-Cultural Research, 28,* 134–190.

Booth, A., & Dabbs, J. M., Jr. (1993). Testosterone and men's marriages. *Social Forces, 72,* 463–477.

Bradley, B. S., & Gobbart, S. K. (1989). Determinants of gender-typed play in toddlers. *Journal of Genetic Psychology, 150*, 453–455.

Bradley, S. J., Oliver, G. D., Chernick, A. B., & Zucker, K. J. (1998). Experiment of nurture: Ablatio penis at 2 months, sex reassignment at 7 months, and a psychosexual follow-up in young adulthood. *Pediatrics, 102*, 1–5.

Breedlove, S. M. (1994). Sexual differentiation of the human nervous system. *Annual Review of Psychology, 45*, 389–418.

Bronstein, P. (1988). Father-child interaction: Implications for gender-role socialization. In P. Bronstein & C. P. Cowan (Eds.), *Fatherhood today: Men's changing role in the family* (pp. 107–124). New York: Wiley.

Bronstein, P., & Cowan, C. P. (Eds.). (1988). *Fatherhood today: Men's changing role in the family.* New York: Wiley.

Brooks, J., & Lewis, M. (1974). Attachment behavior in thirteen-month-old opposite-sex twins. *Child Development, 45*, 243–247.

Brown, R. (1965). *Social psychology.* New York: Free Press.

Buck, R. W., Savin, V. J., Miller, R. E., & Caul, W. P. (1972). Communication of affect through facial expressions in human. *Journal of Personality and Social Psychology, 23*, 362–371.

Bunker, B. B., & Seashore, E. W. (1975). Breaking the sex role stereotypes. *Public Management, 57*, 5–11.

Burley, N., & Symanski, R. (1981). Women without: An evolutionary and cross-cultural perspective on prostitution. In R. Symanski (Ed.), *The immoral landscape: Female prostitution in western societies* (pp. 239–274). Toronto, Ontario: Butterworth.

Burstein, B., Bank, L., & Jarvick, L. F. (1980). Sex differences in cognitive functioning: Evidence, determinants, and implications. *Human Development, 23*, 299–313.

Buss, D. M. (1989). Sex differences in human mate preferences: Evolutionary hypotheses testing in 37 cultures. *Behavioral and Brain Sciences, 12*, 1–49.

Buss, D. M. (1994). The strategies of human mating. *American Scientist, 82*, 238–249.

Buss, D. M. (1999). *Evolutionary psychology: The new science of the mind.* Boston: Allyn and Bacon.

Buss, D. M., & Schmitt, D. P. (1993). Sexual Strategies Theory: An evolutionary perspective on human mating. *Psychological Review, 100*, 204–232.

Bussey, K., & Bandura, A. (1984). Influence of gender constancy and social power on sex-linked modeling. *Journal of Personality and Social Psychology, 47*, 1292–1302.

Bussey, K., & Bandura, A. (1992). Self-regulatory mechanisms governing gender development. *Child Development, 63*, 1236–1250.

Bussey, K., & Bandura, A. (1999). Social cognitive theory of gender development and differentiation. *Psychological Review, 106*, 676–713.

Bussey, K., & Perry, D. G. (1982). Same-sex imitation: The avoidance of cross-sex models or the acceptance of same-sex models? *Sex Roles, 8*, 773–784.

Butcher, J. N., Dahlstrom, W. G., Graham, J. R., Tellegen, A. M., & Kaemmer, B. (1989). *MMPI-2: Manual for administration and scoring.* Minneapolis, MN: University of Minnesota Press.

Butler, D., & Geis, F. L. (1990). Nonverbal affect responses to male and female leaders: Implications for leadership evaluation. *Journal of Personality and Social Psychology, 58*, 48–59.

Byne, W., Tobet, S., Mattiace, L. A., Lasco, M. S., Kemether, E., Edgar, M. A., Morgello, S., Buehsbaum, M. S., & Jones, L. B. (in press). The interstitial nuclei of the human anterior hypothalamus: An investigation of variation within sex, sexual orientation and HIV status. *Hormones and Behavior.*

Byrne, D., & Osland, J. A. (2000). Sexual fantasy and erotica/pornography: Internal and external imagery. In L. T. Szuchman & F. Muscarella (Eds.), *Psychological perspectives on human sexuality* (pp. 283–305). New York: Wiley.

Byrnes, J. P., Miller, D. C., & Schafer, W. D. (1999). Gender differences in risk taking: A meta-analysis. *Psychological Bulletin, 125*, 367–383.

Caldera, Y. M., Huston, A. C., & O'Brien, M. (1989). Social interactions and play patterns of parents and toddlers with feminine, masculine, and neutral toys. *Child Development, 60*, 70–76.

Campbell, D. P. (1971). *Handbook for the Strong Vocational Interest Blank.* Stanford, CA: Stanford University Press.

Carli, L. L. (1982). Are women more social and men more task-oriented? A meta-analytic review of sex differences in group interaction, reward allocation, coalition formation, and cooperation in the Prisoner's Dilemma game. Unpublished manuscript, University of Massachusetts at Amherst.

Carli, L. L. (1990). Gender, language, and influence. *Journal of Personality and Social Psychology, 59*, 941–951.

Carli, L. L. (1991). Gender, status, and influence. In E. J. Lawler, B. Markovsky, C. Ridgeway, & H. A. Walker (Eds.), *Advances in group processes* (pp. 89–113). Greenwich, CT: JAI Press.

Carli, L. L., & Bukatko, D. (2000). Gender, communication, and social influence: A developmental perspective. In T. Eckes & H. Trautner (Eds.), *The developmental social psychology of gender* (pp. 295–331). Mahwah, NJ: Erlbaum.

Carpenter, C. J., & Huston-Stein, A. (1980). Activity structure and sex-typed behavior in preschool children. *Child Development, 30*, 419–424.

Carter, D. B., & Levy, G. D. (1988). Cognitive aspects of early sex-role development: The influence of gender schemas on preschoolers' memories and preferences for sex-typed toys and activities. *Child Development, 59*, 782–792.

Cashdan, E. (1995). Hormones, sex, and status in women. *Hormones and Behavior, 29*, 354–366.

Cejka, M. A., & Eagly, A. H. (1999). Gender-stereotypic images of occupations correspond to the sex segregation of employment. *Personality and Social Psychology Bulletin, 25*, 413–423.

Choo, P., Levine, T., & Hatfield, E. (1997). Gender, love schemas, and reactions to romantic break-ups. In R. Crandall (Ed.), *Handbook of gender research.* Corte Madera, CA: Select Press.

Christensen, D., & Rosenthal, R. (1982). Gender and nonverbal decoding skill as determinants of interpersonal expectancy effects. *Journal of Personality and Social Psychology, 42*, 75–87.

Christiansen, K., & Knussman, R. (1987). Androgen levels and components of aggressive behavior in man. *Hormones and Behavior, 21*, 170–180.

Clark, C., Klonoff, H., & Hayden, M. (1990). Regional cerebral glucose metabolism in Turner syndrome. *Canadian Journal of Neurological Sciences, 17*, 140–144.

Clark, M. & Reis, H. (1988). Interpersonal processes in close relationships. *Annual Review of Psychology, 39*, 609–672.

Cohen, J. (1977). *Statistical power analysis for the behavioral sciences* (Rev. ed.). San Diego, CA: Academic Press.

Colapinto, J. (2000). *As nature made him.* New York: Simon & Schuster.

Collaer, M. L., & Hines, M. (1995). Human behavior sex differences: A role for gonadal hormones during early developments? *Psychological Bulletin, 118,* 55–107.

Collins, W. A., & Russell, G. (1991). Mother-child and father-child relationships in middle childhood and adolescence. *Developmental Review, 11,* 99–136.

Constantinople, A. (1973). Masculinity-femininity: An exception to a famous dictum. *Psychological Bulletin, 80,* 389–407.

Cook, E. P. (1985). *Psychological androgyny.* New York: Pergamon Press.

Cooke, B., Hegstrom, C. D., Villeneuve, L. S., & Breedlove, S. M. (1998). Sexual differentiation of the vertebrate brain: Principles and mechanism. *Frontiers in Neuroendocrinology, 19,* 323–362.

Cox, C. (assisted by Terman, L.) (1926). *Genetic studies of genius, II.* Stanford, CA: Stanford University Press.

Crawford, M. (1988). Gender, age, and the social evaluation of assertion. *Behavior Modification, 12,* 549–564.

Crawford, M., & Unger, R. (2000). *Women and gender: A feminist psychology.* Boston: McGraw-Hill.

Crews, D. (1994). Commentary: Temperature, steroids and sex determination. *Journal of Endocrinology, 142,* 1–8.

Crews, D., Bergeron, J. M., Bull, J. J., Flores, D., Tousignant, A., Skipper, J. K., & Wibbels, T. (1994). Temperature-dependent sex determination in reptiles: Proximate mechanisms, ultimate outcomes, and practical applications. *Developmental Genetics, 15,* 297–312.

Cross, S. E., & Madson, L. (1997). Models of the self: Self-construals and gender. *Psychological Bulletin, 122,* 5–37.

Crouter, A. C., Manke, B. A., & McHale, S. M. (1995). The family context of gender identification in early adolescence. *Child Development, 66,* 317–329.

Dabbs, J. M. (2000). *Heroes, rogues, and lovers: Testosterone and behavior.* New York: McGraw-Hill.

Dabbs, J. M., Jr. (1997). Testosterone, smiling, and facial appearance. *Journal of Nonverbal Behavior, 21,* 45–55.

Dabbs, J. M., Jr., Carr, T. S., Frady, R. L., & Riad, J. K. (1995). Testosterone, crime, and misbehavior among 692 male prison inmates. *Personality and Individual Differences, 18,* 627–633.

Dabbs, J. M., Jr., & Hargrove, M. F. (1997). Age, testosterone, and behavior among female prison inmates. *Psychosomatic Medicine, 59,* 477–480.

Dabbs, J. M., Jr., Hargrove, M. F., & Heusel, C. (1996). Testosterone differences among college fraternities: Well-behaved vs. rambunctious. *Personality and Individual Differences, 20,* 157–161.

Dabbs, J. M., Jr., & Malinger, A. (1999). High testosterone levels predict low voice pitch among males. *Personality and Individual Differences, 27,* 801–804.

Dabbs, J. M., Jr., & Morris, R. (1990). Testosterone, social class, and antisocial behavior in a sample of 4,662 men. *Psychological Science, 1,* 209–211.

Dabbs, J. M., Jr., Ruback, R. B., Jr., Frady, R. L., Hopper, C. H., & Sgoutas, D. S. (1988). Saliva testosterone and criminal violence among women. *Personality and Individual Differences, 9,* 269–275.

Daitzman, R. J., & Zuckerman, M. (1980). Disinhibitory sensation seeking, personality, and gonadal hormones. *Personality and Individual Differences, 1,* 103–110.

Daitzman, R. J., Zuckerman, M., Sammelwitz, P. H., & Ganjam, V. (1978). Sensation seeking and gonadal hormones. *Journal of Biosocial Science, 10*, 401–408.

Daly, M., & Wilson, M. (1983). *Sex, evolution, and behavior* (2nd ed.). Boston: Willard Grant Press.

Daly, M., & Wilson, M. (1988). *Homicide.* Hawthorne, NY: Aldine.

Daly, M., Wilson, M., & Weghorst, S. J. (1982). Male sexual jealousy. *Ethology and Sociobiology, 3*, 11–27.

D'Andrade, R. (1966). Sex differences and cultural institutions. In. E. E. Maccoby (Ed.), *The development of sex differences.* Stanford, CA: Stanford University Press.

Darwin, C. (1859). *On the origin of species.* London: Murray.

Darwin, C. (1871). *The descent of man and selection in relation to sex.* London: Murray.

Dawkins, R. (1986). *The blind watchmaker.* New York: Norton.

Dawkins, R. (1989). *The selfish gene* (New ed.). New York: Oxford University Press.

Deaux, K. (1984). From individual differences to social categories: Analysis of a decade's research on gender. *American Psychologist, 39*, 105–116.

Deaux, K. (1987). Psychological constructions of masculinity and femininity. In J. M. Reinisch, L. A. Rosenblum, & S. A. Sanders (Eds.), *Masculinity/femininity: Basic perspectives* (pp. 289–303). New York: Oxford University Press.

Deaux, K., & LaFrance, M. (1998). Gender. In D. T. Gilbert, S. T. Fiske, & G. Lindzey (Eds.), *The handbook of social psychology* (4th ed., pp. 788–827). Boston: McGraw-Hill.

Deaux, K., & Lewis, L. L. (1983). Components of gender stereotypes. *Psychological Documents, 13*, 25 (Ms. No. 2583).

Deaux, K., & Lewis, L. L. (1984). The structure of gender stereotypes: Interrelationships among components and gender label. *Journal of Personality and Social Psychology, 46*, 991–1004.

Deaux, K., & Major, B. (1987). Putting gender into context: An interactive model of gender-related behavior. *Psychological Review, 94*, 369–389.

Dennett, D. C. (1995). *Darwin's dangerous idea: Evolution and the meanings of life.* New York: Touchstone.

Diamond, M. (1993). Homosexuality and bisexuality in different populations. *Archives of Sexual Behavior, 22*, 291–310.

Diamond, M., & Sigmundson, H. K. (1997). Sex reassignment at birth: Long-term review and clinical implications. *Archives of Pediatric and Adolescent Medicine, 151*, 298–304.

Dindia, K., & Allen, M. (1992). Sex differences in self-disclosure: A meta-analysis. *Psychological Bulletin, 112*, 106–124.

DiPietro, J. (1981). Rough and tumble play: A function of gender. *Developmental Psychology, 17*, 50–58.

Dittmann, R. W., Kappes, M. E., & Kappes, M. H. (1992). Sexual behavior in adolescent and adult females with congenital adrenal hyperplasia. *Psychoneuroendocrinology, 17*, 153–170.

Dittmann, R. W., Kappes, M. H., Kappes, M. E., Börger, D., Meyer-Bahlburg, H. F. L., Stegner, H., Willig, R. H., & Wallis, H. (1990). Congenital adrenal hyperplasis II: Gender-related behavior and attitudes in female salt-wasting and simple-virilizing patients. *Psychoneuroendocrinology, 15*, 421–434.

Dittmann, R. W., Kappes, M. H., Kappes, M. E., Börger, D., Stegner, H., Willig, R. H., & Wallis, H. (1990). Congenital adrenal hyperplasis I: Gender-related behavior and attitudes in female patients and sisters. *Psychoneuroendocrinology, 15*, 401–420.

Dovidio, J. F., Ellyson, S. L., Keating, C. F., Heltman, K., & Brown, C. E. (1988). The relationship of social power to visual displays of dominance between men and women. *Journal of Personality and Social Psychology, 54*, 233–242.

Downey, J., Ehrhardt, A. A., Morishima, A., Bell, J. J., & Gruen, R. (1987). Gender role development in two clinical syndromes: Turner syndrome versus constitutional short stature. *Journal of the American Academy of Child and Adolescent Psychiatry, 26*, 566–573.

Dresselhaus, M. D., Franz, J. R., & Clark, B. C. (1994). Interventions to increase the participation of women in physics. *Science, 263*, 1392–1393.

Eagly, A. H. (1987). *Sex differences in social behavior: A social-role interpretation.* Hillsdale, NJ: Erlbaum.

Eagly, A. H. (1995). The science and politics of comparing men and women. *American Psychologist, 50*, 145–158.

Eagly, A. H., & Carli, L. L. (1981). Sex of researchers and sex-typed communications as determinants of sex differences in influenceability: A meta-analysis of social influence studies. *Psychological Bulletin, 90*, 1–20.

Eagly, A. H., & Crowley, M. (1986). Gender and helping behavior: A meta-analytic review of the social psychological literature. *Psychological Bulletin, 100*, 283–308.

Eagly, A. H., & Diekman, A. B. (1997). The accuracy of gender stereotypes: A dilemma for feminism. *Revue Internationale de Psychologie/International Review of Social Psychology, 10*, 11–30.

Eagly, A. H., & Johnson, B. T. (1990). Gender and leadership style: A meta-analysis. *Psychological Bulletin, 108*, 233–256.

Eagly, A. H., & Karau, S. J. (1991). Gender and the emergence of leaders: A meta-analysis. *Psychological Bulletin, 117*, 125–145.

Eagly, A. H., Makhijani, M. G., & Klonsky, B. G. (1992). Gender and the evaluation of leaders: A meta-analysis. *Psychological Bulletin, 111*, 3–22.

Eagly, A. H., Mladinic, A., & Otto, S. (1991). Are women evaluated more favorably than men? An analysis of attitudes, beliefs, and emotions. *Psychology of Women Quarterly, 15*, 203–216.

Eagly, A. H., & Steffen, V. J. (1984). Gender stereotypes stem from the distribution of women and men into social roles. *Journal of Personality and Social Psychology, 46*, 735–754.

Eagly, A. H., & Steffen, V. J. (1986). Gender and aggressive behavior: A meta-analytic review of the social psychological literature. *Psychological Bulletin, 100*, 309–330.

Eagly, A. H., & Wood, W. (1982). Inferred sex differences in status as a determinant of gender stereotypes about social influence. *Journal of Personality and Social Psychology, 43*, 915–928.

Eagly, A. H., Wood, W. (1999). The origins of sex differences in human behavior: Evolved dispositions versus social roles. *American Psychologist, 54*, 408–423.

Eagly, A. H., Wood, W., & Diekman, A. B. (2000). Social role theory of sex differences and similarities: A current appraisal. In T. Eckes & H. M. Trautner (Eds.), *The developmental social psychology of gender* (pp. 123–174). Mahwah, NJ: Erlbaum.

Eagly, A. H., Wood, W., & Fishbaugh, L. (1981). Sex differences in conformity: Surveillance by the group as a determinant of male non-conformity. *Journal of Personality and Social Psychology, 40*, 384–394.

Eals, M., & Silverman, I. (1994). The hunter-gatherer theory of spatial sex differences: Proximate factors mediating the female advantage in recall of object arrays. *Ethology and Sociobiology, 15*, 95–105.

Eaton, W. O., & Enns, L. R. (1986). Sex differences in human motor activity level. *Psychological Bulletin, 100*, 19–28.

Eccles, J. S., & Jacobs, J. E. (1986). Social forces shape math attitudes and performance. *Signs: Journal of Women in Culture and Society, 11*, 367–389.

Eccles, J. S., Jacobs, J., Harold, R., Yoon, K. S., Arbreton, A., & Freedman-Doan, C. (1993). Parents and gender-related socialization during the middle childhood and adolescent years. In S. Oskamp & M. Costanzo (Eds.), *Gender issues in contemporary society.* Newbury Park, CA: Sage.

Edelman, D. A. (1986). *DES/dethylstilbestrol—New perspectives.* Boston: MTP Press.

Ehrhardt, A. A., & Baker, S. W. (1974). Fetal androgens, human central nervous system differentiation, and behavior sex differences. In R. C. Friedman, R. M. Richart, & R. L. Vande Wiele (Eds.), *Sex differences in behavior* (pp. 33–51). New York: Wiley.

Ehrhardt, A. A., Evers, K., & Money, J. (1968). Influence of androgen and some aspects of sexually dimorphic behavior in women with the late-treated andrenogenital syndrome. *Johns Hopkins Medical Journal, 123*, 115–122.

Ehrhardt, A. A., Greenberg, N., & Money, J. (1970). Female gender identity and absence of fetal gonadal hormones: Turner's syndrome. *Johns Hopkins Medical Journal, 126*, 237–248.

Ehrhardt, A. A., Meyer-Bahlburg, H. F. L., Rosen, L. R., Feldman, J. F., Veridiano, N. P., Zimmerman, I., & McEwen, B. S. (1985). Sexual orientation after prenatal exposure to exogenous estrogen. *Archives of Sexual Behavior, 14*, 57–78.

Eisenberg, N. H., Murray, E., & Hite, T. (1982). Children's reasoning regarding sex-typed toy choices. *Child Development, 53*, 81–86.

Eisenberg, N., & Lennon, R. (1983). Sex differences in empathy and related capacities. *Psychological Bulletin, 94*, 100–131.

Eisenberg, N., Wolchik, S. A., Hernandez, R., & Pasternack, J. F. (1985). Parental socialization of young children's play: A short-term longitudinal study. *Child Development, 56*, 1506–1513.

Eisenstock, B. (1984). Sex role differences in children's identification with counter-stereotypical televised portrayals. *Sex Roles, 10*, 417–430.

Ellis, L., & Ames, M. A. (1987). Neurohormonal functioning and sexual orientation: A theory of homosexuality-heterosexuality. *Psychological Bulletin, 101*, 233–258.

Ellis, L.,& Coontz, P. D. (1990). Androgens, brain functioning, and criminality: The neurohormonal foundations of antisociality. In L. Ellis & H. Hoffman (Eds.), *Crime in biological, social, and moral contexts* (pp. 162–193). New York: Praeger.

Fagot, B. I. (1977). Consequences of moderate cross-gender behavior in preschool children. *Child Development, 48*, 902–907.

Fagot, B. I. (1978). The influence of sex of child on parental reactions to toddler children. *Child Development, 49*, 459–465.

Fagot, B. I. (1985). Beyond the reinforcement principle: Another step toward understanding sex role development. *Developmental Psychology, 21*, 1097–1104.

Fagot, B. I., Hagan, R., Leinbach, M. D., & Kronsberg, S. (1985). Differential reactions to assertive and communicative acts of toddler boys and girls. *Child Development, 56*, 1499–1505.

Fagot, B. I., & Leinbach, M. D. (1989). The young child's gender schema: Environmental input, internal organization. *Child Development, 60*, 663–672.

Fagot, B. I., & Leinbach, M. D. (1993). Gender-role development in young children: From discrimination to labeling. *Developmental Review, 13*, 205–224.

Fagot, B. I., Leinbach, M. D., & Hagan, R. (1986). Gender labeling and the adoption of sex-typed behaviors. *Developmental Psychology, 22,* 440–443.

Fagot, B. I., Leinbach, M. D., & O'Boyle, C. (1992). Gender labeling, gender stereotyping, and parenting behaviors. *Developmental Psychology, 28,* 225–230.

Fagot, B. I., & Patterson, G. R. (1969). An in vivo analysis of reinforcing contingencies for sex-role behaviors in the preschool child. *Developmental Psychology, 1,* 563–568.

Fagot, B. I., Rodgers, C. S., & Leinbach, M. D. (2000). Theories of gender socialization. In T. Eckes & H. Trautner (Eds.), *The developmental social psychology of gender* (pp. 65–89). Mahwah, NJ: Erlbaum.

Fausto-Sterling, A. (1992). *Myths of gender* (2nd ed.). New York: Basic Books.

Fausto-Sterling, A. (2000). *Sexing the body: Gender politics and the construction of sexuality.* New York: Basic Books.

Feingold, A. (1988). Cognitive gender differences are disappearing. *American Psychologist, 43,* 95–103.

Feingold, A. (1990). Gender differences in effects of physical attractiveness on romantic attraction: A comparison across five research paradigms. *Journal of Personality and Social Psychology, 59,* 981–993.

Feingold, A. (1992). Gender differences in mate selection preferences: A test of the parental investment model. *Psychological Bulletin, 112,* 125–139.

Feingold, A. (1994). Gender differences in personality: A meta-analysis. *Psychological Bulletin, 116,* 429–456.

Fiske, S. T. (1998). Stereotyping, prejudice, and discrimination. In D. T. Gilbert, S. T. Fiske, & G. Lindsey (Eds.), *The handbook of social psychology* (4th ed., Vol. 2, pp. 357–411). Boston: McGraw-Hill.

Fitch, R. H., Miller, S., & Tallal, P. (1997). Neurobiology of speech perception. *Annual Review of Neuroscience, 20,* 331–353.

Fivush, R., Brotman, M. A., Buckner, J. P., & Goodman, S. H. (2000). Gender differences in parent-child emotion narratives. *Sex Roles, 42,* 233–253.

Flaubert, G. (1972, originally published in 1857). *Madame Bovary* (L. Bair, Trans.). New York: Bantam Books.

Ford, C. S., & Beach, F. A. (1951). *Patterns of sexual behavior.* New York: Harper & Row.

Forger, N. G., Hodges, L. L., Roberts, S. L., & Breedlove, S. M. (1992). Regulation of motoneuron death in the spinal nucleus of the bulbocavernosus. *Journal of Neurobiology, 23,* 1192–1203.

Freeland v. Freeland, 159 P. 698, 699 (Wash. 1916)

Freud, S. (1905–1962). *Three essays on the theory of sexuality.* New York, NY: Basic Books.

Frey, K. S., & Ruble, D. N. (1992). Gender constancy and the "cost" of sex-typed behavior: A test of the conflict hypothesis. *Developmental Psychology, 28,* 714–721.

Friedman, H. S., Tucker, J. S., Schwartz, J. E., Tomlinson-Keasey, C., Martin, L. R., Wingard, D. L., & Criqui, M. H. (1995). Psychosocial and behavior predictors of longevity: The aging and death of the "Termites." *American Psychologist, 50,* 69–78.

Funder, D. C. (1997). *The personality puzzle.* New York: Norton.

Furnham, A., & Mak, T. (1999). Sex-role stereotyping in television commercials: A review and comparison of fourteen studies done on five continents over 25 years. *Sex Roles, 41,* 413–437.

Gabriel, S., & Gardner, W. L. (1999). Are there "his" and "hers" types of interdependence? The implications of gender differences in collective versus relational interdependence for affect, behavior, and cognition. *Journal of Personality and Social Psychology, 77*, 642–655.

Galton, F. (1874). *English men of science: Their nature and nurture.* London: Macmillan.

Gaulin, S. J. C. (1992). Evolution of sex differences in spatial ability. *Yearbook of Physical Anthropology, 35*, 125–151.

Gaulin, S. J. C., & Fitzgerald, R. W. (1989). Sexual selection for spatial-learning ability. *Animal Behavior, 37*, 322–331.

Geary, D. C. (1998). *Male, female: The evolution of human sex differences.* Washington, DC: American Psychological Association.

Geis, F. L. (1993). Self-fulfilling prophecies: A social psychological view of gender. In A. E. Beall & R. J. Sternberg (Eds.), *The psychology of gender* (pp. 9–54). New York: Guilford Press.

Gergen, M. M., & Davis, S. N. (Eds.). (1997). *Toward new psychology of gender.* New York: Routledge.

Geschwind, N., & Galaburda, A. M. (1987). *Cerebral lateralization: Biological mechanisms, associations, and pathology.* Cambridge, MA: MIT Press.

Geschwind, N., & Levitsky, W. (1968). Human brain: Left-right asymmetries in temporal speech region. *Science, 161*, 186–187.

Gesell, A. L., Halverson, H. M., & Amatruda, C. (1940). *The first five years of life: A guide to the study of the preschool child.* New York: Harper & Brothers.

Gilligan, C. (1982). *In a different voice.* Cambridge, MA: Harvard University Press.

Gillis, J. S., & Avis, W. E. (1980). The male-taller norm in mate selection. *Personality and Social Psychology Bulletin, 6*, 396–401.

Gold, D., Crombie, G., Brender, W., & Mate, P. (1984). Sex differences in children's performance in problem-solving situations involving an adult model. *Child Development, 55*, 543–549.

Gordon, H. W., & Galatzer, A. (1980). Cerebral organization in patients with gonadal dysgenesis. *Psychneuroendrocrinology, 5*, 235–244.

Gottlieb, G., Wahlsten, D., & Lickliter, R. (1998). The significance of biology for human development: A developmental psychobiological systems view. In W. Damon & R. M. Lerner (Eds.), *Handbook of child psychology: Vol 1. Theoretical models of human development* (5th ed., pp. 233–273). New York: Wiley.

Gottman, J. M. (1994). *Why marriages succeed or fail.* New York: Simon & Schuster.

Gottman, J. M., & Levenson, R. W. (1988). The social psycho-physiology of marriage. In P. Roller & M. A. Fitzpatrick (Eds.), *Perspectives on marital interaction.* New York: Taylor and Francis.

Gouchie, C., & Kimura, D. (1991). The relationship between testosterone levels and cognitive ability patterns. *Psychoneuroendocrinology, 16*, 323–334.

Gough, H. G. (1957). *Manual for the California Psychological Inventory.* Palo Alto, CA: Consulting Psychologists Press.

Gould, R. J., & Slone, C. G. (1982). The "feminine modesty" effect: A self-presentational interpretation of sex differences in causal attribution. *Personality and Social Psychology Bulletin, 8*, 477–485.

Graham, K. (1997). *Personal history.* New York: Knopf.

Gray, J. (1992). *Men are from Mars, women are from Venus.* New York: Harper Collins.

Greene, R. L. (1991). *MMPI-2/MMPI: An interpretive manual.* Boston: Allyn and Bacon.

Gross, M. R. (1982). Sneakers, satellites and parentals: Polymorphic mating strategies in North American sunfishes. *Zeitschrift fur Tierpsycholgie, 60*, 1–26.

Guilford, J. P., & Zimmerman, W. S. (1956). Fourteen dimensions of temperament. *Psychological Monographs, 70*, 11–24.

Gurney, M. E., & Konishi, M. (1979). Hormone induced sexual differentiation of brain and behavior in zebra finches. *Science, 208*, 1380–1382.

Haddock, G., & Zanna, M. P. (1994). Preferring "housewives" to "feminists": Categorization and the favorability of attitudes towards women. *Psychology of Women Quarterly, 18*, 25–52.

Hall, J. A. (1984). *Nonverbal sex differences: Communication accuracy and expressive style.* Baltimore: Johns Hopkins University Press.

Halpern, D. F. (1992). Sex differences in cognitive abilities (2nd ed.). Hillsdale, NJ: Erlbaum.

Halpern, D. F. (1997). Sex differences in intelligence: Implications for education. *American Psychologist, 52*, 1091–1102.

Halpern, D. F. (2000). Sex differences in cognitive abilities (3rd ed.). Hillsdale, NJ: Erlbaum.

Hamer, D. H., Hu, S., Magnuson, N. H., & Pattatucci, A. M. L. (1993). A linkage between DNA markers on the X chromosome and male sexual orientation. *Science, 261*, 321–327.

Hamilton, W. D. (1964). The genetic evolution of social behavior. I and II. *Journal of Theoretical Biology, 7*, 1–52.

Hamilton, W. D., & Zuk, M. (1982). Heritable true fitness and bright birds: A role for parasites? *Science, 218*, 384–387.

Hampson, E. (1990a). Estrogen-related variations in human spatial and articulatory-motor skills. *Psychneuroendocrinology, 15*, 97–111.

Hampson, E. (1990b). Variations in sex-related cognitive abilities across the menstrual cycle. *Brain and Cognition, 14*, 26–43.

Hampson, E., & Kimura, D. (1988). Reciprocal effects of hormonal fluctuations on human motor and perceptual-spatial skills. *Behavioral Neuroscience, 102*, 456–459.

Hampson, E., Rovet, J. F., & Altmann, D. (1998). Spatial reasoning in children with congenital adrenal hyperplasia due to 21-hydroxylase deficiency. *Developmental Neuropsychology, 14*, 299–320.

Hare-Mustin, R. T., & Marecek, J. (1988). The meaning of difference: Gender theory, postmodernism and psychology. *American Psychologist, 43*, 455–464.

Harris, J. (1995). Where is the child's environment? A group socialization theory of development. *Psychological Review, 102*, 458–489.

Hartung, C. M., & Widiger, T. A. (1998). Gender differences in the diagnosis of mental disorders: Conclusions and controversies of the DSM-IV. *Psychological Bulletin, 123*, 260–278.

Haslam, N. (1997). Evidence that male sexual orientation is a matter of degree. *Journal of Personality and Social Psychology, 73*, 862–870.

Hathaway, S. R. (1956). Scales 5 (Masculinity-Femininity), 6 (Paranoia), and 8 (Schizophrenia). In G. S. Welsh & W. G. Dahlstrom (Eds.), *Basic readings on the MMPI in psychology and medicine* (pp. 104–111). Minneapolis, MN: University of Minnesota Press.

Hathaway, S. R., & McKinley, J. C. (1951). *MMPI manual.* New York: Psychological Corporation.

Hazzard, W. R. (1990). A central role of sex hormones in the sex differential in lipoprotein metabolism, atherosclerosis, and longevity. In M. G. Ory & H. R. Warner (Eds.), *Gen-*

der, health, and longevity: Multidisciplinary perspectives (pp. 87–108). New York: Springer.

Helgeson, V. S. (1994a). Prototypes and dimensions of masculinity and femininity. *Sex Roles, 31* (pp. 653–682).

Helgeson, V. S. (1994b). Relation of agency and communion to well-being: Evidence and potential explanations. *Psychological Bulletin, 116,* 412–428.

Hellige, J. B. (1993). *Hemispheric asymmetry: What's right and what's left?* Cambridge, MA: Harvard University Press.

Hendrick, C., & Hendrick, S. (1986). A theory and method for love. *Journal of Personality and Social Psychology, 50,* 392–402.

Hendrick, J., & Stange, T. (1991). Do actions speak louder than words? An effect of the functional use of language on dominant sex role behavior in boys and girls. *Early Childhood Research Quarterly, 6,* 565–576.

Henley, N. M. (1977). *Body politics: Power, sex, and nonverbal communication.* Englewood Cliffs, NJ: Prentice-Hall.

Hetherington, E. M. (1967). The effects of familial variables on sex-typing, on parent-child similarity, and on imitation in children. In J. P. Hill (Ed.), *Minnesota Symposium on Child Psychology* (Vol. 1) (pp. 82–107). Minneapolis, MN: University of Minnesota Press.

Hier, D. B., & Crowley, W. F., Jr. (1982). Spatial ability in androgen-deficient men. *New England Journal of Medicine, 306,* 1202–1205.

Hines, M., Alsum, P., Roy, M., Gorski, R. A., & Goy, R. W. (1987). Estrogenic contributions to sexual differentiation in the female guinea pig: Influences of diethyltilbestrol and tamoxifen on neural, behavioral, and ovarian development. *Hormones and Behavior, 21,* 402–417.

Hines, M., & Gay, R. W. (1985). Estrogens before birth and the development of sex-related reproductive traits in the female guinea pig. *Hormones and Behavior, 19,* 331–347.

Hines, M., & Shipley, C. (1984). Prenatal exposure to diethylstilbestrol (DES) and the development of sexually dimorphic cognitive abilities and cerebral lateralization. *Developmental Psychology, 20,* 81–94.

Hoffman, C. D., & Teyber, E. C. (1985). Naturalistic observation of sex differences in adult involvement with girls and boys of different ages. *Merrill-Palmer Quarterly, 31,* 93–97.

Holland, J. L. (1992). *Making vocational choices* (2nd ed.). Odessa, FL: Psychological Assessment Resources.

Holloway, R. L. (1998). Relative size of the corpus collosum redux: Statistical smoke and mirrors? *Behavioral and Brain Sciences, 21,* 333–335.

Holloway, R. L., Anderson, P. J., Defendini, R., & Harper, C. (1993). Sexual dimorphism of the human corpus collosum. *American Journal of Physical Anthropology, 92,* 481–498.

Huang, C. P. (1986). Behavior of Swedish primary and secondary caretaking fathers in relation to mother's presence. *Developmental Psychology, 22,* 749–751.

Hunt, M. (1999). How science takes stock: The story of meta-analysis. New York: Russell Sage.

Huston, A. C. (1983). Sex-typing. In P. H. Mussen (Ed.), *Handbook of child psychology: Socialization, personality, and social development* (Vol. 4, pp. 388–467). New York: Wiley.

Hyde, J. S. (1981). How large are cognitive gender differences? A meta-analysis using ω^2 and *d. American Psychologist, 36,* 892–901.

Hyde, J. S. (1984). How large are gender differences in aggression? A developmental meta-analysis. *Developmental Psychology, 20,* 722–736.

Hyde, J. S. (1986). Gender differences in aggression. In J. S. Hyde & M. C. Linn (Eds.), *The psychology of gender: Advances through meta-analysis* (pp. 51–66). Baltimore: Johns Hopkins University Press.

Hyde, J. S. (1990). Meta-analysis and the psychology of gender differences. *Signs: Journal of Women in Culture and Society, 16,* 55–73.

Hyde, J. S., & Linn, M. C. (1988). Gender differences in verbal ability: A meta-analysis. *Psychological Bulletin, 104,* 53–69.

Ibsen, H. (1961). *Four Major Plays.* New York, NY: Oxford University Press.

Imperato-McGinley, J., Peterson, R. E., Gautier, T., & Sturla, E. (1979). Androgens and the evolution of male-gender identity among male pseudohermaphrodites with 5α-reductase deficiency. *New England Journal of Medicine, 3000,* 1233–1237.

Imperato-McGinley, J., Pichardo, M., Gautier, T., Boyer, D., & Bryden, M. P. (1991). Cognitive abilities in androgen-insensitive subjects: Comparison with control males and females from the same kindred. *Clinical Endocrinology, 34,* 341–347.

International Institute for Strategic Studies. (2000). *The military balance 2000, 2001.* London: Oxford University Press.

Inzlicht, M., & Ben-Zeev, T. (2000). A threatening intellectual environment: Why females are susceptible to experiencing problem-solving deficits in the presence of males. *Psychological Science, 11,* 365–371.

Jacklin, C. N., DiPietro, J. A., & Maccoby, E. E. (1984). Sex-typing behavior and sex-typing pressure in child/parent interaction. *Archives of Sexual Behavior, 13,* 413–425.

Jacklin, C. N., Maccoby, E. E., & Dick, A. E. (1973). Barrier behavior and toy preferences: Sex differences (and their absence) in the year-old child. *Child Development, 44,* 196–200.

Jacobs, D. M., Tang, M. X., Stern, Y., Sano, M., Marder, K., Bell, K. L., Schofield, P., Dooneief, G., Gurland, B., & Mayeux, R. (1998). Cognitive function in nondemented older women who took estrogen after menopause. *Neurology, 50,* 368–373.

Jacobs, L. F., Gaulin, S. J. C., Sherry, D. F., & Hoffman G. E. (1990). Evolution of spatial cognition: sex-specific patterns of spatial behavior predict hippocampal size. *Proceedings of the National Academy of Sciences, USA, 87,* 6349–6352.

Jahoda, G. (1980). Sex and ethnic differences in a spatial-perceptual task: Some hypotheses tested. *British Journal of Psychology, 71,* 425–431.

Janowsky, J. S. (1989). Sexual dimorphism in the human brain: Dispelling the myths. *Developmental Medicine and Child Neurology, 31,* 257–263.

Janowsky, J. S., Oviatt, S. K., & Orwoll, E. S. (1994). Testosterone influences spatial cognition in older men. *Behavioral Neuroscience, 108,* 325–332.

Jensen, A. R. (1998). *The g factor: The science of mental ability.* New York: Praeger.

Johnson, E. S., & Meade, A. C. (1987). Developmental patterns of spatial ability: An early sex difference. *Child Development, 58,* 725–740.

Josephs, R. A., Markus, H. R., & Tafarodi, R. W. (1992). Gender and self-esteem. *Journal of Personality and Social Psychology, 63,* 391–402.

Jussim, L. (1986). Self-fulfilling prophecies: A theoretical and integrative review. *Psychological Review, 93,* 429–445.

Jussim, L, & Eccles, J. (1995). Naturalistic studies of interpersonal expectancies. *Review of Personality and Social Psychology, 15,* 74–108.

Jussim, L., Eccles, J., & Madon, S. (1996). Social perception, social stereotypes, and teacher expectations: Accuracy and the question for the powerful self-fulfilling prophecy. In M. P. Zanna (Ed.), *Advances in experimental social psychology* (Vol. 28, pp. 281–388). San Diego, CA: Academic Press.

Kagan, J. (1964). Acquisition and significance of sex-typing and sex-role identity. In M. L. Hoffman & L. W. Hoffman (Eds.), *Review of child development research* (Vol. 1, pp. 137–167). New York: Russell Sage.

Katz, P. A., & Boswell, S. (1984). Sex-role development and the one-child family. In T. Falboa (Ed.), *The single-child family* (pp. 63–116). New York: Guilford Press.

Katz, P. A., & Boswell, S. (1986). Flexibility and traditionality in children's gender roles. *Genetic, Social, and General Psychology Monographs, 112*, 103–147.

Katz, P. A., & Ksansnak, K. R. (1994). Developmental aspects of gender role flexibility and traditionality in middle childhood and adolescence. *Developmental Psychology, 30*, 272–282.

Kendler, K. S., Thornton, L. M., Gilman, S. E., & Kessler, R. C. (2000). Sexual orientation in a U.S. National Sample of twin and nontwin sibling pairs. *American Journal of Psychiatry, 157*, 1843–1846.

Kenrick, D. T. (1987). Gender, genes, and the social environment: A biosocial interactionist perspective. In P. Shaver & C. Hendrick (Eds.), *Sex and gender: Review of personality and social psychology* (Vol. 7, pp. 14–43). Newbury Park, CA: Sage.

Kenrick, D. T., & Keefe, R. C. (1992). Age preferences in mates reflect sex differences in human reproductive strategies. *Behavioral and Brain Sciences, 15*, 75–133.

Kerns, K. A., & Berenbaum, S. A. (1991). Sex differences in spatial ability in children. *Behavior Genetics, 21*, 383–396.

Kessler, S. J., & McKenna, W. (1978). *Gender: An ethnomethodological approach.* New York: Wiley.

Kester, P., Green, R., Finch, S. J., & Williams, K. (1980). Prenatal "female hormone" administration and psychosexual development in human males. *Psychoneuroendocrinology, 5*, 269–285.

Kimball, M. M. (1986). Television and sex role attitudes. In T. M. Williams (Ed.), *The impact of television: A natural experiment in three communities* (pp. 265–301). Orlando, FL: Academic Press.

Kimura, D. (1987). Are men's and women's brains really different? *Canadian Psychology, 28*, 133–147.

Kimura, D. (1999). *Sex and cognition.* Cambridge, MA: MIT Press.

King, M., & McDonald, E. (1992). Homosexuals who are twins: A study of 46 probands. *British Journal of Psychiatry, 160*, 407–409.

Kinsey, A. C., Pomeroy, W. B., & Martin, C. E. (1948). *Sexual behavior in the human male.* Philadelphia: Saunders.

Kinsey, A. C., Pomeroy, W. B., & Martin, C. E. (1953). *Sexual behavior in the human female.* Philadelphia: Saunders.

Kling, K. C., Hyde J. S., Showers, C. J., & Buswell, B. N. (1999). Gender differences in self-esteem: A meta-analysis. *Psychological Bulletin, 125*, 470–500.

Knight, G. P., Fabes, R. A., & Higgins, D. A. (1996). Concerns about drawing causal inferences from meta-analyses: An example in the study of gender differences in aggression. *Psychological Bulletin, 119*, 410–421.

Kohlberg, L. (1966). A cognitive-developmental analysis of children's sex role concepts and attitudes. In E. E. Maccoby (Ed.), *The development of sex differences* (pp. 82–173). Stanford, CA: Stanford University Press.

Kunda, Z., & Thagard, P. (1996). Forming impressions from stereotypes, traits and behaviors: A parallel-constraint satisfaction theory. *Psychological Review, 103*, 284–308.

Kurdek, L. A., & Schmitt, J. P. (1986). Interaction of sex role self-concept with relationship quality and relationship beliefs in married, heterosexual cohabiting, gay, and lesbian couples. *Journal of Personality and Social Psychology, 51,* 365–370.

Lackey, P. N. (1989). Adults' attitudes about assignments of household chores to male and female children. *Sex Roles, 20,* 271–281.

LaFrance, M., & Henley, N. M. (1997). On oppressing hypotheses: Or, differences in nonverbal sensitivity revisited. In M. R. Walsh (Ed.), *Women, men, & gender: Ongoing debates* (pp. 104–119). New Haven, CT: Yale University Press.

LaFreniere, P., Strayer, F. F., & Gauthier, R. (1984). The emergence of same-sex affiliative preferences among preschool peers: A developmental/ethological perspective. *Child Development, 55,* 1958–1965.

Lalumiere, M. L., Blanchard, R., Zucker, K. J. (2000). Sexual orientation and handedness in men and women: A meta-analysis. *Psychological Bulletin, 126,* 575–592.

Lamb, M. E., Frodi, A. M., Frodi, M., & Huang, C. P. (1982). Characteristics of maternal and paternal behavior in traditional and non-traditional Swedish families. *International Journal of Behavioral Development, 5,* 131–141.

Lamb, M. E., Pleck, J. H., Charnov, E. L., & Levine, J. A. (1987). A biosocial perspective on paternal behavior and involvement. In J. B. Lancaster, J. Altman, A. S. Rossi, & L. R. Sherrod (Eds.), *Parenting across the lifespan.* New York: Aldine de Gruyter.

Langlois, J. H., & Downs, C. (1980). Mothers, fathers and peers as socialization agents of sex-typed play behavior in young children. *Child Development, 51,* 1217–1247.

Lawrie, L., & Brown, R. (1992). Sex stereotypes, school subject preferences and career aspirations as a function of single/mixed sex schooling and the presence/absence of an opposite sex sibling. *British Journal of Education Psychology, 63,* 132–138.

Leaper, C. (2000). Gender, affiliation, assertion, and the interactive context of parent-child play. *Developmental Psychology, 36,* 381–393.

Leaper, C., Anderson, K. J., & Saunders, P. (1998). Moderators of gender effects on parents' talk to their children: A meta-analysis. *Developmental Psychology, 34,* 3–27.

Lee, Y., Jussim, L. J., & McCauley, C. R. (1995). *Stereotype accuracy: Toward appreciating group differences.* Washington, DC: American Psychological Association.

Le Guin, U. K. (1969). *The left hand of darkness.* New York, NY: Ace Books.

Lenney, E. (1991). Sex roles: The measurement of masculinity, femininity, and androgyny. In J. P. Robinson, P. R. Shaver, & L. S. Wrightsman (Eds.), *Measures of personality and social psychological attitudes* (Vol. 1, pp. 573–660). San Diego, CA: Academic Press.

LeVay, S. (1991). A difference in hypothalamic structure between heterosexual and homosexual men. *Science, 253,* 1034–1037.

Levine, J., Fishman, C., & Kagan, J. (1967). Social class and sex as determinants of maternal behavior. *American Journal of Orthopsychiatry, 37,* 397.

Levine, S. C., Huttenlocher, J., Taylor, A., & Langrock, A. (1999). Early sex differences in spatial skill. *Developmental Psychology, 35,* 940–949.

Levy, G. D. (1989). Relations among aspects of children's social environments, gender schematization, gender-role knowledge, and flexibility. *Sex Roles, 21,* 655–667.

Lewin, M. (1984a). "Rather worse than folly?" Psychology measures femininity and masculinity, 1: From Terman and Miles to the Guilfords. In M. Lewin (Ed.), *In the shadow of the past: Psychology portrays the sexes* (pp. 152–178). New York: Columbia University Press.

Lewin, M. (1984b). "Rather worse than folly?" Psychology measures femininity and masculinity, 2: From "13 gay men" to the instrumental-expressive distinction. In M. Lewin (Ed.), *In the shadow of the past: Psychology portrays the sexes* (pp. 179–204). New York: Columbia University Press.

Lewis, L. L. (1985). The influence of individual differences in gender stereotyping on the interpersonal expectancy process. Unpublished doctoral dissertation, Purdue University, West Lafayette, IN.

Lewis, M., & Weinraub, M. (1979). The father's role in the child's social network. In M. E. Lamb (Ed.), *The role of the father in child development* (pp. 157–184). New York: Wiley.

Libby, M. N., & Aries, E. (1989). Gender differences in preschool children's narrative fantasy. *Psychology of Women Quarterly, 13,* 293–306.

Lightdale, J. R., & Prentice, D. A. (1994). Rethinking sex differences in aggression: Aggressive behavior in the absence of social roles. *Personality and Social Psychology Bulletin, 20,* 34–44.

Linn, M. C., & Peterson, A. C. (1986). A meta-analysis of gender differences in spatial ability: Implications for mathematics and science achievement. In J. S. Hyde & M. C. Linn (Eds.), *The psychology of gender: Advances through meta-analysis* (pp. 67–101). Baltimore: Johns Hopkins University Press.

Lippa, R. (1991). Some psychometric characteristics of gender diagnosticity measures: Reliability, validity, consistency across domains and relationship to the Big Five. *Journal of Personality and Social Psychology, 61,* 1000–1011.

Lippa, R. A. (1994). *Introduction to social psychology* (2nd ed.). Pacific Grove, CA: Brooks/Cole.

Lippa, R. (1995a). Do sex differences define gender-related individual differences within the sexes? Evidence from three studies. *Personality and Social Psychology Bulletin, 21,* 349–355.

Lippa, R. (1995b). Gender-related individual differences and psychological adjustment in terms of the Big Five and circumplex models. *Journal of Personality and Social Psychology, 69,* 1184–1202.

Lippa, R. (1997). The display of masculinity, femininity, and gender diagnosticity in self-descriptive photo essays. *Journal of Personality, 65,* 137–169.

Lippa, R. (1998a). Gender-related individual differences and National Merit test performance: Girls who are "masculine" and boys who are "feminine" tend to do better. In L. Ellis & L. Ebertz (Eds.), *Males, females, and behavior: Toward biological understanding.* Westport, CT: Praeger.

Lippa, R. (1998b). Gender-related individual difference and the structure of vocational interests: The importance of the "People-Things" dimension. *Journal of Personality and Social Psychology, 74,* 996–1009.

Lippa, R. (1998c). The nonverbal judgment and display of extraversion, masculinity, femininity, and gender diagnosticity: A lens model analysis. *Journal of Research in Personality, 32,* 80–107.

Lippa, R. A. (2000). Gender-related traits in gay men, lesbian women, and heterosexual men and women: The virtual identity of homosexual-heterosexual diagnosticity and gender diagnosticity. *Journal of Personality, 68,* 899–926.

Lippa, R. A. [2001]. On deconstructing and reconstructing masculinity-femininity. *Journal of Research in Personality, 35,* 168–207.

Lippa, R., & Arad, S. (1997). The structure of sexual orientation and its relation to masculinity, femininity, and gender diagnosticity: Different for men and women. *Sex Roles, 37,* 187–208.

Lippa, R., & Arad, S. (1999). Gender, personality, and prejudice: The display of authoritarianism and social dominance in interviews with college men and women. *Journal of Research in Personality, 33,* 463–493.

Lippa, R., & Connelly, S. C. (1990). Gender diagnosticity: A new Bayesian approach to gender-related individual differences. *Journal of Personality and Social Psychology, 59,* 1051–1065.

Lippa, R., & Hershberger, S. (1999). Genetic and environmental influences on individual differences in masculinity, femininity, and gender diagnosticity: Analyzing data from a classic twin study. *Journal of Personality, 67,* 27–55.

Lippa, R. A., Martin, L. R., & Friedman, H. S. (2000). Gender-related individual differences and mortality in the Terman longitudinal study: Is masculinity hazardous to your health? *Personality and Social Psychology Bulletin, 26,* 1560–1570.

Lippa, R. A. & Tan, F. D. (2001). Does culture moderate the relationship between sexual orientation and gender-related personality traits? *Cross-Cultural Research, 35,* 65–87.

Lippe, B. (1991). Turner syndrome. *Endocrinology and Metabolism Clinics of North America, 20,* 121–152.

Lippmann, W. (1922). *Public opinion.* New York: Harcourt, Brace.

Lish, J. D., Meyer-Bahlburg, H. F. L., Ehrhardt, A. A., Travis, B. G., & Veridiano, N. P. (1992). Prenatal exposure to diethylstilbestrol (DES): Childhood play behavior and adult gender-role behavior in women. *Archives of Sexual Behavior, 21,* 423–441.

Liss, M. B. (1983). Learning gender-related skills through play. In M. B. Liss (Ed.), *Social and cognitive skills: Sex roles and children's play* (pp. 147–167). New York Academic Press.

Lockheed, M. E., & Harris, A. M. (1984). Cross-sex collaborative learning in elementary classrooms. *American Educational Research Association Journal, 21,* 275–294.

Loehlin, J. C. (1992). *Genes and environment in personality development.* Newbury Park, CA: Sage.

Loehlin, J. C., & Nichols, R. C. (1976). *Heredity, environment, & personality: A study of 850 sets of twins.* Austin, TX: University of Texas Press.

Lovejoy, J., & Wallen, K. (1988). Sexually dimorphic behavior in group-housed rhesus monkeys (Macaca mulatta) at 1 year of age. *Psychobiology, 16,* 348–356.

Lubinski, D., & Humphreys, L. G. (1990). A broadly based analysis of mathematical giftedness. *Intelligence, 14,* 327–355.

Luecke-Aleksa, D., Anderson, D. R., Collins, P. A., & Schmitt, K. L. (1995). Gender constancy and television viewing. *Developmental Psychology, 31,* 773–780.

Lunn, D. (1987). Foot asymmetry and cognitive ability in young children. Unpublished master's thesis, Department of Psychology, University of Western Ontario, London, Canada. [Cited and described in D. Kimura. (1999) *Sex and cognition.* Cambridge, MA: MIT Press.]

Lynn, R. (1992). Sex differences in the differential aptitude test in British and American adolescents. *Educational Psychology, 12,* 101–106.

Lytton, H., & Romney, D. M. (1991). Parents' differential socialization of boys and girls: A meta-analysis. *Psychological Bulletin, 109,* 267–296.

Maccoby, E. E. (1966). Sex differences in intellectual functioning. In E. E. Maccoby (Ed.), *The development of sex differences* (pp. 25–55). Stanford, CA: Stanford University Press.

Maccoby, E. E. (1987). The varied meanings of "masculine" and "feminine." In J. M Reinisch, L. A. Rosenblum, & S. A. Sanders, (Eds.), *Masculinity/femininity: Basic perspectives* (pp. 227–239). New York: Oxford University Press.

Maccoby, E. E. (1990). The role of gender identity and gender constancy in sex-differentiated development. *New Directions for Child Development, 47,* 5–20.

Maccoby, E. E. (1998). *The two sexes: Growing up apart, coming together.* Cambridge, MA: Belknap Press.

Maccoby, E. E., & Jacklin, C. N. (1974). *The psychology of sex differences.* Stanford, CA: Stanford University Press.

Maccoby, E. E., & Jacklin, C. N. (1980). Sex differences in aggression: A rejoinder and reprise. *Child Development, 51,* 964–980.

Maccoby, E. E., & Mnookin, R. H. (1992). *Dividing the child: The social and legal dilemmas of custody.* Cambridge, MA: Harvard University Press.

MacLusky, N. J., & Naftolin, F. (1981, March 20). Sexual differentiation of the central nervous system. *Science, 211,* 1294–1303.

Madon, S., Jussim, L., Keiper, S., Eccles, J., Smith, A., & Palumbo, P. (1998). The accuracy and power of sex, social class, and ethnic stereotypes: A naturalistic study in person perception. *Personality and Social Psychology Bulletin, 24,* 1304–1318.

Maguire, E. A., Frackowiak, R. S., & Frith, C. D. (1997). Recalling routes around London: Activation of the right hippocampus in taxi drivers. *Journal of Neuroscience, 17,* 7103–7110.

Maltz, D. N., & Borker, R. A. (1982). A cultural approach to male-female miscommunication. In J. J. Gumperz (Ed.), *Language and social identity* (pp. 196–216). New York: Cambridge University Press.

Mann, V. A., Sasanuma, S., Sakuma, N., & Masaki, S. (1990). Sex differences in cognitive abilities: A cross-cultural perspective. *Neuropsychologia, 28,* 1063–1077.

Manning, J. T., Barley, L., Walton, J., Lewis-Jones, D. I., Trivers, R. L., Singh, D., Thornhill, R., Rohde, P., Bereczkei, T., Henzi, P., Soler, M., & Szwed, A. (2000). The 2nd:4th digit ratio, sexual dimorphism, population differences and reproductive success: Evidence for sexually antagonistic genes? *Evolution and Human Behavior, 21,* 163–183.

Manning, J. T., Scutt, D., Wilson, J., Lewis-Jones, D. I. (1998). The ratio of 2nd to 4th digit length: A predictor of sperm numbers and concentrations of testosterone, luteinizing hormone and oestrogen. *Human Reproduction, 13,* 3000–3004.

Marantz, S. A., & Mansfield, A. F. (1977). Maternal employment and the development of sex-role stereotyping in five- to eleven-year-old girls. *Child Development, 48,* 668–673.

Margolin, G., & Patterson, G. R. (1975). Differential consequences provided by mothers and fathers for their sons and daughters. *Developmental Psychology, 11,* 537–538.

Markow, T. A. (1994). *Developmental instability, its origins and evolutionary implications.* Boston: Kluwer Academic.

Markus, H., & Kitayama, S. (1991). Culture and the self: Implications for cognition, emotion, and motivation. *Psychological Review, 98,* 124–153.

Markus, H., Crane, M., Bernstein, S., & Siladi, M. (1982). Self-schemas and gender. *Journal of Personality and Social Psychology, 42,* 38–50.

Martell, R. F., Lane, D. M., & Emrich, C. (1996). Male-female differences: A computer simulation. *American Psychologist, 51,* 157–158.

Martin, C. L. (2000). Cognitive theories of gender development. In T. Eckes & H. Trautner (Eds.), *The developmental social psychology of gender* (pp. 91–121). Mahwah, NJ: Erlbaum.

Martin, C. L., Eisenbud, L., & Rose, H. (1995). Children's gender-based reasoning about toys. *Child Development, 66,* 1453–1471.

Martin, C. L., & Halverson, C. F. (1981). A schematic processing model of sex typing and stereotyping in children. *Child Development, 52,* 1119–1134.

Martin, C. L., & Halverson, C. F. (1987). The roles of cognition in sex role acquisition. In D. B. Carter (Ed.), *Current conceptions of sex roles and sex typing: Theory and research* (pp. 123–137). New York: Praeger.

Masters, M. S., & Sanders, B. (1993). Is the gender difference in mental rotation disappearing? *Behavior Genetics, 23,* 337–341.

McClearn, G. E., Johansson, B., Berg, S., Pederson, N. L., Ahern, F., Petrill, S. A., & Plomin, R. (1997). Substantial genetic influence on cognitive abilities in twins 80 or more years old. *Science, 276,* 1560–1563.

McFadden, D. (1998). Sex differences in the auditory system. *Developmental Neuropsychology, 14,* 261–298.

McFadden, D., & Pasanen, E. G. (1998). Comparison of the auditory systems of heterosexuals and homosexuals: Click-evoked otoacoustic emissions. *Proceedings of the National Academy of Science, 95,* 2709–2713.

McFadden, D., & Pasanen, E. G. (1999). Spontaneous otoacoustic emissions in heterosexuals, homosexuals, and bisexuals. *Journal of the Acoustical Society of America, 105,* 2403–2413.

McGhee, P. E., & Frueh, T. (1980). Television viewing and the learning of sex role stereotypes. *Sex Roles, 6,* 179–188.

McGlone, J. (1980). Sex difference in human brain asymmetry: A critical survey. *Behavioral and Brain Sciences, 3,* 215–227.

McGue, M., Bouchard, T. J., Jr., Iacono, W. G., & Lykken, D. T. (1993). Behavioral genetics of cognitive ability: A life-span perspective. In R. Plomin & G. E. McClearn (Eds.), *Nature, nurture, and psychology* (pp. 59–76). Washington, DC: American Psychological Association.

McGuiness, D., & Morley, C. (1991). Sex differences in the development of visio-spatial abilities in pre-school children. *Journal of Mental Imagery, 15,* 143–150.

McKnight, J. (1997). *Straight Science: Homosexuality, Evolution, and Adaptation.* New York: Routledge.

McNeely, C. A. (1998, Summer). Lagging behind the times: Parenthood, custody, and gender bias in the family court. *Florida State University Law Review, 25.*

Meany, M. J., Stewart, J., & Beatty, W. W. (1985). Sex differences in social play: The socialization of sex roles. In J. S. Rosenblatt, C. Beer, C. M. Busnell, & P. Stater (Eds.), *Advances in the study of behavior* (Vol. 15, pp. 1–58). New York: Academic Press.

Mendel, G. J. (1866). Versuche Ueber Pflanzenhybriden, *Verhandlugen des Naturforschunden Vereines in Bruenn, 4,* 3–47.

Merriman, W. E., Keating, D. P., & List, J. A. (1985). Mental rotation of facial profiles: Age-, sex-, and ability-related differences. *Developmental Psychology, 21,* 888–900.

Merton, R. D. (1948). The self-fulfilling prophecy. *Antioch Review, 8,* 193–210.

Meyer-Bahlburg, H. (1984). Psychoendocrine research on sexual orientation: Current status and future options. In G. J. De Vries, J. P. C. De Bruin, H. M. B. Uylings, & M. A. Corner (Eds.), *Progress in brain research* (Vol. 61, pp. 375–398). Amsterdam: Elsevier.

Meyer-Bahlburg, H. F. L., Ehrhardt, A. A., Rosen, L. R., Feldman, J. F., Veridiano, N. P., Zimmerman, I., & McEwen, B. S. (1984). Psycho-sexual milestones in women prenatally exposed to diethylstilbestrol. *Hormones and Behavior, 18,* 359–366.

Meyer-Bahlburg, H. F. L., Ehrhardt, A. A., Rosen, L. R., Gruen, R. S., Veridiano, N. P., Vann, F. H., & Neuwalder, H. F. (1995). Prenatal estrogens and the development of homosexual orientation. *Developmental Psychology, 31,* 12–21.

Miller, C. L. (1987). Qualitative differences among gender-stereotyped toys: Implications for cognitive and social development in girls and boys. *Sex Roles, 16,* 473–487.

Miller, E. M. (2000). Homosexuality, birth order, and evolution: Toward an equilibrium reproductive economics of homosexuality. *Archives of Sexual Behavior, 29,* 1–34.

Minton, C., Kagan, J., & Levine, J. A. (1971). Maternal control and obedience in the two-year-old child. *Child Development, 42,* 1873–1894.

Mischel, W. (1966). A social learning view of sex differences. In E. E. Maccoby (Ed.), *The development of sex differences* (pp. 57–81). Stanford, CA: Stanford University Press.

Mischel, W., & Grusec, J. (1966). Determinants of the rehearsal and transmission of neutral and aversive behaviors. *Journal of Personality and Social Psychology, 3,* 197–205.

Mitchell, J. E., Baker, L. A., & Jacklin, C. N. (1989). Masculinity and femininity in twin children: Genetic and environmental factors. *Child Development, 60,* 1475–1485.

Moller, A. P., & Swaddle, J. P. (1998). *Asymmetry, developmental stability and evolution.* New York: Oxford University Press.

Money, J. (1975). Ablatio penis: normal male infant sex-reassigned as a girl. *Archives of Sexual Behavior, 4,* 65–71.

Money, J. & Schwartz, M. (1977). Dating, romantic and nonromantic friendships, and sexuality in 17 early-treated adrenogenital females, aged 16–25. In P. A. Lee, L. P. Plotnick, A. A. Kowarski, & C. J. Migeon (Eds.), *Congenital adrenal hyperplasia* (pp. 419–431). Baltimore: University Park Press.

Montepare, J. M., & Vega, C. (1988). Women's vocal reactions to intimate and casual male friends. *Personality and Social Psychology Bulletin, 14,* 103–113.

Morawski, J. G. (1987). The troubled quest for masculinity, femininity, and androgyny. In P. Shaver & C. Hendrick (Eds.), *Sex and gender: Review of personality and social psychology* (Vol. 7, pp. 44–69). Newbury Park, CA: Sage.

Morgan, M. (1982). Television and adolescents sex role stereotypes: A longitudinal study. *Journal of Personality and Social Psychology, 43,* 947–955.

Mori, D., Chaiken, S., & Pliner, P. (1987). "Eating lightly" and the self-presentation of femininity. *Journal of Personality and Social Psychology, 53,* 693–702.

Moyer, K. E. (1976). *The psychology of aggression.* New York: Harper & Row.

Myers, A. M., & Gonda, G. (1982). Utility of the masculinity-femininity construct: Comparison of traditional and androgyny approaches. *Journal of Personality and Social Psychology, 43,* 514–522.

Newson, J., & Newson, E. (1986). Family and sex roles in middle childhood. In D. J. Hargreaves & A. M. Colley (Eds.), *The psychology of sex roles* (pp. 142–158). London: Harper & Row.

Nicolopoulou, A. (1997). Worldmaking and identity formation in children's narrative play-acting. In B. Cox & C. Lightfoot (Eds.), *Sociogenic perspectives in internalization* (pp. 157–187). Hillsdale, NJ: Erlbaum.

Nicolopoulou, A., Scales, B., & Weintraub, J. (1994). Gender differences and symbolic imagination in the stories of four-year-olds. In A. H. Dyson & C. Geneshi (Eds.), *The need for story: Cultural diversity in classroom and community* (pp. 102–123). Urbana, NY: National Council of Teachers of English.

Nordeen, E. J., Nordeen, K. W., Sengelaub, D. R., & Arnold, A. P. (1985). Androgens prevent normally occurring cell death in a sexually dimorphic spinal nucleus. *Science, 229,* 671–673.

Nordvik, H., & Amponsah, B. (1998). Gender differences in spatial abilities and spatial activity among university students in an egalitarian educational system. *Sex Roles, 38,* 1009–1023.

Norrander, B. (1999). The evolution of the gender gap. *Public Opinion Quarterly, 63,* 566–576.

Nottebohm, F., & Arnold, A. P. (1976). Sexual dimorphism in vocal control areas of the songbird brain. *Science, 194,* 211–213.

Nyborg, J. (1983). Spatial ability in men and women: Review and a new theory. *Advances in Behavior Research and Therapy, 5,* 89–140.

O'Brien, M., & Huston, A. C. (1985). Development of sex-typed play behavior in toddlers. *Developmental Psychology, 21,* 866–871.

Oliver, M. B., & Hyde, J. S. (1993). Gender differences in sexuality: A meta-analysis. *Psychological Bulletin, 114,* 29–51.

Olson, J. M., Roese, N. J., & Zanna, M. P. (1996). Expectancies. In E. T. Higgins & A. W. Kruglanski (Eds.), *Social psychology: Handbook of basic principles* (pp. 211–238). New York: Guilford.

Olweus, D. (1986). Aggression and hormones: Behavioral relationships with testosterone and adrenaline. In D. Olweus, J. Block, & M. Radke-Yarrow (Eds.), *Development of antisocial and prosocial behaviors: Research, theories, and issues.* Orlando, FL: Academic Press.

Olweus, D., Mattsson, A., Schalling, D., & Low, H. (1980). Testosterone, aggression, physical, and personality dimensions in normal adolescent males. *Psychosomatic Medicine, 42,* 253–269.

Ostatnikova, D., Laznibatova, J., & Dohnanyiova, M. (1996). Testosterone influence on spatial ability in prepubertal children. *Studia Psychologica, 38,* 237–245.

Parke, R. O., Slaby, R. G. (1983). The development of aggression. In P. Mussen & E. M. Hetherington (Eds.) *Handbook of child psychology (Vol. 4): Socialization, personality, and social development* (pp. 549–641). New York, NY: John Wiley.

Parsons, T., & Bales, R. F. (Eds.). (1955). *Family, socialization and interaction process.* New York: Free Press of Glencoe.

Pattatucci, A. M. L., & Hamer, D. H. (1995). Development and familiality of sexual orientation in females. *Behavior Genetics, 25,* 407–420.

Pennebaker, J. W., & Watson, D. (1988). Blood pressure estimations and beliefs among normotensives and hypertensives. *Health Psychology, 7,* 309–328.

Pennington, B. F., Heaton, R. K., Kazmark, P., Pendleton, M. G., Lehman, R., & Shucard, D. W. (1985). The neuropsychological phenotype in Turner syndrome. *Cortex, 21,* 391–404.

Peplau, L. A., & Gordon, S. L. (1985). Women and men in love: Gender differences in close heterosexual relationships. In V. E. O'Leary, R. K. Unger, & B. S. Wallston (Eds.), *Women, gender, and social psychology* (pp. 257–292). Hillsdale, NJ: Erlbaum.

Petersen, A. C. (1976). Physical androgyny and cognitive functioning in adolescence. *Developmental Psychology, 12,* 524–533.

Petrie, M., Halliday, T., & Sanders, C. (1991). Peahens prefer peacocks with more elaborate trains. *Animal Behavior, 41,* 323–331.

Phillips, K., & Silverman, I. (1997). Differences in the relationship of menstrual cycle phase to spatial performance on two- and three-dimensional tasks. *Hormones and Behavior, 32,* 167–175.

Phillips, S., King, S., & DuBois, L. (1978). Spontaneous activities of female versus male newborns. *Child Development, 49,* 590–597.

Phoenix, C. H., Goy, R. W., Gerall, A. A., & Young, W. C. (1959). Organizing action of prenatally administered testosterone propionate on the tissues mediating mating behaviors in the female guinea pig. *Endocrinology, 65,* 369–382.

Pillard, R. C. (1991). Masculinity and femininity in homosexuality: "Inversion" revisited. In J. C. Gonsiorek & J. D. Weinrich (Eds.), *Homosexuality: Research implications for public policy* (pp. 32–43). Newbury Park, CA: Sage.

Pillard, R. C., & Weinrich, J. D. (1986). Evidence of familial nature of male homosexuality. *Archives of General Psychiatry, 43*, 808–812.

Porteus, S. D. (1965). *Porteus maze test: Fifty years application.* Palo Alto, CA: Pacific Books.

Pratto, F., Sidanius, J., Stallworth, L., & Malle, B. (1994). Social dominance orientation: A personality variable predicting social and political attitudes. *Journal of personality and social psychology, 72*, 37–53.

Prediger, D. J. (1982). Dimensions underlying Holland's hexagon: Missing link between interests and occupations? *Journal of Vocational Behavior, 21*, 259–287.

Proust, M. (1934). *Remembrance of things past.* New York: Random House.

Pugh, K. R., Shaywitz, B. A., Shaywitz, S. E., Constable, R. T., Skudlarski, P., Fulbright, R. K., Bronen, R. A., Shankweiler, D. P., Katz, L., Fletcher, J. M., & Gore, J. C. (1996). Cerebral organization of component processes in reading. *Brain, 119*, 1221–1238.

Questions féministes. (1977). Publication: Paris: Editions Tierce.

Quigley, C. A., DemBellis, A., Marschke, K. B., El-Awady, M. K., Wilson, E. M. & French, F. S. (1995). Androgen receptor defects: Historical, clinical, and molecular perspectives. *Endocrine Review, 16*, 271–321.

Raag, T., & Rackliff, C. L. (1998). Preschoolers' awareness of social expectations of gender: Relationships to toy choices. *Sex Roles, 38*, 685–700.

Reese, E., Haden, C. A., & Fivush, R. (1996). Mothers, fathers, daughters, and sons: Gender differences in autobiographical reminiscing. *Research on Language and Social Interaction, 29*, 27–56.

Reiner, W. G. (2000). Androgen exposure in utero and the development of male gender identity in genetic males reassigned female at birth. Paper presented at the International Behavior Development Symposium: Biological Basis of Sexual Orientation, Gender Identity, and Gender-Typical Behavior, Minot, ND.

Repetti, R. L. (1984). Determinants of children's sex stereotyping: Parental sex-role traits and television viewing. *Personality and Social Psychology Bulletin, 10*, 457–468.

Resnick, S. M., Berenbaum, S. A., Gottesman, I. I., & Bouchard, T. J., Jr. (1986). Early hormonal influences on cognitive functioning in congenital adrenal hyperplasia. *Developmental Psychology, 22*, 191–198.

Resnick, S. M., Metter, E. J., & Zonderman, A. B. (1997). Estrogen replacement therapy and longitudinal decline in visual memory: A possible protective effect? *Neurology, 49*, 1491–1497.

Ridgeway, C. L. (1982). Status in groups: The importance of motivation. *American Sociological Review, 47*, 76–88.

Ridgeway, C. L., & Diekema, D. (1992). Are gender differences status differences? In C. L. Ridgeway (Ed.), *Gender, interaction, and inequality* (pp. 157–180). New York: Springer.

Riordan, C. (1990). *Girls and boys in school: Together or separate?* New York: Teachers College Press.

Roberts, T. A., & Pennebaker, J. W. (1995). Gender differences in perceiving internal state: Toward a his-and-hers model of perceptual cue use. In M. Zanna (Ed.), *Advances in experimental social psychology* (Vol. 27, pp. 143–176). New York: Academic Press.

Roddy, J. M., Klein, H. A., Stericker, A. B., & Kurdek, L. A. (1981). Modification of stereotypic sex-typing in young children. *Journal of Genetic Psychology, 139*, 109–118.

Roscoe, B., Diana, M. S., & Brooks, R. H. (1987). Early, middle, and late adolescents' views on dating and factors influencing partner selection. *Adolescence, 22*, 59–68.

Rosenkrantz, P., Vogel, S., Bee, H., Broverman, I., & Broverman, D. M. (1968). Sex-role stereotypes and self-concepts in college students. *Journal of Consulting and Clinical Psychology, 32*, 286–295.

Rosenthal, R., & Rubin, D. B. (1982). A simple, general purpose display of magnitude of experimental effects. *Journal of Education Psychology, 74*, 166–169.

Rovet, J. F. (1993). The psychoeducational characteristics of children with Turner syndrome. *Journal of Learning Disabilities, 26*, 333–341.

Rowe, D. C. (1982). Sources of variability in sex-linked personality attributes. *Developmental Psychology, 18*, 431–434.

Rowe, D. C. (1997). Genetics, temperament, and personality. In R. Hogan, J. Johnson, & S. Briggs (Eds.), *Handbook of personality psychology* (pp. 376–386). San Diego, CA: Academic Press.

Rubin, Z., Peplau, L. A., & Hill, C. T. (1981). Loving and leaving: Sex differences in romantic attachments. *Sex roles, 7*, 821–835.

Ruble, D. N., Greulich, F., Pomerantz, E. M., & Gochberg, G. (1993). The role of gender-related processes in the development of sex differences in depression. *Journal of Affective Disorders, 29*, 97–128.

Ruble, D. N., & Martin, C. L. (1998). Gender development. In W. Damon & N. Eisenberg (Eds.), *Handbook of child psychology: (Vol 3). Social, emotional, and personality development.* (5th ed., pp. 993–1016). New York: Wiley.

Rudman, L. A. (1998). Self-promotion as a risk factor for women: The costs and benefits of counterstereotypical impression management. *Journal of Personality and Social Psychology, 74*, 629–645.

Russell, A., & Saebel, J. (1997). Mother-son, mother-daughter, father-son, and father-daughter: Are they distinct relationships? *Developmental Review, 17*, 11–147.

Rust, J., Golombox, S., Hines, M., Johnston, K., Golding, J. & the ALSPAC Study Team (2000). The role of brothers and sisters in gender development of preschool children. *Journal of Experimental Child Psychology, 77*, 292–303.

Sadker, M., & Sadker, D. (1986, March). Sexism in the classroom: From grade school to graduate school. *Phi-Delta-Kappan*, 512–515.

Sadker, M., & Sadker, D. M. (1995). *Failing at fairness: How our schools cheat girls*. New York: Touchstone.

Schwartz, F. N. (1989). Management women and the new facts of life. *Harvard Business Review, 89*, 65–76.

Sears, R. R., Maccoby, E. E., & Levin, H. (1957). *Patterns of child rearing*. Evanston, IL: Row, Peterson.

Sears, R. R., Rau, L., & Alpert, R. (1965). *Identification and child rearing*. Stanford, CA: Stanford University Press.

Sedney, M. A. (1987). Development of androgyny: Parental influences. *Psychology of Women Quarterly, 11*, 311–326.

Serbin, L. A., Moller, L. C., Gulko, J., Powlishta, K. K., & Colburne, K. A. (1994). The emergence of gender segregation in toddler playgroups. In C. Leaper (Ed.), *Childhood sex segregation: Causes and consequences* (pp. 7–17). San Francisco: Jossey-Bass.

Serbin, L. A., O'Leary, K. D., Kent, R. N., & Tonick, I. J. (1973). A comparison of teacher response to preacademic and problem behavior of boys and girls. *Child Development, 44*, 796–804.

Serbin, L. A., Powlishta, K. K., & Gulko, J. (1993). The development of sex-typing in middle childhood. *Monographs of the Society for Research in Child Development, 58* (Serial No. 232).

Seymoure, P., Doll, H., & Juraska, J. M. (1996). Sex differences in radial maze performance: Influence of rearing environment and room cues. *Psychobiology, 24*, 33–37.

Shackelford, S., Wood, W., & Worchel, S. (1996). Behavioral styles and the influence of women in mixed-sex groups. *Social Psychology Quarterly, 59*, 284–293.

Sherwin, B. B. (1988). A comparative analysis of the role of androgen in human male and female sexual behavior: Behavioral specificity, critical thresholds, and sensitivity. *Psychobiology, 16*, 416–425.

Should women be sent into combat? (1991, July 21) *New York Times,* p. E3.

Shute, V. J., Pellegrino, J. W., Hubert, L., and Reynolds, R. W. (1983). The relation between androgen levels and human spatial abilities. *Bulletin of the Psychonomic Society, 21,* 465–468.

Sidanius, J., Pratto, F., & Bobo, L. (1994). Social dominance orientation and the political psychology of gender: A case of invariance? *Journal of personality and social psychology, 67,* 998–1011.

Siegal, M. (1987). Are sons and daughters treated more differently by fathers than by mothers? *Developmental Review, 7,* 183–209.

Signorielli, N. (1993). Television, the portrayal of women, and children's attitudes. In G. L. Berry & J. K. Asamen (Eds.), *Children and television: Images in a changing sociocultural world* (pp. 229–242). Newbury Park, CA: Sage.

Silverman, I., & Eals, M. (1992). Sex differences in spatial abilities: Evolutionary theory and data. In J. H. Barkow, L. Cosmides, & J. Tooby (Eds.), *The adapted mind: Evolutionary psychology and the generation of culture* (pp. 533–549). New York: Oxford University Press.

Silverman, I., Kastuk, D., Choi, J., & Phillips, K. (1999). Testosterone and spatial ability in men. *Psychoneuroendocrinology, 24*, 813–822.

Silverman, I., & Phillips, K. (1998). The evolutionary psychology of spatial sex differences. In C. Crawford & D. L. Krebs (Eds.), *Handbook of evolutionary psychology: Ideas, issues, and application* (pp. 595–612). Mahwah, NJ: Erlbaum.

Singh, D., Vidaurri, M., Zambarano, R. J., Dabbs, J. M., Jr. (1999). Lesbian erotic role identification: Behavioral, morphological, and hormonal correlates. *Journal of Personality and Social Psychology, 76*, 1035–1049.

Skrypnek, B. J., & Snyder, M. (1982). On the self-perpetuating nature of stereotypes about men and women. *Journal of Experimental Social Psychology, 18,* 277–291.

Skuse, D. H., James, R. S., Bishop, D. V. M., Coppin, B., Dalton, P., Aamodt-Leeper, G., Bacarese-Hamilton, M., Creswell, C., McGurk, R., & Jacobs, P. A. (1997). Evidence from Turner's syndrome of an imprinted X-linked locus affecting cognitive function. *Nature, 387*, 705–708.

Slaby, R. G., & Frey, K. S. (1975). Development of gender constancy and selective attention to same-sex models. *Child Development, 46*, 849–856.

Slijper, F. M. E. (1984). Androgens and gender role behavior in girls with congenital adrenal hyperplasia (CAH). *Progress in Brain Research, 61*, 417–422.

Smetana, J. G., & Letourneau, K. J. (1984). Development of gender constancy and children's sex-typed free play behavior. *Development Psychology, 20*, 691–696.

Smith, P. K., & Daglish, L. (1977). Sex differences in parent and infant behavior in the home. *Child Development, 48*, 1250–1254.

Snow, M. E., Jacklin, C. N., & Maccoby, E. E. (1983). Sex-of-child differences in father-child interaction at one year of age. *Child Development, 54*, 227–232.

Snyder, M. (1981). On the self-perpetuating nature of social stereotypes. In D. L. Hamilton (Ed.), *Cognitive processes in stereotyping and intergroup behavior* (pp. 183–212). Hillsdale, NJ: Erlbaum.

Sommers, C. H. (2000). *The war against boys: How misguided feminism is harming our young men.* New York: Simon & Schuster.

Spence, J. T., & Buckner, C. (1995). Masculinity and femininity: Defining the undefinable. In P. J. Kalbfleisch & M. J. Cody (Eds.), *Gender, power, and communication in human relationships* (pp. 105–138). Hillsdale, NJ: Erlbaum.

Spence, J. T., & Helmreich, R. L. (1978). *Masculinity and femininity: Their psychological dimensions, correlates, and antecedents.* Austin, TX: University of Texas Press.

Spence, J. T., & Helmreich, R. L. (1980). Masculine instrumentality and feminine expressiveness: Their relationships with sex role attitudes and behaviors. *Psychology of Women Quarterly, 5,* 147–163.

Spence, J. T., Helmreich, R. L., & Stapp, J. (1974). The Personal Attributes Questionnaire: A measure of sex role stereotypes and masculinity-femininity. *JSAS, Catalog of Selected Documents in Psychology, 4,* 43–44 (Ms. No. 617).

Spencer, S. H., Steele, C. M., & Quinn, D. M. (1999). Stereotype threat and women's math performance. *Journal of Experimental Social Psychology, 35,* 4–28.

Steele, C. M. (1997). A threat in the air: How stereotypes shape intellectual identity and performance. *American Psychologist, 52,* 613–629.

Stern, M., & Karraker, K. H. (1989). Sex stereotyping of infants: A review of gender labeling studies. *Sex Roles, 20,* 501–522.

Stevenson, M. R., & Black, K. N. (1988). Paternal absence and sex-role development: A meta-analysis. *Child Development, 59,* 793–814.

Stoneman, Z., Brody, G. H., & MacKinnon, C. E. (1986). Same-sex and cross-sex siblings: Activity choices, roles, behavior, and gender stereotypes. *Sex Roles, 15,* 495–511.

Strong, E. K., Jr., (1936). Interests of men and women. *Journal of Social Psychology, 9,* 49–67.

Strong, E. K., Jr. (1943). *Vocational interests of men and women.* Stanford, CA: Stanford University Press.

Studlar, D. T., McAllister, I., & Hayes, B. C. (1998). Explaining the gender gap in voting: A cross-national analysis. *Social Science Quarterly, 79,* 779–798.

Stuhlmacher, A. F., & Walters, A. E. (1999). Gender differences in negotiation outcome: A meta-analysis. *Personnel Psychology, 52,* 653–677.

Swann, W. B., Jr. (1999). *Resilient identities: self-relationships and the construction of social reality.* New York: Basic Books.

Swedenborg, E. (1987). *Arcana Coelestia.* (John Elliott, Trans.). London: The Swedenborg Society.

Swim, J., Borgida, E., Maruyama, G., & Myers, D. G. (1989). Joan McKay versus John McKay: Do gender stereotypes bias evaluations? *Psychological Bulletin, 105,* 409–429.

Symons, D. (1979). *The evolution of human sexuality.* New York: Oxford University Press.

Tan, U., & Tan, M. (1998). The curvilinear correlations between total testosterone level and fluid intelligence in men and women. *International Journal of Neuroscience, 94,* 55–61.

Tannen, D. (1990). *You just don't understand: Women and men in conversation.* New York: Morrow.

Tauber, M. A. (1979). Sex differences in parent-child interaction styles during a free-play session. *Child Development, 50,* 981–988.

Taylor, M. C., & Hall, J. A. (1982). Psychological androgyny: Theories, methods, and conclusions. *Psychological Bulletin, 92,* 347–366.

Taylor, S. E., Klein, L. C., Lewis, B. P., Gruenwald, T. L., Gurung, R. A. R., & Updegraff, J. A. (2000). Biobehavioral responses to stress in females: tend-and-befriend, not fight-or-flight. *Psychological Review, 107,* 411–429.

Terman, L. M., & Oden, M. H. (1947). *Genetic Studies of genius:the gifted child grows up* (Vol. 4), Stanford, CA: Stanford University Press.

Terman, L. M., & Miles, C. C. (1936). *Sex and personality: Studies in masculinity and femininity.* New York: McGraw-Hill.

Thomas, E. B., Leiderman, P. H., & Olson, J. P. (1972). Neonate-mother interaction during breast feeding. *Developmental Psychology, 6,* 110–118.

Thomas, J. R., & French, K. E. (1985). Gender differences across age in motor performance: A meta-analysis. *Psychological Bulletin, 98,* 260–282.

Thompson, T. L., & Zerbinos, E. (1995). Gender roles in animated cartoons: Has the picture changed in 20 years? *Sex Roles, 32,* 651–673.

Thompson, T. L., & Zerbinos, E. (1997). Television cartoons: Do children notice it's a boy's world? *Sex Roles, 37,* 415–432.

Thornhill, R., & Palmer, C. T. (2000). *A natural history of rape: Biological bases of sexual coercion.* Cambridge, MA: MIT Press.

Tierney, M. C., & Luine, V. N. (1998). New concepts in hormone replacement therapy: Selective estrogen receptor modulators (SERMS). IV. Effects of estrogens and antiestrogens on the CNS. *Journal of the Canadian Society of Obstetrics & Gynecology, 19,* 46–56.

Trautner, H. M. (1992). The development of sex-typing in children: A longitudinal analysis. *German Journal of Psychology, 16,* 183–199.

Trevor, M. C. (1999). Political socialization, party identification, and the gender gap. *Public Opinion Quarterly, 63,* 62–89.

Trivers, R. L. (1972). Parental investment and sexual selection. In B. Campbell (Ed.), *Sexual Selection and the Descent of Man: 1871–1971* (pp. 136–179). Chicago, IL: Aldirie.

Tyack, D., & Hansot, E. (1990). *Learning together: A history of coeducation in American schools.* New Haven, CT: Yale University Press.

Udry, J. R. (2000). Biological limits of gender construction. *American Sociological Review, 65,* 443–457.

Unger, R. K. (1979). Toward a redefinition of sex and gender. *American Psychologist, 34,* 1085–1094.

United Nations Development Programme. (2000). United Nations Human Development Report, 2000 [On-line]. Available at http://www/undp.org. New York: United Nations.

Urberg, K. A. (1982). The development of concepts of masculinity and femininity in young children. *Sex Roles, 8,* 659–668.

Van Goozen, S. H. M. (1994). *Male and female: Effects of sex hormones on aggression, cognition, and sexual motivation.* Amsterdam: University of Amsterdam.

Van Goozen, S. H. M., Cohen-Ketenis, P. T., Gooren, L. J. G., Frijda, N. H., & van de Poll, N. E. (1995). Activating effects of androgens on cognitive performance: Causal evidence in a group of female-to-male transsexuals. *Neuropsychologia, 32,* 1153–1157.

von Baeyer, C. L., Sherk, D. L., & Zanna, M. P. (1981). Impression management on the job interview: When the female applicant meets the male "chauvinist" interviewer. *Personality and Social Psychology Bulletin, 7,* 45–51.

Voyer, D., Voyer, S., & Bryden, M. P. (1995). Magnitude of sex differences in spatial abilities: A meta-analysis and consideration of critical variables. *Psychological Bulletin, 117,* 250–270.

Wagner, D. G., & Berger, J. (1997). Gender and interpersonal task behaviors: Status expectation accounts. *Sociological Perspectives, 40,* 1–32.

Wallen, K. (1996). Nature needs nurture: The interaction of hormonal and social influences on the development of behavioral sex differences in rhesus monkeys. *Hormones and Behavior, 30,* 364–378.

Warin, J. (2000). The attainment of self-consistency through gender in young children. *Sex Roles, 42,* 209–231.

Watson, D., & Clark, L. A. (1984). Negative affectivity: The disposition to experience negative emotional states. *Psychological Bulletin, 96,* 465–490.

Watson, D., & Clark, L. A. (1997). Extraversion and its positive emotional core. In R. Hogan, J. Johnson, & S. Briggs (Eds.), *Handbook of personality psychology* (pp. 767–793). San Diego, CA: Academic Press.

Weinraub, M., Clemens, L. P., Sockloff, A., Ethridge, T., Gracely, E., & Myers, B. (1984). The development of sex role stereotypes in the third year: Relationships to gender labeling, gender identity, sex-typed toy preference, and family characteristics. *Child Development, 55,* 1493–1503.

White, B. J. (1994). The Turner syndrome: Origin, cytogenetic variants, and factors influencing the phenotype. In S. H. Broman & J. Grafman (Eds.), *Atypical cognitive deficits in developmental disorders: Implications for brain function* (pp. 183–195). Hillsdale, NJ: Erlbaum.

Whiting, B. B., & Edwards, C. P. (1988). *Children of different worlds: The formation of social behavior.* Cambridge, MA: Harvard University Press.

Whitley, B. E., Jr. (1983). Sex-role orientation and self-esteem: A critical meta-analytic review. *Journal of Personality and Social Psychology, 44,* 765–785.

Whitley, B. E., Jr. (1984). Sex-role orientation and psychological well-being: Two meta-analyses. *Sex Roles, 12,* 207–225.

Wiederman, M. W. (1997). The truth must be in here somewhere: Examining the gender discrepancy in self-reported lifetime number of sex partners. *The Journal of Sex Research, 34,* 375–386.

Wiggins, J. S. (Ed.). (1996). *The Five-Factor Model of personality: Theoretical perspectives.* New York: Guilford.

Wilcox, A. J., Maxey, J., & Herbst, A. L. (1992). Prenatal diethylstilbestrol exposure and performance on college entrance examinations. *Hormones and Behavior, 26,* 433–439.

Wilkinson, L. C., & Marrett, C. (Eds.). (1985). *Gender influences in classroom interaction.* Hillsdale, NJ: Erlbaum.

Williams, G. C., & Meck, W. H. (1991). The organizational effects of gonadal steroids on sexually dimorphic spatial ability. *Psychoneuroendocrinology, 16,* 155–176.

Williams, J. E., & Best, D. L. (1982). *Measuring sex stereotypes: A thirty-nation study.* Beverly Hills, CA: Sage.

Williams, T. J., Pepitone, M. E., Christensen, S. E., Cooke, B. M., Huberman, A. D., Breedlove, N. J., Breedlove, T. J., Jordan, C. I., & Breedlove, S. M. (2000). Finger length patterns and human sexual orientation. *Nature, 404,* 455–456.

Willis, S. L., & Schaie, K. W. (1988). Gender Differences in spatial ability in old age: Longitudinal and intervention findings. *Sex Roles, 18,* 189–203.

Wilson, E. O. (1975). *Sociobiology: The new synthesis.* Cambridge, MA: Harvard University Press.

Wilson, E. O. (1978). *On human nature.* Cambridge, MA: Harvard University Press.

Wilson, E. O. (1998). *Consilience.* New York: Vintage Books.

Wilson, J. D. (1999). The role of androgens in male gender role behavior. *Endocrine Reviews, 20,* 726–737.

Wilson, J. D., Griffin, J. E., & Russell, D. W. (1993). Steroid 5α-reductase 2 deficiency. *Endocrine Reviews, 14,* 577–593.

Wisniewski, A. B., Migeon, C. J., Meyer-Bahlburg, H. F. L., Gearhart, J. P., Berkovitz, G. D., Brown, T. R., & Money, J. (2000). Complete androgen insensitivity syndrome: Long-term medical, surgical, and psychosexual outcome. *The Journal of Clinical Endocrinology and Metabolism, 85,* 2664–2669.

Women Enter German Combat Forces. (2001, January 3). *Los Angeles Times.*

Woolf, V. (1957, originally published in 1929). *A room of one's own.* New York: Harcourt Brace Jovanovich.

Yalcinkaya, T. M., Siiteri, P. K., Vigne, J., Licht, P., Pavgi, S., Frank, L. G., & Glickman, S. E. (1993). A mechanism for virilization of female spotted hyenas in utero. *Science, 260,* 1929–1931.

Youniss, J., & Smollar, J. (1985). *Adolescent relations with mothers, fathers, and friends.* Chicago: University of Chicago Press.

Zahavi, A., & Zahavi, A. (1997). *The handicap principle: A missing piece of Darwin's puzzle.* New York: Oxford University Press.

Zanna, M. P., & Pack, S. J. (1975). On the self-fulfilling nature of apparent sex differences in behavior. *Journal of Experimental Social Psychology, 11,* 583–591.

Zeman, J. & Garber, J. (1996). Display rules for anger, sadness, and pain: It depends on who is watching. *Child Development, 67,* 957–973.

Zhou, J. N., Hofman, M. A., Gooren, L. J. G., & Swaab, D. F. (1995). A sex difference in the human brain and its relation to transsexuality. *Nature, 378,* 68–70.

Zucker, K. J., Wilson-Smith, D. N., Kurita, J. A., & Stern, A. (1995). Children's appraisals of sex-typed behaviors in their peers. *Sex Roles, 33,* 703–725.

Zuckerman, D. M., Singer, D. G., & Singer, J. L. (1980). Children's television viewing, racial and sex role attitudes. *Journal of Applied Social Psychology, 10,* 281–294.

Author Index

Subject Index

A

aggression, 15–16, 78, 117, 187–88, 201
  absolute rates of, 118
  biological factors and, 119
  d value statistic of, 10–11
  physical aggression, 10–11, 116, 117–19
  testosterone and, 108, 109, 110, 117, 118–19
Albright, Madeleine, 226
American Psychiatric Association, 26, 42
American Psychologist, 166
androgen-insensitive males, 104–5, 173, 189
androgyny, 45–49, 53, 67, 92
  "androgyny is best" concept, 48, 50
  behavioral flexibility and, 49
  bipolar M-F model and, 51
  combination theory of, 50
  conformity and, 48
  gender aschematic individuals and, 52, 92

gender aschematic society, 53
gender schema theory and, 52
masculine gender roles and, 48–49, 57
masculinity and feminity concepts in, 52
M-traits in, 50
PAQ M scale and, 50
sex role "liberation" and, 52
sex-typed individuals and, 48, 49
stereotypically feminine behaviors and, 48–49, 57
traditional gender roles and, 49
undifferentiated individuals, 48
Attitude Interest Analysis Survey, 37

B

"Baby X" studies, 186
Bandura, Albert, 87, 88
Barrow, Robert H. general, 228, 229
behavior differences of men, women, 157–58, 160
behavior geneticists, 126